RODRIGO DUTERTE

*An author-selfie, beside a cardboard cut-out of
President Rodrigo Duterte in Davao City.*

Jonathan Miller was born in the north of Ireland and has spent much of his life in Southeast Asia, where his family lived for 25 years. As a foreign correspondent, he gravitated back, devoting nearly half his 30-year career to reporting from across Asia. This resulted in an abiding fascination with the region and an incurable addiction to chillis. After more than a decade as London-based Foreign Affairs Correspondent with Channel 4 News, he took up the post of Asia Correspondent just as Rodrigo Duterte rose to power. He soon found himself covering the calamitous consequences. Jonathan has won four Royal Television Society awards for his journalism and four Amnesty International TV News awards.

RODRIGO DUTERTE

Fire and Fury
in the Philippines

JONATHAN MILLER

SCRIBE

Melbourne • London

Scribe Publications
18–20 Edward St, Brunswick, Victoria 3056, Australia
2 John St, Clerkenwell, London, WC1N 2ES, United Kingdom
3754 Pleasant Ave, Suite 100, Minneapolis, Minnesota 55409 USA

Published by Scribe 2018

Set in Sabon LT
Typeset by Avon DataSet Ltd, Warwickshire, B50 4JH

Printed and bound in the UK by CPI Group (UK) Ltd, Croydon
CR0 4YY

Scribe Publications is committed to the sustainable use of natural
resources and the use of paper products made responsibly from
those resources.

9781947534346 (US edition)
9781925693409 (e-book)

scribepublications.com

CONTENTS

FOREWORD:
ADDICTED TO KILLING

At about the time I was assigned as Asia correspondent for Channel 4 News and arrived back in the region, a foul-mouthed maverick mayor from Mindanao — an island in the far south of the Philippines — announced that he was going to run for president. Rodrigo Duterte possessed street charisma and had engagingly bad manners. Filipinos called this 'gangster charm', and swooned. When Duterte called Pope Francis a 'son of a whore' and got away with it in a country almost as staunchly Catholic as the Vatican, I began to pay more serious attention. This Mayor Duterte seemed like he could get away with murder. He presented himself as a man of the people, an insurgent outsider with no time for the corrupt oligarchs and dynastic elites of what he disparaged as 'imperial Manila'. He loved guns and girls and motorbikes, and hated drugs and crime and protocol.

The Philippines, a tropical archipelago of over 7000 far-flung islands and 100 million people — a quarter of whom live in poverty — was on the look-out for a saviour. The mayor's rough-edged appeal cut across both class and wealth divides. Duterte's brazen, cavalier style made Filipinos laugh and feel good about themselves. In his own words, he did not 'give a shit' about what people thought — particularly when it came to human rights. After years of feckless liberal leadership and decades of deference to America — the former colonial ruler — here at last was a straight-talking politician with simple solutions to national problems. Duterte claimed to be a socialist, but didn't peddle ideology: he spoke the gutter language of the poor and was a shameless populist authoritarian at the vanguard of an emerging new world order, way ahead of Donald J. Trump. Duterte promised that, as president, he would do just as he had done as mayor of Davao City: rid the place of bad guys and do society a favour. He revelled in his *nom de guerre*, 'Duterte Harry', after Clint Eastwood's shoot-first-ask-questions-later vigilante cop, 'Dirty' Harry Callahan.

'I am your last card,' he told an electorate in his thrall. 'I promise you, I will get down and dirty just to get things done … All of you who are into drugs, you sons of bitches, I will really kill you. I have no patience. I have no middle ground. Either you kill me, or I will kill you idiots.'

Rodrigo Duterte cleaned up all right. He won by a landslide and immediately began to deliver on his promises. On day one, he launched a Latin America-style 'Dirty War', and with it introduced the darkest of Latino shadows: the death squad. By the end of year one, he was presiding over the largest loss of civilian lives in Southeast Asia since Pol Pot took Cambodia back to Year Zero: 10,000 in just 12 months, most of them dirt poor. In Duterte's reign of terror, death squads roam the slums, and, within months of his coming to power, these vigilantes had killed three times as many Filipinos as died in nearly a decade of martial law under the disgraced dictator Ferdinand Marcos during the 1970s and 1980s.

Duterte set about rehabilitating the reputation of Marcos and his clan. To many, this felt like a frontal assault on the collective memory of a still-unresolved national trauma, but the president declared it was time to bury the past. He approved the reinterment of Marcos' body in the national Cemetery of Heroes, set about abolishing the agency still trying to recoup most of the US$10 billion plundered by Marcos and his cronies, and supported an electoral challenge which could yet engineer the installation of Ferdinand Marcos Jr as his vice president. Ferdinand Jr and his sister, Imee Marcos, governor of the family's home province of Ilocos Norte, began to accompany Duterte on foreign trips, most notably on a state visit to China in October 2016. A year later a new 12-peso stamp was issued bearing the smiling face of the dead despot. Many Filipinos were aghast. A meme circulated on Facebook: 'New Marcos stamps won't stick. People are spitting on the wrong side.'

With the daily bloodbath splashed across the headlines, in February 2017 Duterte jailed Senator Leila de Lima, the former justice secretary and his leading critic. The charges against her were condemned as 'pure fiction' and politically motivated by human rights groups, and had followed a vicious campaign of harassment. He aggressively attacked the Catholic Church, his chief justice, and world leaders who criticised his drugs war — including then US president Barack Obama who, like the Pope, was awarded the 'Order of Son of a Whore'. Duterte turned his back on America, the Philippines' strongest ally, in favour of Beijing and Moscow. Across Asia, a region where cultural rules of behavioural etiquette are strictly observed, people were struck dumb by Duterte's recalcitrance and effrontery, and watched events unfold with an uncomprehending and embarrassed fascination.

In May 2017, Duterte declared martial law in Mindanao, and gave the army a free hand to wage wars against Islamists and communists. Dissenting voices were drowned out by the president's army of cyber-trolls on Facebook, and, by the end of his tumultuous first year in office, he was more popular than when he had been elected. Duterte basked in the sort of approval ratings usually associated with totalitarian regimes. Congress has since acquiesced in backing the extension of martial law in Mindanao until the end of 2018.

Every fresh profanity directed at world leaders would prompt demands for 'more Duterte!' from my London newsroom, and although I would happily oblige — because he was indeed good fodder — friends and contacts in the Philippines saw in him a much more menacing figure than the entertaining cardboard cut-out loudmouth he was initially portrayed as abroad. Among the Filipino cognoscenti, aware of what had really happened when he was mayor of Davao City, the mood was dark. From the start, they had shuddered at the prospect of what he would do as president — like the frisson that rippled through liberal America when Trump announced his intention to run for office, but worse. Much worse. The little already written about Duterte was buried in local Davao newspaper stories, leaked US diplomatic cables, and decade-old reports by a UN investigator and a human rights group. These painted him as a violent authoritarian, the Godfather of the dreaded Davao Death Squad, a cocksure mayor sincere in his belief that he was right — for whom the end justified the means.

I grew up in Southeast Asia and first visited the Philippines a few months after Marcos declared martial law. I remember the edgy atmosphere, and listening in to urgent conversations between my school-teacher parents and their Filipino and foreign colleagues in Manila and Baguio City, the summer capital of the Philippines, as they grappled with the anxieties and fears that come with living under military dictatorship. It was along the Marcos Highway on the way up to Baguio that a much-hated 100-foot-high concrete bust of the dictator was later built. The statue was bombed by communist rebels in 1989, the year Marcos died in exile. As a student, back in 1983, I had read with horror of the assassination of Benigno 'Ninoy' Aquino, the most outspoken opponent of martial law, just after he had landed, after three years in exile, at the international airport in Manila which now bears his name. In remarkable television footage from inside the aircraft, Aquino told reporters: 'I cannot allow myself to be petrified by the fear of assassination and spend my life in a corner.' Minutes later, he was shot dead as he was escorted from the plane.

Three decades on, I could not help but wonder whether Filipinos in Duterte's Philippines would still be as shocked as they were then by such a killing. I had begun to doubt they would be until the murder, in August 2017, of Kian Loyd delos Santos, a 17-year-old boy whose blatant extra-judicial killing at the hands of plain-clothes police nauseated Filipinos and began to galvanise opposition to the drugs war — and to Duterte. It felt like a watershed moment. In one snapshot of national public opinion following Kian's killing, the president's net approval rating appeared to have slid to under 50 per cent for the first time, prompting headlines suggesting his political honeymoon might be over. Although another opinion poll contradicted this — indicating that Duterte's approval and trust ratings remained at 80 per cent

— the dawning of Duterte's downfall might one day be traced back to the teenager's sordid back-alley execution, just as the fall of Marcos was triggered by the assassination of Aquino.

The month after Kian's killing, the powerful Catholic Church found its voice, ordering that church bells be rung at 8 pm every evening across the archipelago for the next 40 days in protest at the killings. At the end of January 2018, a Philippine court filed charges against three officers over the murder of Kian Loyd delos Santos. By then, Duterte's war on drugs had been raging for more than 18 months. As this book goes to press, only a handful of homicide cases arising from the war on drugs have made it to the courts and there has not been a single conviction. Because the judicial system had proved unable or unwilling to bring the killers to justice, the chief prosecutor of the International Criminal Court in The Hague announced in February 2018 that she would launch a preliminary examination of the killings linked to the war on drugs since Duterte became president. He responded by denying he had ever given an order to police to kill drug suspects, and his spokesman dismissed the move as a 'waste of the court's time and resources'.

As a journalist, I based myself for a decade in Southeast Asia, living between Malaysia, Singapore, Cambodia, and Thailand, and covering the region. In 2001, three months after 9/11, I was the reporter on a documentary for Channel 4 on the war against Abu Sayyaf and other Islamist insurgent groups in Mindanao. It was there I first began to understand the depth of the bitterness felt by Filipino Moro Muslims after centuries of oppression by Spanish, then American, colonial invaders, land-grabs by Catholic Filipino settlers, and decades of insurgency. It would be another 15 years before the Philippines elected Duterte as the country's first-ever Mindanaoan president. He seemed to offer fresh hope … but only to begin with.

I had the first of several personal encounters with Duterte in Davao City six weeks into his presidency, when martial law in Mindanao was still months away. The numbers murdered in his war on drugs had yet to reach 2000, but the killing spree already had the world's attention. At a midnight news conference attended by the travelling presidential press corps and local journalists in Davao, I asked him to respond to accusations that he had unleashed a national death squad. As the only foreign correspondent present, it was easier for me to ask such questions. He retorted angrily, boasting of how, when he'd been mayor, he had ordered his courageous police to shoot to kill. Thinking I was an American, he railed against US hypocrisy; police over there, he said, were shooting black men — 'what's the difference?' I pointed out that these killings weren't sanctioned by the president, but he ignored this. The news conference was broadcast live on several TV channels and our exchange notched up 13 million views on YouTube. The verdict? Foreign reporter trounced! Like others with the impertinence to ask such stupid questions, I received threats from Duterte trolls on social media.

A few weeks later, I returned to Duterte's lair in Davao. This time, the president was fresh off a plane from meeting his professed hero, Vladimir Putin, at a summit. It was November 2016 and his other hero, Marcos, had been furtively reburied with military honours in his absence. Duterte took a few moments to eulogise the late dictator and then reverted to his favourite theme, his drugs war, issuing threats and justifying the killings which by then were approaching 6000. The Philippines, he declared, was a narco-state, 'as if we are now a country in Latin America', and he warned those playing 'narco-politics' that they would be killed. Standing at the microphone, I pointed out that the Latin American narco-states he mentioned were associated with death squads and said that in his first five months in power, death squads in the Philippines had already killed far more people than even Marcos managed. This provoked another anti-American diatribe, covering the US invasions of Panama and Iraq, the killing of children, adults, 'even the dogs and the goats', and the hypocrisy of the United States in criticising him about human rights. 'You destroyed countries!' he said.

The official transcript of that news conference, released by Malacañang Palace, did not record his final comment to me, but it was this that made national newspaper and television headlines the following day. The president asked if I had any more questions. As his communications secretary, a former TV journalist, physically pulled me away from the microphone by my shirt tails, Duterte said: 'You cannot think of a question?' He muttered something about hypocrisy, and then, under his breath, he added '*putang ina mo*' ('you son of a whore'), but the microphones all caught it. The '*mo*' tagged on to the end made this particularly personal, I learned, one up on Pope Francis and Obama. As I returned to my seat in the roomful of journalists, he said, in the Tagalog language, 'Look at him, running off like a coward.'

Back in Manila the following night, I joined a freelance Filipino photographer, Luis Liwanag, on what was known as 'the night shift' — on the front line of Duterte's drugs war. This was the second time I had been out with the 'night crawlers', but by now the national kill-rate stood at more than 20 a day. Not long after 10 pm we arrived at the scene of a death squad killing, within minutes of the shooting. Two masked men on a motorbike, we were told. A gaggle of teenagers had gathered outside a Dunkin' Donuts. They were staring sullenly at the body of a man sprawled on his back in the gutter right in front of them. A crimson rivulet of blood, oozing from the exit wound on the back of his head, was starting to mingle with rainwater in a kerbside puddle. Police arrived and tied some yellow tape to nearby railings. They were practised and unhurried in their routine. Traffic continued to move up and down the street and all seemed normal — apart from the dead man in the gutter. A young woman in a passing jeepney taxi leant out and took a snapshot on her smartphone as a small crowd looked on; no one, it seemed, particularly shocked, just mawkishly transfixed.

Luis had cut his teeth as a photojournalist during the final years of Marcos, and his dramatic pictures of the protests that led to the dictator's overthrow were emblematic of an era. A Leica camera was tattooed on his forearm, two Canon SLRs slung round his neck. Now in his fifties — and respectfully referred to as 'Sir Luis' by fellow snappers — he was back, documenting the rise of a new authoritarian, and trying, he told me, to humanise the horror.

'They're getting bolder. It used to be just in dark alleys, now it's right in the centre of a busy street,' he said, breaking briefly to snatch a few more frames. 'People are getting used to it … they are becoming desensitised. It's like a regular event now. A rampage of nightly killings. It's really horrible the way people are being killed like insects.'

Like insects.

In the months that followed, these two words kept coming back at me as I delved ever-deeper into Duterte's past and the systematic extermination programme he had launched. He was, it seemed, addicted to killing. He might not have called drug addicts cockroaches, but he had questioned whether they were human and said he would be 'happy to slaughter them'.

'If Germany had Hitler, the Philippines would have …' he said, pointing to himself.

It seemed to me that the Philippines had a much larger problem than drugs. It had a new dictator in the making.

Months later, I spent an hour in conversation with Miguel Syjuco, the award-winning Filipino novelist who shared my obsession with the Philippines' new strongman. Syjuco was working on another novel and had recently been out on the night shift in Manila, too. After writing several op-eds for *The New York Times*, he had received threats of violence and been subjected to character assassinations. When we spoke, events had been unfolding fast and the drugs war's body count inexorably rising. Duterte had declared 'partial martial' in the south and had mused in public about extending military rule across the Philippines.

'History is repeating itself,' Syjoco said. 'Even the names of the past are back. It's dangerous not just because it's happening, but because we are letting it happen. Duterte represents what results when you allow democracy to be perverted, when the people consider it acceptable to have as ruler someone who is willing to discard the democratic checks and balances and any laws he feels inconvenienced by. What scares me most,' he said, 'is what our democratic institutions will look like at the end of this. The legislature, courts, media, the church, the opposition. He has gone after anyone who has stood up to him and he has very effectively used his mob of trolls and propagandists.'

'Democracy isn't just the majority voting in whoever we want,' he said. 'Democracy is ensuring that even the minority is represented and granted equal rights. Thirty years is an entire generation over which the people of the Philippines have forgotten the lessons of dictatorship.'

Within a few weeks of our speaking, Duterte's allies in Congress moved to impeach the chairman of the election commission, the chief justice, and the independent government ombudsman. Under the pretext of his war on drugs, Duterte had declared war on the rule of law, replacing it with justice from the barrel of a gun. When I sought answers from the presidential palace about exactly what was happening, my questions were dismissed as 'malicious'. The president was 'decisive', I was told. 'He doesn't pander to western liberal perspectives.'

I have an aversion to western foreign correspondents 'parachuting' into countries and pontificating sagely about what they think is going on. That is why this book is drawn almost entirely from what Filipinos have told me about what they think is happening in their country. I have listened to Duterte's critics and to members of his family, to ministers in his cabinet, and to other loyal supporters, including priests, civil servants, newspaper editors, and close associates. And, of course, I have listened to Duterte … for hours and hours and hours. I brought this on my own head having taken on this book. *Putang ina!* It has been a form of self-inflicted, slow, and painful torture.

My observation is that, while Filipino journalists continue to document the killings and the president's pursuit of ever-greater powers, the noose will tighten in Asia's oldest democracy. An atmosphere of intimidation has enveloped the Philippines under Duterte's increasingly authoritarian regime and his heavy-handed style of governance has been enthusiastically endorsed by Donald J. Trump. I personally know journalists, human rights defenders, lawyers, opposition activists, and politicians who have been threatened — some with death. Many I spoke to requested anonymity because they were so fearful of the repercussions.

For Filipinos who keep their heads below the parapet, life just goes on. They're aware, of course, of the killings, and still intrigued by the antics of Duterte Harry and his iconoclastic outbursts. But if you're middle class and educated, the closest you're likely to come to Duterte's death squads is when you chance across a paragraph in a paper reporting some slaying in a slum you've never been to, or your eye is drawn to the photograph of a five-year-old who's been shot and whose killer will never be caught. The writer Margaret Atwood captured well such collective insouciance in her 1985 book *The Handmaid's Tale*:

> We lived, as usual, by ignoring. Ignoring isn't the same as ignorance, you have to work at it.
>
> Nothing changes instantaneously: in a gradually heating bathtub you'd be boiled to death before you knew it. There were stories in the newspapers of course, corpses in ditches …

Over the months I spent researching and writing this book, that's how it felt in Duterte's republic of fear. But, as the temperature rose, a growing number of ordinary Filipinos began to show signs of discomfort, distress. It just became harder and harder to ignore what was happening.

Jonathan Miller
Bangkok, March 2018

1

CARDBOARD CUT-OUT

In a disappointed country, where the promise of a half-forgotten people's revolution had been squandered, and memories of dictatorship and Imelda's shoes had faded, they were finally ready for another strongman. The Age of Anger was dawning in the Philippines, the fuse was lit, and, as the presidential election of May 2016 approached, 'Duterte Harry' swaggered into the political arena, threatening to blow punks' heads clean off.

'Kill them,' he'd say. Make my day.

Rodrigo Duterte reassured his audience that killing criminals was nothing new to him. 'If I have to kill you, I will kill you. Personally,' he said. This became his rhetorical refrain, which he delivered in such an informal, understated, poker-faced way that no one could be sure if he was joking. It turned out that he wasn't: the core election pledge of the law-and-order candidate for Sixteenth President of the Philippine Republic was mass murder, pure and simple.

The shameless self-comparisons to Idi Amin and Hitler would

come later. He had never killed an innocent human being, Duterte said, as he vowed to exterminate a species of sub-humans: the 'sniff-dogs' and dealers at the heart of what he claimed was a national methamphetamine pandemic. This had been allowed to fester for far too long, he declared, to the point that it posed an existential threat. Filipinos had long known that their country had a drug addiction problem. Until now, though, they hadn't realised that it threatened national security. But when Duterte assured them that it did, they believed him. The broken justice system could not fix things, he told the people — and, in that, he was not wrong. But he had a Final Solution of his own: there will be blood, he said, and promised carnage. 'God will weep if I become president.'

Bombast and bravado dominated his obscenity-laced campaign speeches, in which Duterte raged and swore to kill the vermin of the drugs trade. 'These sons of whores are destroying our children,' he said, repeatedly. He promised to dump so many bodies in Manila Bay that the fish would grow fat feeding on them. Every speech contained murderous threats, and, later, often included incitements for ordinary citizens to take up arms themselves, as vigilante killers. The funeral parlours would be packed, he predicted; accurately.

Duterte's filthy mouth made him headline news. The more he cursed, the more media attention he won, and the more his growing army of supporters laughed and loved him. To lighten up his menacing invective, he boasted of his philandering and cracked jokes about rape. There were, of course, many Filipinos who baulked at his boorishness, appalled by his unfiltered outbursts and vulgarity. He had the bearing and behaviour of a gangster warlord, and sold himself as an outsider from the far south, where, as a local mayor, he claimed he had sorted out a troubled city's woes. His master plan as president was simple:

to nationalise the franchise he had founded. He said he had a winning formula.

In crime-infested shanties across the archipelago, his take-no-prisoners style made him wildly popular. He was a tough-guy-hero who had *cojones* — or, as they say in the Tagalog language, '*may bayag*' ('he's got balls'). He spoke the salty language of the poor; uncouth, unvarnished, like nothing they had ever heard before from someone with his sights set on Malacañang, the grand colonial-era presidential palace on the banks of Manila's Pasig River. But Duterte — a lawyer by profession — shrewdly played to the fears of richer Filipinos, too, and their perception that violent criminality was rampant.

For those who swore allegiance to him — and he inflamed fierce loyalty — Duterte Harry was a revenge fantasy come true. Nothing was sacred. In a devout Catholic country that idolised America, he called both the Pope and Obama '*putang ina*' and discovered that this did not dent his popularity at all. He warned the Roman Catholic Church, the Philippine national media, foreign governments, and anyone with the temerity to suggest his methods were unsound: 'Don't fuck with me.'

'He is being used as a vehicle of the Holy Spirit,' his elder sister, Eleanor, explained. 'The country is in such turmoil and is so dark, we have to cleanse it. You cannot see the light until you clear the path of darkness. If it is your destiny, it is your destiny.'

Long ago, she said to me as we climbed the creaking staircase of what she grandly called 'the ancestral home' (to which the family had actually only moved when Rodrigo was a child), a clairvoyant told their mother that all that has now transpired had been written in the stars. 'One of your sons,' she'd said — and Eleanor stressed that she obviously meant Rodrigo — 'will, by destiny, assume a very high position.'

'What made him president?' she asked me, rhetorically. 'Destiny. The Father's will. Lucifer will never win.'

In Eleanor's messianic vision, anyone who challenged her brother was an emissary of Satan.

We reached the top of the panelled staircase and there, from a gold and dark-wood frame, a cocky-looking kid stared out from a fading sepia-tinged photograph, printed onto canvas. His right hand was resting on his hip, and with his left arm he made the pretence of leaning rakishly on a badly drawn, ornate column on the set.

'See that young boy with the cap on his head? That's Rodrigo. That's him! Five years old.'

The recalcitrant glare of the young Rodrigo Duterte is a vaguely menacing look which the Filipino people have all now come to know. His expression, though, is hard to read — then, as now. Those who love him see it as defiance; to others, it is the sneer of cold command.

His sister, three years his senior, sighed. 'Typical mama's boy. He gets away with murder.'

Eleanor always used the present tense, even when referring to events from long ago.

Those who've tracked Duterte's long and blood-soaked journey from that 'ancestral home' to the Malacañang Palace with ever-growing alarm would not argue with Eleanor's unwitting verdict. On election day, Duterte won 16.6 million votes, 6.6 million more than his closest rival, and more than any other president in Philippine history, bar the rigged re-election of Ferdinand Marcos in 1981. He built a government on the back of his anti-criminality campaign, and he launched his dirty war well before his inauguration. Within his first six months in office, more than 7000 people had been gunned down, twice as many as were killed during the entire nine-year-long military dictatorship of Marcos. To give this a sense of comparative scale, this was double the number killed in Northern Ireland's Troubles, over a period of 30 years. After that, the numbers in the Philippines just kept on going up.

'Suspects' whose names had appeared on 'watch lists' were shot dead in supposed encounters with the police, or by death squads — armed men on motorbikes in ski-masks — who roamed towns and cities across the country with a licence from the president to kill. These 'vigilantes' were widely suspected of being off-duty cops or hired hitmen who took orders directly from the police. The killings were called 'deaths under investigation', but there was never a real investigation and, until the end of January 2018, when three police officers were charged with murdering the teenager Kian Loyd delos Santos, not a single prosecution.

Even while president-elect, Duterte placed bounties on the heads of suspected drug dealers and addicts, inciting a killing spree by offering cash rewards to ordinary citizens. He scoffed at threats by human rights lawyers to hold him to account for 'command responsibility' in what they said could amount to crimes against humanity. He marshalled social media and mobilised an army of die-hard acolytes and trolls — branded 'the Dutertards' by those they attacked. They fervently supported his drive to cleanse the Philippines of what they derided as 'scum'. Once president, Duterte said there would be a price to pay for 'safety', and that price, he said, was human rights. Human rights activists and lawyers were both classed as legitimate targets for assassination. In May 2017, he even threatened to behead human rights advocates who criticised his drugs war.

Duterte sought to burnish his personal credentials as someone who killed bad guys, although the lawyer in him liked to keep claims vague. Eight months before he declared his candidacy, he told the magazine *Esquire Philippines* that he had first killed when he was 17, 'maybe' stabbing somebody to death in what he said was a drunken beach brawl. 'I have never in my life killed an innocent person,' he reassured them. He made the same claim in November 2017, while addressing expatriate Filipinos in Vietnam, although on that occasion he said he was 16. The *Esquire* article was accompanied by striking black-and-white photographic portraits of him, posing in a combat jacket, cradling a long-arm weapon with a telescopic sight. He wore an identical, ambiguous expression to the one in the childhood photograph: sniper's eye and the trademark defiant sneer.

In the months following his election, Duterte made many other boasts about his willingness to pull a gun and fire at bad guys: he said he had shot a fellow student while at law school and shot dead three suspected criminals while mayor of a distant place called Davao City. He even claimed he'd hurled a rape-and-murder suspect from a helicopter, mid-flight, narcos-style. He'd done it before, he said, and would have no qualms about doing it again. He won a standing ovation at a national business leaders' forum in Manila after he told them how, as mayor, he had patrolled his city at night on a Harley Davidson, 'looking for an encounter so I could kill'. During his campaign, he referred to Davao City as his 'Exhibit A', and said he staked his credibility on his record there as mayor.

When he burst onto the scene, as if from nowhere, as a presidential candidate, few in the capital and across the biggest island of Luzon, on which Manila stands, knew much — if anything — about the foul-mouthed iconoclastic firebrand from the south. He had lived, since childhood, on Mindanao, the southernmost large island in an archipelago of more than 7000

— most of which have yet to be named.

To the northerners, Mindanao is a far-away place where wars happen; the Philippines' 'wild south' for centuries, untamed, and now beset by blood-thirsty jihadists, separatist insurgencies, kidnap gangs, pirates in the Sulu Sea, and, in the mountains, guerrillas of the communist New People's Army; all of them either killing or making a killing — or both. Mindanao was, and still is, regarded as a cauldron of Islamist violence, where Luzon Catholics fear to tread; a land where gun-law rules. Its *de facto* coastal capital is Davao City, once the murder capital of the Philippines. For 22 years, it was ruled by a gun-toting mayor who, it turned out, had repeatedly been investigated for his alleged links to a death squad. The mayor gloried in the nickname Duterte Harry. And he had another name: The Punisher.

In Davao City, a Pyongyang-style personality cult today surrounds their mayor-president. In hotel lobbies, shops, restaurants, the airport, and in local businesses, the man they just call 'Rody' — but pronounce as Rudi — skulks, in person, sporting a slightly unsettling half-smile. The cardboard cut-outs are life-sized, and, although the president is small of stature, it can be alarming when you suddenly become aware of a figure lurking silently behind you and when you spin round, it's him. Sometimes he's wearing a trademark red-checked lumberjack shirt, sometimes a black Polo shirt, and always jeans. Making these Duterte icons has become an industry in Davao: the cardboard cut-out Rodys are everywhere, and come with identical weighted frames to prevent the mayor from toppling over and falling on his face.

The city's streets are clean and ordered, and it's said to be completely safe to wander around at night. There's a building boom, the local economy is thriving, speed limits are rigorously enforced, smokers are banished, and children aren't allowed out alone past curfew at 10 pm, or their parents face fines. And, like everywhere else in the Philippines these days, the 'scum' get shot ... although, actually, that's always happened here.

Today, the city's 1.6 million residents are too timid to admit what they know to be the truth about Rodrigo Duterte's lengthy reign of terror because, for three decades, they blindly acquiesced and kept their heads down. Many, including the local press, are literally indebted to the former mayor, beneficiaries of his largesse. Davaoeños will tell you that they love him. Local surveys put Duterte's approval rating at 96 per cent. Surprisingly though, even some his most fervent admirers don't deny there's a climate of fear.

'Yes, there is,' one conceded, privately. 'But it's fear with respect. Fear with love. In Davao, we are very proud of him.'

Over many years, the people of Davao grew to understand that resistance was futile. Those who openly opposed Duterte's tactics did not fare well; for some, their life expectancy proved short. Those supporting him found life improved immeasurably because, if there was ever a problem, the mayor was sure to help. Stories abound of his 'personal' generosity. Duterte always stood in mayoral elections as the law-and-order candidate. He promised zero-tolerance on drugs and criminality. In City Hall, he kept a loaded, gold-plated revolver on his desk.

During the seven terms of Mayor Duterte, the bodies of hundreds of street-kids and petty criminals, as well as addicts and dealers of crystal-meth, or *shabu*, as it is known in the Philippines, were found dumped in Davao's back streets. Often their corpses were discovered with their faces wrapped in masking tape. Their hands were tied and hand-written signs were hung around their necks: 'addict,' 'pusher,' 'thief'. The people of Davao City came to realise that these murders would all remain unsolved. They had watched their mayor's Hugo Chavez-style Sunday morning TV talk show, 'From the Masses, For the

Masses', where he would brandish 'watch lists' containing hundreds of named suspects. They knew that having your name on that list was as good as having a target painted on your back.

Davao City was Duterte's laboratory for killing. It was to become his template, a political model for his brand of governance, for replication on a national scale. Between 1998 and 2015, more than 1400 Davaoeños were murdered, some by .45 calibre handguns, others just by butchers' knives. The perpetrators of these unsolved murders were euphemistically labelled 'unknown vigilante killers'. But everybody knew this to be the handiwork of what was ubiquitously referred to as the 'Davao Death Squad'.

Filipino and foreign human rights investigators venturing to Davao in those days linked the extra-judicial killings to the Heinous Crimes Division of the city police, and pointed the finger firmly at Mayor Duterte Harry. He talked openly of criminals being 'legitimate targets of assassination', but denied any criminal liability himself. Locally, it was, of course, an open secret that Duterte was the Godfather of the Davao Death Squad. He usually denied that, too, although on occasion, he would boast of personal complicity. Once, on 'From the Masses', he made an admission which took people by surprise. 'They say I am the death squad? True, that is true,' he said.

With President Duterte ensconced in Malacañang Palace, members of that death squad — one, a retired senior police officer who claimed to have been the leader of that infamous Davao Heinous Crime Division — broke cover to testify under oath in the Philippine Senate. All that had been alleged was true, they said. The Davao Death Squad really did exist and they had been in it. The mayor, the now contrite former killers said, had personally carried out summary executions, ordered countless other murders, and paid for hits in cash. These claims were summarily rejected by Malacañang, and no effort was spared to discredit his accusers. One fled into exile, the other went on the run.

As president, the mercurial Rodrigo Duterte has, at times, proved erratic. But almost everything about the style and direction of his governance has been uncannily predictable, if not quite written in the stars. His personality traits, his patterns of behaviour — observable since his teenage years, throughout a 25-year marriage, and through his seven terms as mayor — presaged exactly how he would behave as president.

Duterte's attitudes to drugs and criminality, his methods for dealing with his critics, his views on Catholicism and communism, his opinion of America, the chip on his shoulder over historical injustice in Mindanao ... it was all foretold; there are antecedents. Foreign governments, and, at home, his political opponents, need only examine this past to gain an insight into what Duterte is likely to do next. And, if the doomsayers prove right — among them, a former classmate who's tracked Duterte's record for more than 50 years, senior lawyers, journalists, activists, priests, and politicians — the joining of the dots is a trail that leads to darkness.

Within months of coming to power, Duterte controversially ordered the reburial of Ferdinand Marcos in the Cemetery of Heroes — a 'hero' who had overseen the murder, imprisonment, and torture of thousands of Filipinos, and plundered US$10 billion from Philippine national coffers. The president regularly threatened to do away with *habeas corpus* (which allows for arrest without warrant) and repeatedly floated the possibility of his being 'forced' to declare martial law, before declaring it across Mindanao in May 2017 to contain a small jihadist insurrection in the city of Marawi. Having failed to do so, he used the supermajority he commands in Congress and the Senate, to extend this to the end of 2017, as concern inevitably grew that he would soon extend it geographically as well. Then, in December 2017, martial law in Mindanao and the suspension of *habeas corpus* was again extended, this time until the end of 2018, with Congress voting 240–27 to approve Duterte's request.

The president used his allies in both houses to push legislation reintroducing capital punishment. His 'eye-for-an-eye' bill stalled in the Senate, but he has continued to press Congress to pass the legislation, which, if it is approved would make the Philippines the first and only country in the world to renege on the abolition of the death penalty, in violation of international law. Duterte announced that he wanted to put 'five or six' prisoners to death every day for various 'heinous crimes', including drug offences.

The new authoritarian political order he established placed both the Philippine National Police and communists in commanding roles. He launched a brutal 'lock her up' campaign against his leading critic, the former justice minister and human rights investigator Senator Leila de Lima, who was then arrested and detained inside national police headquarters. As the months went by, he launched further attacks and threats against the handful of remaining senators who dared to question, criticise, or condemn his ever-more despotic governance. By October 2017, seemingly convinced of a plot to oust him, he warned he would declare what he called 'a revolutionary government' and would arrest all his critics — amid growing concern that the Philippines was returning to dictatorship. The declaration of what's been dubbed 'RevGov' would allow for 'extraordinary measures' to cure a 'failed system'. This would include the scrapping of the 1987 post-Marcos constitution, the introduction of a tough new Internal Security Act, and the introduction of a federal system, something Duterte has long campaigned for. Critics claim it would be nationwide martial law in all but name.

From day one of his presidency, fear and violence emerged as

Duterte's favoured tools for imposing order. Abroad, he quickly gained a toxic reputation as an authoritarian strongman. The violence he embraced to wage his war was condemned by many western governments, but in Donald J. Trump, Duterte found a friend. Unlike his predecessor in the White House, Trump not only endorsed Duterte's drugs war, but, to the reported consternation of the US State Department, invited a leader the American press had long-dubbed 'the Trump of Asia' to the White House. A foreign correspondent friend, who spent years reporting out of Washington DC observed: 'Duterte behaves like Trump's inner demon.'

At the end of May 2017, a classified confidential document was leaked — or possibly hacked — from the Americas division of the Philippine Department of Foreign Affairs. It contained a verbatim transcript of a telephone conversation between Trump and Duterte. Its contents were confirmed as accurate by a senior official in the Trump administration. The US president's opening gambit went like this: 'I just wanted to congratulate you because I am hearing of the unbelievable job on the drug problem. Many countries have the problem, we have a problem, but what a great job you are doing and I just wanted to call and tell you that.'

Duterte thanked him, calling drugs 'the scourge of my nation'.

Trump told him he understood, adding that 'we had a previous president who did not understand that'.

Having praised his war on drugs, Trump went on to consult Duterte about a paranoid, malignant narcissist who was causing him some trouble. He was referring to North Korea's rogue dictator, Kim Jong-un. 'What's your opinion of him, Rodrigo?' Trump asked. 'Are we dealing with someone who [is] stable or not stable?'

'He is not stable, Mr President, as he keeps on smiling when he explodes a rocket,' opined Duterte. 'Every generation has a madman,' he said, and Trump agreed.

'We can't let a madman with nuclear weapons on the loose like that.'

Then Trump twice invited his Filipino friend to the Oval Office — 'Any time you want to come.'

Their alpha-male bromance finally blossomed when Trump came to Manila for a summit in November 2017. In contrast to the animus Duterte directed at Obama, he serenaded Trump at a banquet with his favourite ballad.

'You are the light in my world,' he crooned. 'You are the love I've been waiting for,' before informing his audience that he had sung 'upon the orders of the commander-in-chief of the United States.' The next day, prior to Trump's speech on regional security, the president told Duterte that his performance at the previous night's gala 'talent show' had been 'fantastic'. Duterte's spokesman later said that during their 40-minute one-to-one meeting, Trump made no mention of human rights or what he called 'extra-legal killings', adding that the US president had once again been appreciative of Duterte's efforts in his war on drugs.

At home, Duterte and his supporters set about cultivating a contrived mythology of this iron-fisted mayor-turned-president, a fiction surrounding both the man and his achievements. It's a narrative mix of half-truths and untruths, corroborated by invented or exaggerated statistics and crowd-sourced surveys in which voters were members of his fanatical fan club. In mid-2017, an Oxford University study into social media manipulation by politicians in 28 countries analysed Duterte's use of this cyber-army to disseminate his alt-facts and to round on his critics. It claimed his keyboard-trolls were paid £150,000 during the course of the previous year to pump out his message. Duterte claimed he had only paid people to defend him on social media during his election campaign, but evidence — including personal experience — flies in the face of this. The president was dismissive of the study: 'Oxford University? That's a school for stupid people,' he said.

But the Duterte social media machine has proved devastatingly effective in a country which, according to a digital trends survey by Hootsuite and UK-based consultancy We Are Social Ltd, now leads the world in terms of time spent on social media. Filipinos, it seems, are hooked and on average, spent four hours and 17 minutes each day on sites such as Facebook, Snapchat, and Twitter — more than half an hour longer than their nearest rivals, Brazilians. This might well be down in part to the hopelessly sluggish internet speeds in the Philippines, which ranks just above Afghanistan according to an Akamai Tchnologies report in May 2017. For a while, mobile broadband speeds were among the fastest in Asia though, and the number of social media users grew by a quarter during Duterte's election year alone. Malacañang judges its success by the number of followers, likes, and shares scored by Duterte's most avid fans. But the troll farms are accused of employing fake accounts and algorithmic bots (automated response computer programs) to artificially inflate numbers and create the impression of a trend-wave in public opinion. Pro-Duterte propaganda and fake news is nonetheless widely reported and apparently widely believed by clever people in the media and politics and the law, as well as by the millions of Filipinos who voted for Duterte (and doubtless millions more now too scared to admit they didn't).

One example of the government's use of fake news was a viral post by Duterte's campaign spokesman Peter Tiu Laviña which defended the war on drugs. Laviña cited a report about a nine-year-old girl who was raped and murdered. He lambasted 'human rightists, bishops and presstitutes (sic)' for their failure to condemn what he called 'this brutal act'. They, he said, were 'derailing the government's war against drugs and crime'. In Trumpian style, he went on: 'Our righteous battles ... are fierce and relentless because we face the Devil himself. We cannot be soft or let our guards down lest we ourselves ... be devoured and be defeated!' Below this, he posted a graphic and distressing photograph purporting to show the dead child and her weeping mother. As the online news website, *Rappler*, would later point out in a series of articles which showed how the government was 'weaponizing the internet', the photograph was taken in Brazil, not the Philippines.

But few stopped to challenge the Duterte propaganda machine's assertions or to dig into the president's record as Davao City mayor — or, indeed, question whether his policy of 'ultimate deterrence' had actually worked.

It hadn't. National crime statistics contradict Duterte's claims that the city is transformed and safe. They show, for example, that Davao City remains the murder capital of the Philippines today, first among 15 cities, with more than 1000 recorded murders committed between 2010 and 2015. The murder rate there is roughly twice that of New York City, a metropolis five times the size. In the Philippines, Davao also ranked number two for rape.

In the city's slums, methamphetamine addiction remains rife, 30 years after the former mayor set out to cleanse the place of *shabu*. 'It's there, like candy,' a Davao resident who is an authority on this, but who requested anonymity, told me. And if more evidence were needed that Duterte's 'neutralisation' policy had failed to end the drug addiction problem, there's the fact that in the course of just 10 days — the first 10 days of his presidency — 17,211 drug users surrendered to police in the Davao region fearing they would be shot by roving national death squad hitmen. Former addicts I met in Davao reckoned there were at least as many more who had not surrendered.

Meanwhile, the statistics cited by the president to justify his war on drugs proved dramatically inflated, and his claim that the Philippines was in the throes of 'a drugs pandemic' was overstated. When Reuters news agency in Manila ran a report questioning the 'exaggerated, flawed or non-existent' numbers cited to justify Duterte's drugs campaign, Martin Andanar, the president's communications secretary, dismissed the story as 'malicious' and referred Reuters to the Philippine National Police.

The drugs war has always had more to do with Duterte's personal ambitions than it has had to do with drugs. Dealers and addicts proved a popular and easy target. The self-confessed leader of the Davao Death Squad said that among its members, the mayor had always been referred to by his codename: 'Superman'. It fitted with Duterte's own projection of himself as a self-styled superhero, saviour of Davao. Today, Duterte runs a national salvation project in which he has promised the restoration of national pride and deliverance from evil. An instant hagiography was published immediately after his election: *DU30, Man of Faith and Fate*. DU30 was his campaign nickname; the clenched fist his motif. The book's cover depicts Rodrigo as a knight, clad in shining armour. His helmet is removed to reveal his downcast face, and from one of the knight's dark, soulful eyes, a solitary tear rolls down his cheek.

Duterte's band of loyal supporters, who hail him as a messiah, choose to overlook the inconvenient evidence of the mounting national death-toll as the result of internecine feuding between the murderous gangs and rival drug lords. One of these Duterte devotees is Leo Villareal, a former local radio reporter who went on to work as Mayor Duterte's chief information officer at Davao City Hall for many years. We met at a downtown restaurant in a renovated Spanish colonial villa. He was just back from Manila and could not resist telling me his news as we sat down. Villareal had just been appointed chief communications officer at a government ministry in the capital, and was already working out the logistics of moving his family up there from Davao. Duterte has always rewarded loyalty.

Villareal insisted that the crime rate in the city had come down. He cited a crowd-sourced global online survey that in 2015 had ranked Davao City as the ninth safest city in the world.

'It's one of the safest! It compares with Singapore!' he laughed. 'It's one of the best. He made it like this!'

Davaoeños must have voted in droves in that online survey, but that's exactly the sort of thing Duterte's online army does. Now that the former mayor is president, Villareal said, 'he will solve the law-and-order problem. In Davao we have experienced that. True, many do not like his style, or his bad mouth, or the killings. But after two years, we understood. And now, after two years, Filipinos, too, will understand what is his direction.'

Like other disciples in Davao, who had long ago drunk the Duterte Kool-Aid, Villareal spoke with genuine conviction of his love and loyalty. It was as though he had been completely brainwashed: 'He [Duterte] said, "If I become president, it really will be bloody. If you aren't ready for my leadership, do not elect me. I will kill all criminals and addicts. I will bring a war against drugs and against corrupt people. I will kill them!" And the people chanted "Yes!"' he said. With a triumphal final flourish, the zealous civil servant added: 'I will die for my leader. I will die for him.'

But not everyone in Davao shared such unflinching loyalty. Virgilio P. 'Ver' Bermudez edits *Tribune News*, a small local newspaper, and has reported on the mayor-turned-president for very nearly three decades. I met him at an outdoor bar in central Davao City, set back off the road and attached to a small hotel owned by one of the president's ex-girlfriends. There was a life-sized cardboard cut-out of Duterte in reception to remind guests who was boss. Armed with ice-cold bottles of San Miguel Pale, Bermudez and I discussed the unsettling sense I had in Davao, which had the veneer of a normal, functioning, busy city. I was surrounded by friendly people who did all the things normal people do … except ask searching questions about Rodrigo Duterte. We talked of the pride which Davaoeños naturally felt now that their mayor was in Malacañang, and how they felt entitled to ringside seats which had, for decades, centuries even, been denied to the southerners from Mindanao. Bermudez was bold in his observations, but cautious, too, and was quick to defend Duterte and members of his family from wilder allegations which he had no evidence to support. He leant towards me, across the table.

'Those who are loyal to him are all his beneficiaries and they are all afraid,' he said. 'If you ask the child of a murderer whether they still hold their father in esteem, they will tell you that their father kills so that they can survive. All of us knows that if you pull a trigger, you can kill. But few of us have the stomach for this. He does.'

2

SON OF A ... GOVERNOR

He's in trouble. Again. Sometimes, when this happens, he goes on the run for three days in the hope that by the time he gets home it will have blown over. But he knows this time it won't end well; he's brought dishonour to the family name and he's going to be crucified. You can't fire a stone at a priest from your catapult as he's mowing the lawn at your school, spray ink from a water pistol on the back of another priest's cassock, then play truant for two months, and not bargain on suffering for your sins. He will have to face his beloved mother, The Punisher. She makes no secret of the fact that he is her favourite. Often he can sweet-talk her. Not this time. His normally soft-spoken father is furious. It's he who lays down the law, but it's his mother who is the enforcer. He doesn't feel remorse for what he's done, but it hurts him that he's hurt her, and, being stoic and honourable, he'll take the rap.

Horsewhip or crucifixion. It's not his choice. He hates the crucifix, but his mother is pious and devout, and when it's felt he needs to really contemplate his transgressions, this is her way.

'In the name of the Father ...'

Upstairs, in the spare room, in front of the altar; Jesus, the son of God, in agony, hangs there from the cross, suffering for the sins of this teenaged priest-tormentor. It's in his face. He is kneeling on mung beans, scattered on the hard wooden floor of the guest bedroom. Christ. His mother has ordered him to kneel with his arms outstretched, mirroring Jesus.

And that's pretty much exactly as he told it to his best friend, Jesus. Duterte's oldest friend, Jesus 'Jess' Dureza, his mucker-in-chief at Holy Cross High School in Digos City, Davao; Jesus, the journalist-turned-lawyer-turned-peace-negotiator, turned cabinet minister in the Duterte government. Jesus was waxing lyrical to me in his ministerial chambers in Manila.

'I'll tell you another story,' he chortled.

He was in full flow, and his young communications secretary, Basha, was smirking as she recorded and noted the drift of conversation.

'We would stay in the dormitory of the Brothers of the Sacred Heart, so we had to pray. He would say the rosary. One time he said: "Oh, you're always praying, Jess." At that time I was planning to become a Brother, too. Planning. He would playfully say: "You're always bonding with Jesus." He said "I had my bonding with Jesus. It took a long time. When Mother punished me, I was able to bond with Jesus Christ."' She was an amiable, sweet person, his mother, but very, very strict, his old friend said. And he was an *enfant terrible*. This particular form of bondage scarred Duterte — for life. Now in his seventies, he still talks about it.

If the mixed signals of this act of penitence were hard for the diminutive, 14-year-old Duterte to comprehend, so too are those he sends today as president. In his head, Duterte has always been on the side of the angels. He has always placed himself at the heart of the salvation story he invented as the narrative for his life. As law student, state prosecutor, mayor, and, now, as president, he has raged against injustice and stood up to the bullies, on the side of the oppressed and the weak. But for all the noble convictions and the compassion those who love him say that he embodies, it is not what his victims, enemies, and detractors see. They see a cold-hearted tyrant, armed with an Uzi.

In 2016, Duterte said he 'hadn't entirely abandoned his faith'. A small wooden crucifix still hangs on the wall of the bedroom of the simple house he shares with Honeylet Avanceña, chief among his mistresses, the 'First Girlfriend' in Davao. But he chose an audience of local industrialists to confide that he couldn't perform his duties and be a devout Catholic at the same time. Perhaps he detected a possible conflict of interest with the Duterte Harry style of governance. Having attended two Catholic high schools, been whipped by the deans of discipline, and lashed and crucified by his mother at home, Duterte today has little time for fornicating priests, hypocritical bishops, or the Church in general — or, for that matter, the Pope. (It was his old friend Jesus Dureza who was eventually dispatched to St Peter's in Rome to make peace with the pontiff on behalf of the president, in the wake of the son-of-a-whore-gate scandal.)

While seeking to explain that notorious papal slur, Duterte revealed that he been 'fondled' as a 14-year-old schoolboy, during confession, by a now long-dead American Jesuit priest, Father Mark Falvey. When Falvey returned to his native California in the late 1950s, he is alleged to have continued abusing children at a church on Sunset Boulevard, Hollywood, although he was never charged. In 1975, the year before Falvey died, the Jesuit Order reportedly shelled out US$16 million to settle claims of abuse involving nine American children, over a 16-year period.

It was probably the tip of the iceberg. Duterte later said that the abuse he allegedly suffered had 'to a large extent' shaped his character, his politics, and his view of the world.

'That's how we lost our innocence,' he said, adding that other former classmates at Ateneo de Davao High School had been molested by Falvey, too. Duterte said he hadn't reported being abused out of fear of what might happen.

'How could we complain?' he said. 'We were scared.'

Other experiences in those critical teenage years would profoundly mould Duterte's character. Contrary to the mythology he has assiduously fostered as the People's President — a leader who understood the problems and spoke the language of the poor — Duterte was probably the most privileged teenager in Mindanao; a spoiled brat, in many ways. For all his railing against those he branded the 'oligarchs' of Luzon's political elite, he belonged to Mindanao's political aristocracy. The man who would become the world's most vulgar, foul-mouthed head of state was none other than the son of the governor of the vast province of Davao.

Vicente Duterte, a lawyer and former city mayor from Cebu City in the Philippines' Central Visayas region, moved to Davao City and was elected to the most prominent political position in Mindanao when his son, Rodrigo, was 14. Within six years, Vicente would ascend to an even higher calling, joining the cabinet of President Ferdinand Marcos himself. As the family of the governor of Davao, the Duterte offspring — there were four of them — had it pretty good, with a household full of staff, including a cook, a driver, and a 'boy'. And there was 'security': bodyguards, with Rodrigo assigned one personally. As time went by and his busy parents increasingly absented themselves from family life, it was the bodyguard fraternity with which their eldest son increasingly spent his time.

The bodyguards were drawn from the ranks of the Philippine Constabulary, in those days a notorious unit, under the command of the Armed Forces of the Philippines and answerable to the Minister of Defense. From them, he learned the language and ways of the street, and ran wild, skipping school, sometimes for weeks on end, his absent parents apparently oblivious. What he studied instead was the coarse fighting talk, values, and mannerisms of the paramilitary cops he spent his time with. He adopted the persona of a *bugoy*, the term for 'hoodlum' in his local Bisaya language. He developed what was to become a life-long obsession with guns. He drank and smoked and slept around; often he didn't come home at all, and, if he did, he'd slip in at 4 am. He became increasingly nocturnal — and remains so to this day; he holds press conferences that begin at 1 am, and he appears groggy when he has to attend a morning function.

A large painting of the president now hangs at one end of the former dining room in the family home, down a quiet suburban street in Davao City. Duterte is posed sitting in a wood-panelled room, presumably in Malacañang Palace, and has struck a self-consciously casual position, his right hand held up to his face — a Duterte mannerism. He says he has to massage a nerve to relieve persistent neck and spinal pain from an injury he apparently sustained in a motorcycle accident — for which he also uses Fentanyl patches, a powerful synthetic opioid. He's wearing a traditional Barong Tagalog shirt with the left cuff unbuttoned, blue jeans, and Chelsea boots. His legs are crossed. The Philippine flag stands over his right shoulder, the presidential seal above his left.

The portrait lacks artistry and has the appearance of having been copied from a photograph, but it dominates the room where, long ago, his conservative governor-father ruled — and his authoritarian mother interpreted the law and meted out punishment. Duterte's sister, Eleanor, sat directly under the picture, nostalgically recalling the beatings. We had been talking about the crucifix punishment. 'My mother did the whipping, too. Flogging! Today you can't discipline your child any more. If you spank him, they call it child abuse! What child abuse? What was my mother supposed to do with him?'

'One day we are eating lunch. My father is sitting here,' said Eleanor, gesturing to the top of the family dining table. 'The phone rings. Someone answers it and says "Sir, there's a Father so-and-so who wants to talk to you."' It turned out to be no less than the director of Ateneo de Davao High School himself.

'"Governor," he says, "would you happen to know where your son is? Rodrigo. Governor, I need to tell you that he hasn't been at school for the past two months."' Eleanor's voluminous attempt to mimic her father's response was startling.

'"WHAAAAAT?"' she screeched. It had the feel of a practiced rendition of a family favourite; today this story features prominently in the presidential apocrypha.

The governor called his security chief, she said, a high-ranking officer in the Philippine Constabulary, and ordered him to go and find his son. They went to Davao police headquarters, but no one there knew anything.

'They went all over the city,' Eleanor said. 'They asked all his friends. They don't know.'

Presumably, at their suggestion, they went to every cock-fighting gallery and billiard hall. Still they couldn't find him. The governor reckoned Rodrigo would be somewhere in the city, roving round, and ordered the police to make a public announcement in city cinemas.

'So someone put a notice up and it said, *Rodrigo, if you see this notice, your father says "Go home this minute."* Finally, he shows up. It's already dark. My mother looks at him and says

"You had better answer your father to his satisfaction or you will reeeeally, reeeeeeally be in trouble." My mother is only good at making him kneel down.'

That night, the eldest son of the governor of Davao was sentenced to kneel on mung beans.

The spare room with the altar is on the right at the top of the stairs. Downstairs, in an extension of the original house, a private chapel was created for their mother, Soledad, better known as Nanay Soling, who died in 2012, aged 95. The chapel's walls are festooned with Catholic iconography, electric candles, plastic sunflowers, and statuettes of angels, Jesus, and the Blessed Virgin. Dark-wood prayer-kneelers stand on an ersatz Persian rug, and, on the wall, above the candle-cluttered altar — crowded with yet more statuettes — a clunky mural has been painted. It features the Holy Book, opened to the Ten Commandments.

'Honour thy father and they mother,' it reads. 'Thou shalt not kill. Thou shalt not commit adultery.'

Compared to such heinous crimes, Rodrigo's boyhood misdemeanours really seem quite trivial. But, after catapult-gate and the black ink on white cassock affair, it seems Rodrigo's prolonged absence from Ateneo de Davao High School was the straw that broke the camel's back. In his own version of the story, he was expelled. It sounds better to tell it like that. What seems to have actually happened is that the school, wary of the fact that they were dealing with the governor's son, begged his parents to find another school. Which, finally, they did.

'My dad was the kind of person who would never want to be humiliated or embarrassed,' said Jocelyn, the younger of the two Duterte sisters, three years Rodrigo's junior. She remembers the fallout from the incident as though it happened yesterday, and reckons it must have been at least the third time the school had called to scold the governor.

'I can remember my father turning red and going looking for him,' she said. 'He was the only one in the family who had a taste of my father's temper. He tried to give my dad time to cool off. I used to like it when my dad was so angry at him. I never saw my dad that way.'

Jocelyn told me she was a daddy's girl.

'I remember he was so angry and was holding him by the neck and practically …' She didn't finish her sentence, but instead held out her rigid, shaking, strangling hands.

Jocelyn never referred to her brother by name, only as 'the mayor' or 'the president'.

'He became a very street-smart kid,' she said. 'The mayor was exposed to the street by his bodyguards. He had his police buddies and his bodyguards, and they looked after him. He's very knowledgeable. You cannot fool him. He knows what's happening.'

Jocelyn is *bijou*, slightly built, like her brother, and unmistakably his sister. When we met, in a Manila Spanish tapas bar, she strode onto the terrace with a small entourage of 30-somethings. They comprised her own silent male bodyguard, an equally taciturn young woman in a leather jacket, and a gay 'aide' called Vince. All three wore black. Jocelyn, however, was elegantly dressed in a cream suit, forest-green blouse, diamond necklace, diamond earrings, diamond ring; every bit the governor's daughter. She had her brother's temperament, she said.

'He was bossy. A prankster. We used to fight most of the time.' She even described him as 'quite a dictator'. This, when she said it, had the same effect on me as when her elder sister told me how her brother had 'always got away with murder'. I had spontaneously guffawed as though they had made some cringe-worthy faux pas. Neither sibling registered this. Jocelyn continued, oblivious.

'We had a love-hate relationship,' she said. Jocelyn remembers her brother scaring off his sisters' would-be suitors at the gate of the family home by waving a pistol at them from inside the property. Most turned and fled. Today, Jocelyn and her brother have apparently buried the hatchet in the name of national unity, but the antipathy reached such a point that, in 2001, she went so far as to stand against him in the Davao mayoral election. Two Dutertes on the ballot. Not for the first time, big brother won. Those who know the family well say Rodrigo and Jocelyn remain sporadically at war.

Soledad Roa Gonzales, their mother, was close to many priests in the city, particularly the Jesuits. She was a teacher, and, although warmly remembered, she had a fearsome reputation — one former student said misbehaviour in class was often punished by being forced to stand outside 'and made to feel the heat of the sun'. Nanay Soling was heavily involved in both religious and civic activities; there were few local societies to which she did not belong.

Jocelyn said her mother always spoiled her brother: 'She would always defend him. But he also feared her.'

The day I met her, Jocelyn's brother had hit the national headlines for berating police who'd taken his nebulous orders in his war on drugs a stage too far. Kidnap-for-ransom rackets had been exposed.

'I was laughing,' Jocelyn told me, 'because I saw those errant policemen and he was punishing them! I saw the influence of my mother.'

The name 'Roa' is Maranao, one of the 18 indigenous tribes that comprise the largely Muslim Moro people of Mindanao. Rodrigo Roa Duterte is fiercely proud of this ancestry; less so of the Gonzales bit, which is Castilian. Nanay Soling gave Duterte his principles, Eleanor said, and his temper: 'That's the Spanish.' And he was devoted to her. In the run-up to the presidential election, he said he could not sleep without a comfort blanket given to him by his mother when he was a baby.

In Davao, Duterte keeps a personal seamstress who has worked for him since 1992 as a cook and housekeeper. Her name is Flor de Lisa Mercade Sepe; unlike her grand name, Flor is tiny, tough, rumbustious, and adoring of the man she too still calls 'the mayor'. I bumped into her by accident one evening and she regaled me with stories for more than an hour. It turned out it wasn't just one comfort blanket: they were sheets and there were several. It was Flor de Lisa's job to mend them if they tore. She pulled one of them, which she was working on, from her bag. In places, it was tissue thin, and had been mended so often that it resembled a delicate embroidered lace patchwork, meticulously and lovingly stitched.

'The mayor takes them wherever he goes in the world,' she said. 'This one's more than forty years old!'

At 3 am on 10 May 2016, as early presidential election results indicated he had an unassailable lead, the first thing Duterte did was to head straight to the family mausoleum, in Wireless Cemetery, a congested graveyard in central Davao City. He visited the tomb often, Eleanor said, 'whenever he feels like pouring his heart out to his mother, as though she's still around.'

She raised her Duterte chin and rolled her eyes. 'Mama's boy. I told you.'

There is mobile phone video footage of the tearful president-elect inside the white-walled shrine. A four-foot-high wooden crucifix stands on a small, protruding, spot-lit altar, with a little white porcelain Jesus hanging from it, crown of thorns around his head, arms outstretched, nailed to the cross. To Jesus' left, in an alcove, a portrait of Duterte's illustrious governor-father, Vicente, who'd died young of a heart attack in 1968, while serving as a member of the Marcos cabinet. To Jesus' right, the grave of Duterte's mother, Soledad Roa Gonzales Duterte. A large, gold-framed photograph of her, hanging on the wall.

It was at his mother's grave that Duterte, soon-to-be president-elect, fell apart. His Filipino fans found it extremely moving. What might have been a private moment was crowded by the press, murmuring, clattering, falling over each other inside the cramped shrine. Cameras were flashing, and his daughter, Sara — now, herself, the mayor of Davao City — filmed the scene and posted it on social media.

After crying quietly for some time, her father, dressed in his favourite red-checked, short-sleeved lumberjack-style shirt, pulls a white handkerchief from his pocket and mops his eyes as camera shutters reach a crescendo. Duterte is leaning on the altar, mumbling. His words are barely distinguishable: 'Mother, I am just a nobody,' he sobs, in Bisaya.

In the video, someone's mobile phone played a silly ring tone and broke the spell. The president-elect gathered himself, cracked a joke, then briefly rested his head on the marble slab covering the grave of his father, his quiet father, who never cursed but who had once taken him by the throat and called him '*bugoy*'. Hoodlum. The father for whom he was never going to be good enough.

When Duterte was 'expelled' from Ateneo de Davao High School he was then enrolled in Holy Cross High School in Digos, 50 miles down the road, where he lived in exile, boarding in a small, shared room, beneath the lodgings of the Canadian Brothers who ran the school. By this time, he had acquired a rebel heart. Dureza recalled the first time he had seen him — 'a young man being dragged by his father from the governor's car into the Brothers' House' — on his arrival at the school in Digos. Duterte did not excel academically. He scraped through, taking seven years to complete his secondary education. Records at the school show blank spaces in several subjects, where he was not awarded grades at all. Contemporaries from Holy Cross remember him as quiet, uninvolved in class discussions, and not interested in sports or other extra-curricular activities. The school was nothing short of a Spartan religious garrison, and the Brothers were known to be extremely strict. A young Canadian teacher was assigned to personally 'monitor' the teenaged Duterte, but his father ensured that his wayward son had an even more fearsome guardian, a former army officer-turned-mayor of Digos City, Nonito Lianos. He was a longstanding friend of the Duterte family, had four boys himself, and was feared locally for his authoritarian ways.

'Military men know discipline,' said Eleanor, 'so my father asks him, "Can I leave him with you so that he will not monkey around?" And Mayor Lianos, knowing my father like a brother, said he would treat him like his own.'

'Nonito Lianos was the disciplinarian of Digos,' said Nelson Tandug, the affable alumni affairs officer at Duterte's former school. 'He is probably where he [Duterte] got his methods from. Lianos would personally patrol the streets at night and would break the hoodlums' ribs if he caught them.'

'One night,' according to Eleanor, 'Mayor Lianos had to call on his policemen to go after Rodrigo. He had escaped! He would jump the fence,' she said. 'Where would he go? God only knows.' She said he'd told the mayor he'd gone out chasing girls.

But Duterte broke out of his Digos prison for other reasons, seemingly inspired by his no-nonsense local guardian, Nonito Lianos, to go and catch some bad guys. Dureza said there were gang wars in Digos at that time: 'We were not involved at all, we were not part of it,' he said, but Duterte was determined to find out what was going on. He wanted to track down the ring-leaders responsible for terrorising the neighbourhood. 'When he got the gang leader's name, one evening, we sneaked out, scaled the fence, and went to look for the guy who'd led the gang war.'

Dureza still seemed incredulous that he'd actually done this.

'Seriously! When he approached him — and of course he didn't know us — Rody just slapped him and said: "Do not do this again." He has always been the type who wants to punish bad guys. Even when we were not involved!'

Duterte turned tail, according to Dureza, and, with his terrified friend in tow, sprinted back to Holy Cross.

The absent parents, the horsewhip, the crucifix, and the child-abusing priest; the paramilitary bodyguards, the disciplinarian Mayor Liaños, and the simple fact that he was the governor's son, proved a volatile combination of precursors for the explosive character of Rodrigo Roa Duterte. These days, psychotherapists would speak in terms of childhood trauma and how the absence of positive male role models would have distorted the teenaged Duterte's notion of masculinity. But in those days there were no psychotherapists in Davao. By the time he'd left school, Duterte was adrift, unsure of who he was, and when he went in search of himself, no matter how noble his instincts might have been, he had a worrying set of tools at his disposal. This was a young man cut off from his own humanity; desensitised to suffering.

Many years later, in 1998, when his then wife, Elizabeth Zimmerman, a former Philippine Airlines flight attendant, was seeking annulment of their marriage, a clinical psychologist called Natividad Dayan was commissioned as part of the proceedings, to assess Duterte's character. Dr Dayan had a distinguished professional record as a former president of the International Council of Psychologists. The report she produced was an official court document, and although it was drawn from Elizabeth's own testimony, many of the observations and analyses her report contains chime with those who have studied Duterte closely over decades and who include old friends, priests, politicians, human rights activists, lawyers, and his many victims. They believe that Duterte's behaviour has always been, and remains, consistent with her diagnosis.

'He is suffering from a Narcissistic Personality Disorder, with aggressive features,' Dr Dayan concluded, citing what she characterised as 'his gross indifference, insensitivity, and self-centredness, his grandiose sense of self and entitlement, his manipulative behaviors, his lies and his deceits, as well as his pervasive tendency to demean, humiliate others and violate their rights and feelings.' In summary: 'Rodrigo's personality disturbance, which constitutes his psychological incapacity, is deemed serious, incurable and with antecedents.'

In other words, the document acknowledges that his condition was judged to have existed prior to his marriage to Elizabeth. A section of the conclusion of this clinical analysis, which stated that his indifference to others was 'heightened by lack of capacity for remorse or guilt' was leaked to a Philippine national TV news station a month before the 2016 presidential poll. It caused widespread alarm about Duterte's mental health; newspaper commentators warned that the Philippines, if it were not careful, would end up with a psychopath as president.

The full report describes Duterte as 'a highly impulsive individual who has difficulty controlling his urges and emotions. He is unable to reflect on the consequences of his actions ... For all his wrongdoings, he tends to rationalize and feel justified. Hence, he seldom feels a sense of guilt or remorse.'

The document details Duterte's 'exploitative' and 'manipulative' behaviour within his 'miserable and unhappy' 25-year marriage. It claims he acted in his own 'self-serving interests' to 'boost his political career'. It talks of his volatile temper, argumentativeness, and his provocative, bullying nature. Elizabeth testified that he 'blackmailed' her when he learned of a previous relationship she had had before their marriage, in which she alleged her then 'boyfriend' had raped her. This, she said, was despite her husband's own well known philandering and a string of extra-marital affairs. As mayor of Davao, Duterte, she said, would 'flaunt his affairs and would bring his girlfriends to public and social functions' while continuing to deny his infidelities. He 'humiliated Elizabeth' by revealing the secrets of her past to his friends.

Duterte did not contest the contents of the document or that it was genuine. His supporters pointed out that for the annulment to proceed and for the marriage to be terminated, 'he acted chivalrously in permitting his reputation to be trashed'. His only daughter, Sara, who was to succeed him as Mayor of Davao, but is known to be much closer to her mother, Elizabeth, than to her father, defended him by saying that nowhere in the court documents did it say that Duterte was not fit to lead. It sounded a little half-hearted.

When I raised the annulment papers with his sister, Jocelyn, her response was: 'The mayor accepted everything, the talk about abuse — the mayor accepted everything.' It was as though she too agreed that there wasn't much to contest. The conversation drifted back to their mother, Soledad.

'If my mother was around, he would never [have] become president,' she said. 'My mother would never agree. Because of his character. Because of his character,' she repeated. 'Because of the personal aspects, you know.'

She paused, then laughed.

'It's bad enough being politically exposed, but in the presidency, that is something else. I mean, they dig deeper and deeper and deeper. My mother said, "No. You are not the kind [to be] president." But his being president is a matter of destiny.' On that point, the two Duterte sisters saw eye to eye.

Hillary Clinton had claimed Donald Trump was 'temperamentally unfit' to be the US president, and leading American psychologists came forward to offer their analysis confirming this assessment. He, too, showed signs, they said, of 'malignant narcissism'. By way of character, there are striking common denominators between the two men. Particular temperamental attributes — all warning signs of a narcissistic or sociopathic personality — surfaced again and again in conversation with Filipinos who had known, worked with, tangled with, or been crushed by Duterte; a master-manipulator, mercurial, scheming, impulsive, and ruthlessly ambitious; a misogynist. These descriptors came up repeatedly, supported by sometimes chilling stories. Many pointed to a superiority complex, but the same people talked of how thin-skinned Duterte was too, unable to take criticism, lashing out at anyone unfortunate enough to deliver a perceived slight. Much can be ascribed to nature, but, in Duterte's case, nurture — or absence of it — had a clear and critical impact in the shaping of the man who would be king.

The political populism of the US and Philippine presidents might be of a different brand, but Duterte has appealed to fear and anger in a remarkably similar way to Trump, if taking it a few steps further. Duterte specialises in a similar politics of anxiety, building on collective fears — and popular demand to punish bad guys. The US media, covering the Philippine presidential election, quickly found a journalistic shorthand for comparing the two leaders: Duterte Harry was adorned with a new title: 'the Trump of Asia'. Whether they read him as a messiah or as a tyrant, he made great copy, and, like Trump, he rarely disappointed.

3

TWO SMOKING BARRELS

At the vanguard of the People Power Revolution that toppled Ferdinand Marcos was the spiritual leader of Filipino Catholics, the late Archbishop of Manila, wickedly named Cardinal Sin. This was his real name and he revelled in it, reportedly greeting people at his home with 'Welcome to the house of Sin!' Most Filipinos are known by their nicknames, and to use someone's given name usually sounds ludicrously formal. The Philippines does nicknames like nowhere else on earth. Some are contractions or corruptions of their actual names, others refer to what someone looks like, the circumstances of their birth, their foibles, character traits, or their gender, some sound as though they're onomatopoeic, others are just random.

There's Bongbong Marcos, the ex-president's son, a former senator who challenged the result of the 2016 vice-presidential election, where he came a close second. There's president Duterte's personal gatekeeper at Malacañang Palace, who's just Bong, but combined with his surname, he becomes Bong Go.

Secretary Bong Go , a selfie-king who has now photobombed just about every occasion in which his political master meets someone famous, from Trump to Xi Jinping. There are BimBims, TingTings, Bing-Bongs, Ding-Dongs, and Pings. And plain Dongs. One of the president's two younger brothers is Blue Boy, indicating a possible problem at birth.

Girlie is common, as is Boy. Sometimes you bump into Boys in their seventies. There are Inkys and Pinkys and Ballsys and Babes — and don't think the latter is exclusively female; Babe was probably just the youngest in a big family. In the last administration, there was a male cabinet secretary called Babes Singson, a grandfather. Apple Pie is not that uncommon; there's Honey Pie, Honey Boy (more unusual, but true), Honeylet (the president's main girlfriend), Honey Rose (Bongbong's press secretary), Daffodil, Pepsi, BumBum, and Boo. People are so used to these names that it's only foreigners who find them amusing. In March 2017, Sara Duterte, Mayor of Davao and the president's daughter, nicknamed her newborn baby 'Stonefish' — apparently because she likes the sea. His real name, Marko Digong, will never get a look-in.

President Rodrigo Roa Duterte is never referred to as 'Duterte Harry' or 'The Punisher' in everyday speech. He is the original Digong — not to be confused with the curious, rare marine mammal, the dugong, found in the pirate-infested waters off Mindanao. Newspaper headlines announce that Digong's done this or Digong's done that ... 'Digong threatens martial law.' His supporters call him Tatay Digong (Father Digong), which is mischievously twisted to Katay Digong by his opponents. In Tagalog, *katay* means 'butcher'.

For a while, on Facebook and Twitter, Filipinos toyed with other possible monikers for President Rodrigo 'Digong' Duterte, including P-Rod, P-Gong, and P-Diggy. The previous president,

Benigno Aquino III, is called Noynoy, but when president was rechristened P-Noy by his supporters, a play on *Pinoy*, the demonym for all Filipinos. It was a little bit clever; P-Rod just sounded rude. At high school, Duterte was known as Dut, but Duts has now been sequestrated by his opponents, delivered with sardonic chumminess ... 'Did you hear what Duts has gone and said now?' One sobriquet that did stick was DU30, which his electioneering team came up with. Phonetically, it only really works if you're from County Kerry, but still, you see it everywhere, from bumper stickers (where it's accompanied by his tough-guy clenched fist logo) to the embroidered monogram on presidential Polo shirts.

P-Diggy (unfortunately, that one never did catch on) hates being called 'Sir'. For someone who thrives on adulation, he eschews reverential titles and detests sycophancy. He prefers to be addressed as 'Mayor', and, in press conferences, was still insisting on this well into his presidency: the Mayor of Malacañang.

In the flesh, the mayor of the Philippines is diminutive. When he eventually strolls nonchalantly into a news conference, three hours after it was meant to have started, he slouches and looks stooped. His body language is Putin-esque; he appears permanently bored. He adopts, consciously or otherwise, a devil-may-care posture, as though weary at having to do this at all. He is almost always informally dressed, with an open-neck shirt and jeans. A retinue of palace staff and officials tend to occupy the front row to clap, laugh at his jokes, and frown at perceived disrespect from journalists; communications staff fuss around the fringes. Usually (in possible homage to Colonel Gaddafi), a beauty queen who is also a cop, called Sophia Loren Deliu, will be keeping an eye on things, too. Sophia Loren (who entered a beauty pageant as a serving police woman, and won) is one of several female officers in the presidential security detail.

But what Digong lacks in stature, he more than makes up for in garrulous feistiness, and, once he starts, he doesn't stop. What attracts attention to him is not really charisma; it's more a macabre fascination about who he is going to target now or what sweeping statement he will come out with next. Yet Duterte's supporters talk of how, in Mindanao storytellers' tradition, 'he can mesmerise a room'. There is certainly an assumption that his audience hangs on his every word. It's hard to tell, given that traditions of Asian filial piety demand that courtesy be shown to elders even if, in Duterte's case, his vulgar outbursts are about as un-Asian as it's possible to be.

Journalists assigned to these press conferences are required to arrive at the appointed time, then wait. The president is always, at the minimum, an hour late. At a press conference in Davao City, scheduled to start at 10 pm, Duterte turned up three hours later. Another, in Malacañang, began at 3 am. Reporters are then required to sit through at least an hour, sometimes two, of Duterte ad-libbing about his thoughts on life, drug lords, colonialism, women, insurgencies, corruption, and the universe. He threatens to kill people, curses, and drops in smutty jokes, rambling like a drunk in a bar. In a jumbled mixture of English and Tagalog, he meanders randomly between subjects as diverse as martial law and plate tectonics, then segues between the benefits of Viagra and angry expletive-ridden sideswipes at critics of his drugs war. Only when he finally runs out things to say unprompted are the press permitted to ask focused questions. These rarely elicit a focused response — and, again, the Q&A phase will last an hour or more. If a western politician were to act in this manner, holding court like some medieval monarch, journalists would vote with their feet after 20 minutes. Not in the Philippines. Presidential 'speeches' are later transcribed by some unfortunate minion in Duterte's communications team and are made available online, for all to marvel at.

As Channel 4 News Asia correspondent, it fell to me to cover a number of these dire, but sometimes entertaining, events, both in Manila and in Davao, where the atmosphere is markedly different. After winning the presidency, Duterte continued to spend most weekends in Davao, where he is on home turf, with a pliant, respectful local press corps, long used to his habits and his style. The national press are more hostile, although they too deferentially sit it out, long into the night. They began on a similar footing to their American counterparts under President Donald J. Trump. In the early days, things were tense with Digong threatening to 'kill journalism', and casting the profession as corrupt, characterising journalists as 'vultures'. Duterte felt, to some degree justifiably, that the Filipino vultures had failed to pay sufficient attention to his election campaign until he belatedly topped the opinion polls. As to the foreign press, his friends and his sisters all said he felt maligned, misrepresented, and misunderstood.

Once, when a respected Filipino journalist inquired into Duterte's health after persistent rumours had circulated that the president had a serious illness, he lashed out at what he believed to be impertinence, declaring journalists 'sons of whores'.

He asked of the reporter: 'How is your wife's vagina? Is it smelly? Or not smelly? Give me a report.'

This got a good laugh from his audience, at a gathering in a crocodile farm in Davao. A few days earlier, he had said that journalists who took bribes deserved to die.

'Just because you're a journalist, you are not exempted from assassination, if you are a son of a bitch.'

On that occasion, he was responding to a question about what he would do to protect journalists in a country where nearly 180 have been killed since Marcos was ousted, making the Philippines one of the most dangerous places in the world to work as a journalist. While not apologising, he did later backtrack: 'I never said that killing journalists is justified.' By the end of October 2017, five journalists had been murdered since Duterte's inauguration. The motives proved hard to establish, but at least one had been planning to file a newspaper report on the drugs war.

Like Trump, Duterte is highly sensitive to bad reviews. After months of being relentlessly lambasted by the president over critical coverage of his drugs war, in November 2017, the *Philippine Daily Inquirer* — one of the leading broadsheet newspapers in the Philippines — was sold to Ramon Ang, a business tycoon and friend of the president. The liberal newspaper's coverage of the war on drugs has continued and its more outspoken commentators have not softened their tone. The pro-Duterte Congress also threatened not to renew the franchise of the biggest TV network ABS-CBN, which had allegedly refused to air his political advertisements before the 2016 election. The same network had been shut down by Marcos in 1972 and its president imprisoned; the station finally went back on air again during the People Power revolution 14 years later. In January 2018 the Security and Exchange Commission revoked *Rappler*'s licence, accusing the online news site of violating laws over foreign ownership. Maria Ressa, its CEO, denied this and condemned the SEC's decision as 'a concerted effort to turn journalism into a crime'. *Rappler* had previously accused the government of 'weaponising' the internet through the deployment of pro-Duterte bloggers and trolls. The president had, in turn, branded *Rappler* a 'fake news outlet', and his spokesman said he had every 'right to be angry and curse the press'.

But Duterte's disgruntlement with sections of the Philippine press are not entirely without basis: some Filipino reporters have indeed been corrupted and are susceptible to influence peddlers. Journalism is a very poorly paid profession in the Philippines. As one newspaper editor, with decades in the business, but who asked to remain anonymous, put it: 'In this country, we have a culture of "envelopmental journalism". Often, at press conferences, there is a little envelope, containing a "gift", in return for promotional favours. The temptation is not easy to resist.' They're all at it, the editor said — congressmen, senators, governors, and mayors. And Mayor Duterte Harry, it is widely alleged by insiders, was no exception, with scores of Davao journalists in his pocket, offered exclusive access or foreign trips in exchange for favourable coverage.

The foreign press is not, I discovered, entirely without blame — although their pecuniary dilemmas come in a different guise. Unlike other countries in this region, 'chequebook journalism' prevails in the Philippines, where interviewees are not always minded to divulge something for nothing and past precedent has now made things harder. On one notable and unbelievably frustrating occasion, I was forced to walk away from a well-placed contact, a whistle-blower I had sought to cultivate, because of a last-minute demand for a fistful of dollars in exchange for information. Over the months, I was to learn of other questionable transactions between foreign journalists (from various countries) and their sources. 'Reimbursements' to sources are a grey area, however, and some journalists take a less Manichean view when it comes to reimbursing 'costs' to sometimes extremely poor people. The danger is when reimbursements for time, travel, and expenses mutate into paid inducements to talk, which, in the view of most journalists, crosses a professional ethical boundary and undermines the credibility of claims made. To the best of my knowledge, none of the reports I have cited draws on the testimony of paid sources.

There were no Manila envelopes stuffed full of pesos on show in Malacañang Palace late one night, when President Duterte called a news conferences after a notoriously grim episode in his war on drugs. Predictably, the president was running late, so, as the Philippine press corps gossiped and cameramen elbowed for position, there was time to take in the surroundings. We had been ushered into the grand wood-panelled Heroes' Hall, a large reception room decorated with elaborate glass chandeliers, ornate mirrors, and portraits of the 16 presidents of the independent Philippine Republic, independent from the United States since the Treaty of Manila was signed in 1946.

On the wall to my immediate right was an oil painting of a beaming, fresh-faced Ferdinand Marcos, who, after his overthrow, died ignominiously in exile in Hawaii in 1989. The dead despot spent the next 27 years in a glass box in his home province, attended by his loving widow, Imelda (whose nickname for her husband was 'Andy'). His badly embalmed body had reportedly begun to 'melt' by the time Duterte ordered his burial in Manila, in the Cemetery of Heroes, five months into his presidency. (It's now believed that the body on display for all those years was actually a wax effigy, not actually Andy's corpse, as the family have always claimed.)

The decision to glorify such a controversial and disgraced figure, and caving in to the wishes of the Marcos family, sent shock waves around the country and triggered protests in Manila, but Duterte got away with it. He has openly expressed admiration for Marcos, once describing him as the country's best president, and on another occasion saying that martial law under Marcos had been 'very good'.

Back in the pantheon of heroes, and incongruously juxtaposed next to Marcos, was the portrait of Corazon 'Cory' Aquino, who described herself as a simple housewife, but who became the face of the popular revolt that forced the US-backed dictator to flee. In the painting, she's wearing yellow, the symbolic colour of her revolution. In the dark days of martial law, yellow was the colour of courage. Cory was the widow of Benigno 'Ninoy' Aquino Jr, a prominent senator who led opposition to martial law and who was famously assassinated making his way down the steps from a plane at Manila airport in 1983. Their son, Benigno 'Noynoy' Aquino III was, like his mother, president of the Philippines, and his portrait also hangs in the hall.

At the front of Heroes' Hall, to the right of the long white-clothed table set up in anticipation of Digong's eventual arrival, the next portrait was of President Fidel Ramos. FVR, as he's popularly known, was Marcos' military chief-of-staff. As Marcos began to look vulnerable, Ramos had bravely switched sides to join Cory's People Power insurrection. When she became president, he became her army chief-of-staff.

Duterte was known to hold Ramos in high regard, and craved his endorsement, which in the run-up to the election he received. He appointed Ramos his special envoy to China but then, not long into the Duterte regime, the much-venerated FVR switched sides again, calling Duterte a 'huge disappointment and a let-down'. Ramos attacked him over his war on drugs, the extra-judicial killings, his handling of US relations, and his uncivilised language. Later, the ageing turncoat condemned Duterte for what he called 'the sneaky burial' of Marcos as well. FVR was careful to tell Filipinos that, regardless, they should continue to support Duterte; however, the criticism must have stung.

Across the room hung the portrait of Joseph 'Erap' Estrada, the actor-turned-president, posing with the air of a *bon viveur*, grinning raffishly down at our assembled pack of journalists from behind his thin, black, mobster-moustache. Erap had been a film star who played tough guys. As a politician, he was also a populist who turned out not to be as popular as he'd thought. After just over two years in office, he was ousted by a second People Power revolt before his impeachment trial in the Senate was over. Estrada was eventually sentenced to life in prison for plunder, but was pardoned by his successor, Gloria Arroyo. Estrada ran for the top job again in 2010, but lost to Cory Aquino's son, Noynoy. So instead Erap stood for mayor of Manila, and won. Erap's son, Jose 'Jinggoy' Estrada, a senator, was also charged with plunder, and was jailed in 2014.

Digong was now two hours late and the journalists were growing restless and hungry. Packs of lukewarm chicken rice were eventually handed out by palace staff. A member of the Presidential Communications Office was doing the rounds, finding out who was planning to ask questions. I was asked twice if I would, but on this occasion, I declined. Past experience of being a lightening rod for presidential invective had made me wary. This time, as the only foreign correspondent in the room, I wanted to listen and observe, surrounded by these portraits of past presidents that illustrated what Duterte meant when he'd talked acerbically of the Manila-centric dynastic elites who had come to dominate national politics in the decades since Philippine independence. No wonder he was welcomed as an outsider from the south. Fresh blood.

President Arroyo was the next hero along from the pardoned plunderer, Estrada. In her portrait, she's wearing a white dress with such excessively large shoulder pads that she looks like an angel. The daughter of another Philippine president, whose portrait hangs diametrically opposite hers, Gloria grew up in Malacañang Palace. As president, her government was repeatedly accused of corruption, and she survived two bizarre mutinies that had sought to draw public attention to this issue. After leaving office, Gloria, while serving in Congress, was accused of electoral fraud, indicted, bailed, and then re-arrested on charges of plunder while serving as president. She spent five years in 'hospital detention' before being acquitted by the Supreme Court. She remains an elected congressional representative.

Arroyo and Duterte get on swimmingly. In 2002, as president, she had appointed him the presidential anti-crime consultant. Human Rights Watch openly criticised her for 'taking security advice from someone who openly advocates murder'. Once, President Arroyo had visited Davao, where she rode pillion on the mayor's low-slung motorcycle and squealed in delight like an excited teenager, according to one witness. He, in turn, was guest of honour at her seventieth birthday dinner in April 2017, which he attended with his girlfriend, Honeylet, and their daughter, Veronica. Duterte quickly became the centre of attention, serenading the former president with a rendition of his favourite song, 'Ikaw', the same drippingly sentimental Filipino love-ballad with which he would later serenade Trump. There are numerous versions of President Duterte crooning this available on YouTube. He continued to hog the limelight at Gloria's bash by giving an impromptu speech which promoted his war on drugs. Strangely, the former president used her big occasion to present Duterte with a cake — he had turned 72 the previous week. On top of it was a 10-inch-high icing sculpture of a helmetless easy rider bearing a striking resemblance to the president. His motorbike had the number plate DU30.

Cory's son Noynoy separates Gloria from Digong on the august wood-panelled walls; his portrait hangs directly opposite that of his mother. Noynoy, a liberal, stood on an anti-corruption ticket. It is said that his election victory was buoyed by collective nostalgia, as it followed the death of his revered mother. He remained fairly popular, in part due to the Philippine economy growing faster during his time in office than that of any other country in the region. But his administration was hit by a super-typhoon (which it was slow to respond to), a massacre (of Philippine police in Mindanao, at the hands of Islamist rebels), and, most damaging for a president who had championed 'good governance', a corruption scandal. Rodrigo Duterte, circling above like a vulture himself, detected the unmistakable olfactory essence of political decay.

Duterte made much of a showy police raid ordered by Noynoy and executed by his justice secretary, Leila de Lima, on the national Bilibid Prison complex in late 2014. It turned out that inside the prison, convicted drug lords were 'living like kings', as she put it, Escobar-style, in luxury air-conditioned cells — or 'villas' as some described them. They had stripper joints, Jacuzzis, and marble-tiled bathrooms; there was a live-music stage and a mirror ball, expensive whisky, stacks of cash, and a ready supply of methamphetamines. De Lima's raiders found mobile phones, computers, guns, and grenades; the drug lords even had sugar-gliders — tiny flying foxes — as pets, as well as a supply of inflatable sex-dolls, which was particularly disturbing, given the fact that they could smuggle prostitutes in and out of Bilibid at will. Meanwhile, petty criminals and drug addicts were crammed into squalid cells and had no blow-up sex-dolls to play with.

The justice secretary claimed that the Bilibid prison raid illustrated her determination to crack down on a corrupt system, but her investigation into these drug lords' incarcerated high life would come back to haunt her and eventually lead to her downfall. Leila de Lima, in a previous incarnation, had headed the national Human Rights Commission, and investigated Duterte's links with the Davao Death Squad. Being a vindictive man, Digong did not forget. Even though it was de Lima who had exposed the Bilibid jail scandal, Duterte painted it as the prime example of how Noynoy Aquino's government was soft on crime, inept, and in league with the criminal drug lords themselves. This chimed with public perception. They were the drug lords, Duterte claimed, Noynoy and de Lima.

Duterte's freshly painted portrait is the last one in the heroes' collection. A gold-plated statue of a bucking bronco sits below it, on a console. Like the others, it is framed in mahogany, with a gold laurel trim, and is topped with a golden presidential seal. The mayor of the Philippines, Rodrigo Roa Duterte, is standing, arms folded, sleeves rolled up, surveying the scene. For once, he's actually grinning — and no wonder. A Davao bugoy had actually made it to Malacañang Palace.

At 11.30 pm, a frisson of expectancy spread through Heroes' Hall; cameramen jumped to attend to their equipment, a hush descended, and in walked the president, scowling. He wore jeans, a black fleece over a white t-shirt, and, on top, an unbuttoned cowboy-style blue denim shirt, sleeves rolled up. This was intended to be quite a show, a 'joint-command' press conference; he was accompanied by two cabinet ministers and the chiefs of the army and police. His hefty executive secretary, Salvador 'Bingbong' Medialdea, sat to Duterte's right, and next to Bingbong, former army intelligence officer and feted scourge of communist rebels, General Eduardo 'Ed' Año — known to everyone just by his surname. Flanking Digong on his left, his defence secretary, General Delfin 'Del' Lorenzana. Next to Del, the chief superintendent and director general of the Philippine National Police, Ronald 'Bato' dela Rosa, the mayor's former top cop from Davao, where, like others before him, he had failed to solve a single one of the 1400 death squad murders in the city.

Duterte clearly wasn't happy, and kicked things off in style.

'Dumlao, you son of a whore!' he snarled into the live-TV cameras. 'You've got 24 hours to surrender, then the bounty comes into effect. Dead or alive. Dead better.'

This performance was ripe for satire and impersonation, but there's no equivalent of 'Saturday Night Live' in the Philippines. Duterte is even more thin-skinned than Trump, and some of those who've caused offence to him in days gone by have ended up with a bullet in their head, rather than simply being the target of a snarky tweet. The cast of men behind the long table sat stony-faced, glaring, except the burly, bald Bato (whose nickname means 'rock'). His eyes were pinned on the ceiling, staring intently at one of the chandeliers.

'I will not sacrifice Bato,' the sheriff of Malacañang was saying, emphatically. Bato had had the sense to tender his resignation — for good reason.

The president said he had been 'embarrassed' by the actions of corrupt cops in his war on drugs and was going to call the whole thing off. This was big news indeed. He put a 5 million peso (US$100,000) price on the head of the anti-drugs police superintendent, that son of a whore, Raphael Dumlao. He was said to have been the instigator and ringleader of the abduction and murder — inside the anti-narcotics building at national police headquarters — of a South Korean business executive, Jee Ick-joo.

The Korean's widow, unaware that her husband was dead — strangled, cremated at a funeral parlour owned by a former policemen, his ashes flushed down a toilet — paid a 5 million peso ransom to his 'kidnappers'. She was also unaware that these supposed kidnappers were all serving policemen. There was no evidence that Mr Jee had anything to do with illegal drugs. The sordid story made headlines for days. Bato's 'sacrifice' had never seemed that likely, though; shortly after the sordid story broke, Digong attended Bato's birthday bash at police HQ, right next to where Mr Jee had been killed. Accompanying the president were cabinet ministers, the house speaker of Congress, and Senator Manny Pacquiao, the boxer. They were photographed laughing and toasting each other, and posing for selfies. You got the impression they were going to tough-out the bad PR.

At the press conference, Duterte accused Dumlao of 'putting the reputation of the police in shambles' [sic]. Later, after a stab at the Americans, he again called Dumlao a son of a whore and re-publicised the offer of 5 million pesos for his scalp.

'I'll give it to anybody who can bring him in. Dead. That's okay. Son of a bitch,' the sheriff said.

None of the reporters batted an eyelid. The tough-guy talk was just washing over them now. As the president spoke, the 'beleaguered' Superintendent Bato levered himself out of his chair and approached Digong, from the left. Leaning down, he spoke quietly into the president's ear, but what he said was picked up by a microphone. Bato informed him that Raphael Dumlao was already in police custody. Duterte's expression did not change. As Bato slipped back to his seat, the president continued to rant about drug lords, corrupt cops, and killing. '*Putang ina*', he said, '*putang ina*'. Son of a whore. It wasn't directed at anyone.

Duterte said his 'success' as mayor of Davao had rested on good men like Bato, and that making him the fall guy for what the press now tagged the 'Korean kidnap-slay' debacle would not help his planned purge of the police, who, he said, were rotten to the core. Bent cops were up to their necks in the drugs trade, he said. Operation Double Barrel, as the police operation in his war on drugs was known, would be put on ice until tainted personnel had been cleansed. It wasn't to be the last time he would buckle to public alarm and suspend operations ... temporarily. Duterte said a new Narcotics Command would be set up to weed out bad cops, who would be rounded up and dispatched to fight jihadists in Mindanao — a threat that would put the fear of God into them. He said he would issue an executive order bringing the Armed Forces of the Philippines onto the front line of his war on drugs, the biggest national security threat the country faced. But, he said, there was no need for him to declare martial law. I had a sense, like almost everyone else in the room, that he'd just forgotten to say the word 'yet'.

Duterte said he had been over-optimistic when he promised to eradicate the drugs menace in three months or even six. Pressed by a persistent Filipina reporter as to how long his drugs war would continue, he said it would last until his last day in office. The temporary suspension meant deaths in police 'shoot-outs' stopped straight away; 'vigilante' hits continued as before, and the body count rose, remorselessly. Within less than a month, Jee Ick-joo's 'kidnap-slay' was largely forgotten, Bato's boys were back out of the sin-bin, and the war was back on, relaunched, like a blockbuster Hollywood sequel, as Operation Double Barrel Reloaded.

In April 2017, the Philippine human rights commission was tipped off about an unofficial secret jail, concealed behind a bookcase in a police station in Tondo slum, which I had once visited. A dozen men and women had been held there for more than a week in disgusting, overcrowded conditions without sanitation, lighting, or any ventilation. The photographs were horrendous, showing the detainees crammed into a narrow, dank, dark corridor. They claimed they had been abducted and held as drugs suspects, tortured by police who, they said, had demanded bribes of between US$800 and US$4000 to secure their freedom. Human rights groups said the discovery was just the latest indication that police were exploiting Duterte's war against drugs for their personal gain. The response of the national police chief, Bato, to the discovery of the secret cell was nothing short of extraordinary.

'My officers have done nothing wrong,' he said, before criticising the human rights commission investigators for raiding the police station 'for show'. Bato said that as long as his officers hadn't hurt or extorted money from the detainees, 'it's okay by me'. Sure enough, the following month, a police internal affairs investigation concluded that it hadn't been a secret cell at all, that none of the detainees had been tortured, and that the cell was only being used as a spill-over from the overcrowded holding cells.

In the case of the secret jail, the police station commander had been temporarily suspended while the internal affairs investigators did their work. Duterte was reported to have said he would 'look into it', too — but nothing appears to have come of that at all. Following Jee Ick-joo's kidnap and murder, Duterte had gone to some lengths to make it appear as if the police had been punished, staging a shaming stunt for the media. A group of allegedly 'rogue' policemen were assembled by Bato and then publicly humiliated by the president, in front of live TV cameras. For the 13 minutes of this savage dressing down, Rodrigo Duterte became his mother, who he had recently consulted at her tomb. There were meant to have been 400 'errant cops', but only 228 turned up at Malacañang to be yelled at.

The president said he would order them to clean up Manila's filthy Pasig River; he called them 'idiots' and 'sons of bitches', and drew on his most colourful epithets. The men stood in formation, heads bowed, concentrating on holding in their bulging paunches. Duterte challenged them to a gunfight, warned they would be next on the hit list for street executions, then said they would be sent to an island off Mindanao which is the stronghold of Islamist militants as punishment. The 54 'crooked cops' who were eventually flown to the jihadist hotbed down south complained that the only crime they were guilty of was turning up late for work. The Pasig River remains filthy and polluted.

Operation Double Barrel Reloaded, meanwhile, was now to be led by the Philippine Drug Enforcement Agency — which had just 1800 officers, nationwide — and backed up by Bato's 170,000-strong Philippine National Police, less the 54 unfortunates in Mindanao. Under Duterte's revised strategy, the military, whose job was to contain these jihadist insurgencies, would now be brought into the war against drugs to provide support in 'hostile' situations.

General Año, commander of the Armed Forces of the Philippines (until October 2017), had remained completely silent and poker-faced throughout the Malacañang news conference. In the days that followed, he is understood to have requested the president's orders in writing — twice — which suggested a serious level of concern in military high command about the army's looming embroilment in civilian policing. Nonetheless, he began work on setting up a battalion-sized military task force of up to 5000 troops. This move was watched warily by Duterte's own army of critics, who warned that it was the thin end of the wedge. The Philippine Armed Forces has a long and undistinguished record in regard to extra-judicial killings, particularly involving the violent deaths of cadre from the communist New People's Army.

During his early presidency, Duterte visited more than 20 army camps in quick succession; more, in fact, than any other leader in Philippine history. It was an all-out charm offensive. If he really did have a plan up his sleeve to declare martial law, a notion he had begun to float, he was going to need his generals on side. In February 2017, President Duterte, as their commander-in-chief, was the guest of honour of the alumni association at the Philippine Military Academy in the northern mountain city of Baguio. Thousands of current and former PMA students were there to salute Duterte, who was perched in the stand, surrounded by top brass. Those marching past him included officers who had implemented martial law under Marcos, and those who'd helped end it — and others, serving now. National TV stations carried the whole event live. The bracing mountain morning air meant Duterte could wear his big black leather jacket, which he accessorised with aviator shades. He looked less like an airman than a cross between a biker and a drug lord. He also looked bleary. Digong is a creature of the night. He does not do mornings.

General Año was there, of course, as were Bingbong, Del, and the former army chief, now national security advisor, the grandly named General Hermogenes Esperon, or 'Jun' for short. On his tour of army bases, Duterte made sure he spoke to troops about his anti-drugs offensive, as though on an evangelical mission to convert them to his cause and convince the army's rank and file that his was the only war in town (well, at that stage, at least). His Baguio Military Academy speech predictably followed suit: the first thing he said was that illegal drugs was the biggest threat facing the nation. It was always the same message, ramrodding home the 'staggering' dimensions of the drugs 'pandemic'. In another address to newly appointed senior officers, Duterte repeatedly told them how proud he was of them. He actually stated, doubtless aware of the perception, that when he'd toured the military camps, 'I was not cultivating or propagating any loyalty for me'. But that, as everybody knew, was exactly what Duterte Harry had been doing — and for good reason.

His known links as mayor of Davao with communist insurgent leaders, together with his political 'pivot' away from America — and his hostility to continued close cooperation with the US military — had led to an uneasy relationship between the commander-in-chief and his army commanders, who generally hate communists and love America. Because of his political proximity to prominent leftists, Duterte had sold himself as uniquely positioned to strike a peace deal with the Communists after 50 years of war, during which time an estimated 30,000 had been killed. But he had to be careful not to appear too close.

Duterte's political enemies — including an ex-military senator, one of the ringleaders of both mutinies against former President Gloria Arroyo — were already hard at work trying to convince the army brass that their new commander-in-chief was a communist plant, a mole inside Malacañang itself. The on-off nature of ceasefires and peace talks began to look choreographed, stage-managed, as though designed to dispel such conspiratorial nonsense and to help cement relations with General Año. With Año in particular, the president had a lot of work to do.

Less than a year before he became president, Duterte hosted a 'hero's funeral', as it was described in the local press at the time, in Davao City, for the New People's Army leader Leoncio 'Parago' Pitao, who also had a 5 million peso bounty on his head. As incredulous armed forces commanders looked on, the then mayor permitted thousands of NPA insurgents to remove their weapons and enter the city to attend the funeral — which he then spoke at, feting the dead communist insurgent leader. He was even quoted in a local newspaper as saying that he shared Parago's political views. Parago had been killed in a jungle ambush by scout rangers belonging to the army's 10th Infantry Division, whose commander was a certain Major General Eduardo Año.

Shortly after coming to power, Duterte requested and received a record five-fold increase in the presidential Intelligence Fund, a kitty intended for intelligence gathering and which can be used confidentially, at presidential discretion, for things like bounties and undercover operations. Disbursements from the Intelligence Fund are not itemised, and unless reported by agencies in receipt of the money, they are not audited. The huge increase requested by the president was ascribed, by Secretary Bingbong, to security costs associated with hosting a regional summit — and to the war on drugs. The US$50 million Intelligence Fund, augmented by a US$110 million contingency fund, essentially operates as the president's personal slush fund. In the view of western diplomats in Manila and Filipinos alarmed at the lack of transparency, it has enabled Duterte to buy goodwill and lavish 'gifts', rewards, and bonuses to buy the loyalty of those he needs onside. This is the way he has always worked.

Duterte's rising confidence in the support of the Armed Forces of the Philippines was accompanied by ever more frequent references to martial law in his rambling speeches. One in particular stood out. It took place at the Marco Polo Hotel in Davao City, owned by Carlos 'Sonny' Dominguez, another of Duterte's old schoolmates. Sonny is now his finance secretary. That evening, early in 2017, the hotel was hosting an event for the Davao City Chamber of Commerce and Industry. The former mayor was keynote speaker. He looked particularly stooped and bored, but livened up when he reached the podium. He improvised from the very start, discarding the speech his team had prepared for him, and homed straight in on drugs, crime, and law and order.

In a scattered archipelago, he said, you have to have a strong president. His audience was nodding. All these people talking about me lengthening my stay, talking about martial law — 'It's bullshit,' Duterte said, claiming he really didn't even want to be president at all, as though it was a burden he had reluctantly shouldered for the good of the nation he loved. He had no need to declare martial law, he said. And then came one of those Duterte 'buts'. Having mused publicly about martial law several times before, he had clearly decided that now was the moment to push the boat out a little further.

'You know I have to protect the Filipino people,' he said, patriotically. 'It's my duty. And I tell you now, if I have to declare martial law, I will declare it. I will declare martial law to preserve my nation, period.' He linked it to the *shabu* crystal meth pandemic, claiming there were, as he put it, 'Four million slaves ... That's why I said "Do not go into this thing or I will kill you." *Putang ina*, son of a whore. I will really kill you.' He said if the situation continued to deteriorate, he would declare martial law if he wanted to. His audience of industrialists stared straight ahead, their expressions giving nothing away about what they felt about this Davaoeño hero's demagogic inclinations.

The former mayor didn't stop there. Next, he pointed out his favourite 'loophole' in Cory's 1987 constitution, which had sought to safeguard the Philippines from another future would-be Marcos. He asked what would happen if Congress and the Supreme Court — which would be required to approve (and extend) any declaration of martial law — took different positions. He said if the scale of the drug problem demanded it, he would ignore the Supreme Court ruling. 'I don't care about the Supreme Court,' he said, 'because I have the right to preserve ... my nation. My country transcends everything.' The 1987 constitution stipulates that martial law can only ever be declared if national security is threatened by insurrection or invasion, and if both Congress and the Supreme Court approve the declaration.

Duterte has always claimed that he believes in the rule of law. His critics have long accused him of thinking he is above the law. As a trained attorney and former public prosecutor, Duterte has used his understanding of the law, and its loopholes, to his personal advantage. Often, he has challenged his opponents to bring a case against him, confident that there will be insufficient evidence to secure conviction. When boasting about having shot people dead himself, he has been careful never to provide exact details of specific incidents — or in some cases, to ensure the evidence conveniently disappears. He has also protected himself as mayor and president by distancing himself from explicit orders and maintaining a veneer of what he considers to be plausible deniability. He expresses his desires and things just get done, his critics say. While they cling to hopes that one day he may face charges of crimes against humanity in the International Criminal Court (ICC), Duterte has never actually been charged with any crime. When the chief prosecutor of the ICC announced in February 2018 that she was to launch a preliminary examination into killings linked to Duterte's war on drugs, the president responded by denying he had ever issued an order to police to kill drug suspects. He questioned whether the court had jurisdiction.

The campus of San Beda College of Law in Manila, where Duterte studied, is a stone's throw from Malacañang Palace — up Jose Laurel Street and left at the shrine of St Jude, patron saint of lost causes. The college overlooks Chino Roces Bridge, named after a journalist jailed by Marcos for having led protests against martial law on that spot. Duterte qualified as a lawyer the very year Marcos declared military rule. His roommate from that time, Perfecto Yasay (who, 50 years on, he appointed his first foreign secretary) recalled how the two of them had watched in trepidation as tanks rumbled over nearby Ayala Bridge, close to the YMCA where they roomed. From his account, it seems Duterte, then in his mid-twenties, was at the time opposed to Marcos' totalitarian ambitions.

'He looked at me and said "this could be it",' Yasay said.

They had peered into the streets below from their third floor window in Room 324.

'Martial law was declared that evening. 21 September 1972. We were scared. It was very clear to me from very early on where he stood on this matter. He disliked the whole idea of dictatorship, of declaring martial law. We were concerned we might be arrested, so we left quickly.'

Duterte, he said, went to live with relatives in Quezon City, Manila, and stayed there until his bar exams — postponed because of the military takeover — had been rescheduled.

As it happens, Duterte actually missed his San Beda graduation ceremony. He had been barred from attending the occasion by college authorities because he had just shot one of his classmates in the leg. Duterte mentioned this incident in a pre-election rally, in which he admitted to having ambushed his fellow student — later identified by another former student as Octavio Goco, who died in the United States years later — in order 'to teach him a lesson'. Duterte claimed Goco had bullied him because he was a southerner, as well as other Muslim students.

He told his supporters: 'I said, "You son of a bitch, if I get hit, I will shoot you." I was hit in the nose. Aaaah! Bang!' They enthusiastically applauded. Other former San Beda classmates later accused Duterte of hyperbole, but newspapers reported that the incident had indeed been hushed up by college officials who did not want a scandal. The case was settled out of court, and Duterte's former school classmate and later cabinet colleague,

Jesus Dureza, told me that one of the law professors helped him settle it. It was with personal anecdotes like these, Dureza said, that Duterte had been able 'to capture the imagination of the Filipino voters'.

Dureza, a trained lawyer himself, said: 'People do not understand him. They think he is too cavalier about the law and that he runs roughshod over the law. But I know him. He's a stickler for the application of the law. He has very deep adherence for the law. He is a lawyer. He knows exactly how to conduct himself.' Dureza repeatedly thumped the table in his ministerial office as he insistently drove his point home. It was as though he was trying to convince me that the jury was still out on Duterte Harry.

The reality is that, having gone on to work as state prosecutor in Davao, Duterte had long ago lost faith in the Philippines' broken legal system — where cases take years to even come to court — and opted instead for the Dirty Harry style of summary justice. As president, he has repeatedly shown contempt for the judiciary. Early on, he lashed out at the chief justice of the Supreme Court who had challenged his naming and shaming of judges who he had claimed were complicit in drug trafficking. He told her to get back in her box and threatened to declare martial law if she continued to stir what he called 'a constitutional crisis'.

Now, in Davao, he was musing about martial law again, declaring that he'd do it if he wanted to. As he railed against the drug lords and brandished his infamous thick 'Narco List' (the one the chief justice had criticised), I looked around the room at other journalists — all Filipino, some from the local press, some national — to gauge their reaction to his threat. None looked particularly alarmed, so I wondered if I'd understood. A reporter I spoke to confirmed I'd heard it straight. 'He is sowing confusion,' they said (the reporter cannot be named for obvious reasons). 'So many contradictions. He's going to declare martial law; he's not going to declare martial law. We have the impossible job of having to interpret this stuff. Now he is saying "If I want to declare martial law, I will." The fact that we have to argue about what he actually said is just ridiculous. He should be able to deliver a clear message. We have to report this stuff, but it will just be bashed.'

Next day, sure enough, front page headlines blazed 'Duterte: I will declare martial law if I want to.' Others read: 'Duterte revives martial law fears' and 'Duterte: No one can stop me declaring martial law.' The international media picked up the story, but just as the journalist I'd spoken to had predicted, the president's men quickly scrambled to downplay his threats, haranguing the Philippine media for 'misreporting' the remarks I too had heard him make in Davao.

'The President has categorically said no to martial law,' said his communications secretary, Martin Andanar, a little-known former anchorman, who had thoroughly earned the opprobrium of his erstwhile colleagues. He is to Duterte what Kellyanne Connway is to Trump: the author of alternative facts. On this occasion, Andanar described the offending journalists as 'irresponsible'. Duterte's justice secretary weighed in, too, texting reporters individually to accuse them of quoting the president 'out of context'.

The media hit back. The Malacañang press corps launched all-out war on Andanar. They republished the president's remarks, verbatim.

'We are disturbed,' they announced in a statement, 'by the propensity of the officials of this administration to blame the media whenever the inflammatory statements of the president stir controversy or draw flak. This trend should stop.' The Philippine National Union of Journalists called Andanar 'utterly dishonest', for falsely accusing his former colleagues in the media and for 'peddling brazenly outrageous lies. That is so beneath you.' This was heartening. It seemed the Philippine fourth estate was showing some mettle. Digong might have raised the spectre of declaring martial law and licensed a policy of shoot-to-kill, but they'd be damned if they were going to let him shoot the messengers.

A few months later, while on a visit to see Vladimir Putin in Moscow, President Duterte declared martial law in Mindanao. His decision was triggered by the takeover of Marawi, a town in the northwest of the island, by an alliance of jihadist groups, but prompted, he said, by the beheading of a local police chief by the militants. His claim, which made headlines around the world, was debunked two days later by the *The Washington Post*, whose reporter interviewed the 'decapitated' policeman and found him to be alive and well. Romeo Enriquez told the newspaper he had been 'shocked' to learn of his demise. The siege of Marawi was not fake news, however; it was bloody and deadly, and dragged on for many months. But Philippine Supreme Court judges, in debating what was known as Duterte's Proclamation No. 216, voiced grave concerns about the president's ultimate game plan, and raised the ominous spectre of his declaring martial law nationwide.

4

LOS NIÑOS

It's approaching 5 am on a Sunday morning before Christmas, and in the Santo Niño (Christ child) district of Pasay City, Domingo Mañosca is already up and about. His heavily pregnant wife, Elizabeth, is still fast asleep. Sprawled beside her, in a tangle of little arms and legs, lie their three children: five-year-old Francis is wedged up against their shanty's plywood wall, the hint of an early morning breeze wafting through the gaps between the boards next to him; their eldest, nine-year-old Juliebeth, small for her age, curled up round her 18-month-old sister, Erika, the baby who never stops smiling.

Their second-floor room is rough-hewn, windowless, pokey, nailed together in a patchwork of scavenged shards of planking and ply. All five sleep together on rattan mats, spread over a lino-covered wood platform; none has ever known creature comforts. Upstairs, Domingo's brother, his wife, and their two children are crammed into another partitioned room just off the shared space where they all live and cook. His widowed mother, Maria, also sleeps there.

Domingo cannot and does not make ends meet. To make some kind of living, he rents a sidecar, a bicycle-taxi designed for two passengers — but which usually carries more, whole families, sometimes, in addition to their bags and boxes stacked high. He works gruelling hours, yet what he earns does not even cover his family's outgoings. Often he doesn't get back until late; sometimes he works through the night. The early mornings belong to him, though; Domingo slips out, descends three makeshift ladders into the darkness of the alleyway below, and wends his way to the stalls to buy a coffee. He has to be out on the bike by seven. Renting it costs him 60 pesos (US$1.20) a day. After that, the money's all his. One trip earns around eight or 10 pesos. On a good day, he can clear 140 after the cost of the rental, but that's on a good day. He'd love to have his own second-hand sidecar, but at 5000 pesos it's nothing more than a pipe dream.

In recent months, Domingo's taken the odd toke of *shabu* to help him pedal harder for longer; it messes with your head, but it's like downing a hundred cups of coffee at once. Loads of his fellow sidecar boys do it, too; it's pedi-cab turbo, poor man's cocaine. When he needed to really push himself, to earn a bit extra, like when one of the children was ill and he had to buy medicine, *shabu* seemed heaven-sent. And, like manna, it helped keep hunger at bay; life's worries also miraculously disappeared. Yet the price of a hit had rocketed since the tough-talking candidate he'd voted for became president and launched this drugs crackdown. The small plastic sachets were still affordable, though; and smoking it had always paid off: afterwards he wouldn't need to sleep for two days. But now his *shabu* nights were over: the community *barangay kapitan* had been compiling lists of local users. Somehow, he'd ended up on the 'watch list' and last week he'd had a *tokhang* warning visit from the cops. Word was he'd been shopped by a dealer.

Wanting to do the right thing, and after talking it over with Elizabeth, he had decided to go down to the police station and sign their 'surrender book' undertaking not to touch the stuff again — and he hadn't. In a neighbourhood where so many were at it, he was one of the few who'd fessed up. Better safe than sorry, he'd thought. Supposedly, signing the book would provide him with state-sponsored rehab, although that had yet to happen. The surrender experience had made him feel a bit anxious though, and his pregnant wife, too, especially when they'd heard from a neighbour that a stranger had since been asking around for him.

Santo Niño is a densely packed neighbourhood in the heart of Metro Manila, a conurbation made up of 16 cities and one municipality. The district is a maze of alleyways, some just shoulder-width; its residents live on top of one another in a heap of impoverished humanity, focused on the art of survival. For much of the year, this warren is insufferably hot and airless, but December is cool and bearable, and at this time of day, before dawn, it's still quiet, too; just the rustling sounds of a community beginning to stir.

Returning with his two plastic bags of sweet, milky coffee Domingo, in the light of a naked 40-watt bulb, grabs a screwdriver and starts fiddling with the family's broken DVD player. He's good with electronics, and he had promised Elizabeth that he would fix it. It's still only just gone five and Domingo is squatting on the edge of the raised platform, beside his slumbering family. As he sucks a warm strawful of coffee, there's a knock on the door at the foot of the ladder.

'*Sino yan?*' he calls. Who's there?

No answer. Again, a knock; again no answer. He stops what he's doing, listens, and looks around. All is quiet. At this point, Domingo Mañosca has roughly two minutes left to live.

From just behind him, there is a brief scraping sound, metal on wood. Then, before he can even wheel round, a shot. There were two, in fact. Domingo would have heard the first one, which missed him, but he would not have heard the second.

Elizabeth Navarro opens her eyes in blind panic and, as she does, her husband lands heavily on top of Juliebeth's tiny frame. The left side of his face had been blown off. She recoils in horror. Her first thought is for her daughter, pinned beneath him, and as his hot, sticky blood begins to ooze over everything, she wrenches the little girl from under Domingo's heavy, limp body. Emerging, smeared in her father's dark blood, Juliebeth stares as she takes in the scene, her father's blood and brains spattered everywhere.

Erika, the happy baby, is screaming, and as Elizabeth scoops her up, her eyes dart to five-year-old Francis lying strangely motionless. He, too, she's now noticed, is drenched in blood, and, fighting a rising hysteria, she realises it isn't blood from his mortally wounded father. It is his. Handing the baby to Juliebeth, she reaches for him just as her brother-in-law bursts through the door. The gun had been fired through the gap in the wall just behind Francis, and the first shot had hit Elizabeth's only son in the head. Yet the little boy was still breathing; perhaps, she hoped, the bullet had just grazed him. She thrust Francis at his uncle, Roberto, who, realising there was no hope for his brother, clambered back down the ladder and raced on his own rented bicycle sidecar, towards Pasay City General Hospital, his wounded nephew unconscious on the passenger seat beside him.

At a few minutes past 5 am on that Sunday morning, just before Christmas, Domingo Mañosca, 44, sidecar 'boy', bread-winner, Duterte-supporter, father, husband, and sometime *shabu* user became another statistic in the president's war on drugs, summarily executed inside his own home by an unknown killer. Two hours later, Elizabeth would learn that her little

Francis was now also just a statistic. Roberto returned alone and despondent.

Time magazine published a photo-essay on Duterte's drugs war by the renowned photojournalist James Nachtwey; the last picture in his devastating black-and-white collection showed Elizabeth, her belly swollen, sitting barefoot on the floor of a Pasay funeral parlour. In Philippine funereal tradition, it's considered bad luck for a woman who is pregnant to attend a wake or look upon the dead, but Elizabeth had little choice. In the picture, baby Erika is stretched out asleep on a flattened-out cardboard box at her feet. Elizabeth is wearing a casual white cotton dress patterned with an incongruous printed design of frolicking whales. Her expression, as she observed her lonely wake, is the quintessence of hopelessness. The sides of her mouth are cast down in an almost clown-like demeanour and she's gazing vacantly at a distant point, several light years away.

Beside her, there's a baby bottle, a solitary church candle dripping wax down a stand, and a small electric fan on the floor, aimed at the sleeping child. In the Philippines, when someone dies, their body is never left alone; family members sleep beside the coffin. The Pasay City funeral parlour is cluttered; neon candles blaze from candelabras and sconces, and, on the wall, an electric-candlelit Christ hangs crucified against a backdrop of pleated white damask. It's three days since the killings and the two white coffins containing Domingo and Francis, one big, one pitifully small, rest on gurneys. Next to them, right of frame, lilies, draped in white ribbon printed in standard florists' funereal calligraphy: 'DEEPEST CONDOLENCES'. Just visible in Nachtwey's picture are two tiny yellow chicks, placed on the glass window in the coffins' lids to peck at grains of rice. This widely practised superstition is reserved for murder victims. The pecking chicks symbolise the pricking of the unknown killer's conscience so as to hasten justice. The custom has persisted despite the impunity enjoyed by the henchmen of Duterte's drugs war. The two coffins have ornate scalloped handles and embossed designs down their sides. The cheapest coffin costs four times what Domingo's pipe-dream sidecar would have. A low-end cremation package comes in at 35,000 pesos. About US$700. And that's just for one, although there are discounts for children.

A few days later, the freshly cremated ashes of father and son are interred together at Pasay City Cemetery, a graveyard as chaotic and crowded as the slums its residents had left behind. There have been so many extra-judicial killings in Pasay City that local reporters had sardonically re-christened this 'Patay City': City of the Dead. The municipal cemetery in the 'City of the Dead' has been filling up fast since Duterte Harry came to town; a whole section, in fact — in another example of that same dark humour — has been unofficially renamed 'The Duterte Compound', a stack of high-rise tombs in a four-storey concrete matrix along the back wall of the cemetery.

Because so many families have proved unable to cover the prohibitive costs of coffins and cremation, the Catholic Church has set aside a special fund at the famed local Baclaran Redemptorist Catholic Church, Our Mother of Perpetual Help. The urns containing the ashes are covered by small plaques spelling out the names and lifespans of those they commemorate, but there are no lengthy epitaphs. In some of these open-fronted concrete boxes, bouquets of withered flowers, still in their cellophane wrappers, lean against the bare concrete walls. Many graves have no names at all and are simply numbered. No. 116, scratched into the wet concrete with a stick. No. 265. These are the unknown drugs war dead, the doomed youth who die as cattle.

———

It's a dreary, wet Sunday, several weeks later. Elizabeth's just had her baby, a boy she's called Franc Dominic, and I've gone to Pasay to see them. I've been dropped off on Narra Street in the heart of Barangay 45, the Santo Niño warren. In these labyrinthine squatter colonies, Duterte's war on drugs has increasingly been seen as a war on the urban poor. Confronted by the scale of the slums, and the sheer number of people crammed into them, it's hard to believe government statistics claiming that in the Metro Manila conurbation, fewer than one in ten people live in extreme poverty. There is even a Tagalog slang word for food scavenged from other people's rubbish: *pagpag*, a survival staple. Garbage chicken, beef from bins, assorted delicacies of discarded scraps; washed, recycled, bagged, and sold from hand-pulled *pagpag* carts. That's how poor these people are: in the national capital alone, maybe a million Filipinos are unable to afford to feed their families or themselves. And it's their communities that have been targeted by and suffered the most in police anti-drug operations. The vast majority of those killed in the drugs war have been from the very poorest tier of society.

A steady stream of dead bodies comes from areas like Santo Niño, where people lack the most basic housing, stacked on top of each other without sanitation or access to clean water and power. Few have proper jobs with regular salaries, but because there are no unemployment benefits, everybody works, for if they don't, they starve, even if that means that all they do is scavenge *pagpag*, push a cart, cycle a sidecar ... or sell *shabu*. Rodrigo Duterte, who had a comfortable upbringing (despite the story he spins), does not believe that criminality is rooted in poverty; he thinks all that's required for good behaviour is discipline. But ask a criminal in Manila why they steal things or deal drugs? It's always all about poverty.

The concrete overpass up above, taking light rail-traffic

towards the nearby Ninoy Aquino International Airport, is dripping liquid grime, which trickles down into Narra Street. Huddled underneath are the food stalls where Domingo bought his last coffee. The dank air is suffused with sweet smoke billowing from the grills of industrious street-chefs as they barbecue chicken satay and fish. Sidecars circle puddled potholes, touting for fares. Children roam and toddle everywhere. 'Hey, Joe,' they call — you still hear this throwback to US colonial times all over the Philippines. It's early but the streets are thronging. There's a Well Life pharmacy and small 'sari sari' stores selling everything from fizzy drinks to pirated DVDs, instant noodles, and SIM cards. Motorbikes — entire families on board — weave organically through the pedestrians. Competing sound systems pump out rap and rock medleys. Freddie Mercury's distinctive strains win through: 'Bohemian Rhapsody' fires up from a giant speaker 10 feet away. Freddie crooningly asks whether this is real life or just fantasy. To me, it felt like these people were indeed caught in a landslide and that there was no escape.

Slum junction. Alleyways lead off the street at all angles. An infeasible tangle of electric wires radiating from a solitary lamp-post, power illegally tapped off the main. For all the high growth-rates of recent years (GDP surged by nearly seven per cent in 2016) — which have resulted in a forest of skyscrapers springing up in the well-heeled next-door district of Makati (including a Trump Tower, no less) — Manila's underwhelmed underclass have developed a weary fatalism, an assumption that there will never be any monetary trickle-down and that they were just condemned to their hand-to-mouth existence in one of the most unequal societies in Asia. Many families here will have waved farewell to mothers or fathers or children who'll have joined the great 'OFW' exodus, the millions of Overseas Filipino Workers, many of them maids and mariners, whose annual US$25 billion in cash remittances have long been a mainstay of the national economy. Their overseas votes were also the mainstay of Rodrigo Duterte's electoral landslide.

Most of the houses in Santo Niño are three storeys, with some rising even higher, cabins teetering precariously on aerial extensions, themselves balanced on foundationless walls below. These aren't just your average lean-to *barrio* dwellings — this is a fully-fledged three-dimensional slum. A few of the buildings are concrete, but most are cobbled together from cinder blocks, asbestos, and plywood, topped with rusting roofs of wriggly tin — deafening in typhoon season. Aesthetics don't count for much when survival's at stake. Apart from weeds taking root in gutters, there's no greenery, but amid the shanty-squalor, there are splashes of colour: vibrant t-shirts and dresses hang drying on wires, rainbow-umbrellas cover the food stalls; a blood-red billboard advertising Fortune cigarettes; and, on a bamboo frame that straddles the street, STO NIÑO is spelled out in three-foot-high block capital letters in pink, green, red, and yellow. On closer inspection, it turns out the letters are lanterns, surrounded by coloured stars, which are lighted up at night using re-routed electricity.

Everyone has a curious, but welcoming, smile for the random foreigner, a species not frequently seen in these parts. Most *kano* — a collective term derived from Amerikano — transit Pasay City, at speed, en-route to the international airport, less than two miles away, and they remain unaware of the microcosm of real life lurking below. Yet when their planes take off, they can look down on Pasay's chaotic, but picturesque, poverty. It looks better from the air.

Elizabeth's brother-in-law, Roberto, has arrived.

'*Mabuhay*!' he smiles, the most common of Filipino greetings; it's a jaunty 'hello', and a toast over drinks; a word embracing life. And that's what it literally means: 'Live!' — in the imperative.

'*Mabuhay*!' I return, as we shake hands, although I am in Pasay to talk about death. Leading the way, the dead boy's uncle heads straight into the narrowest gap between houses as Queen's overplayed melancholic ballad fades slowly behind us: gun, head, trigger, dead.

The claustrophobic, muddy passageways are strewn with rubbish and crowded with parked motorbikes and women washing laundry in cheap plastic buckets. Builders, carrying scaffold and rusting reinforced steel, negotiate a tight corner, and locals stop to advise. There are roosters, cockroaches, and cats. Scabby dogs bark as we pass, and, as we move deeper into the maze, it gets darker. We duck into an aperture just two feet wide, between plywood walls, where an uneven staircase leads straight up, around a corner, and then up again, even steeper; it's a ladder now, and so dark you can't find your feet without torchlight; the ceiling so low your head gets bashed each time you climb an uneven rung. At the top, a dog barks frenetically. It isn't the sort you calm by petting it. When the gunshots went off at 5 am in the room just downstairs, the dog must have gone crazy. The entire neighbourhood would have woken up.

The advantage of living on the top floor is the light; despite the greyness of day, we emerge into a bright, open room, and there is Elizabeth, cradling her tiny new baby. She's had her hair cut into a neat bob and wears a hand-me-down oversized t-shirt, emblazoned with 'Lyceum', the university where Duterte had studied political science. Side-lit by a window, she is looking out over the tin roofs and washing lines. Baby Franc Dominic sleeps. There are doodles and sums and a couple of love hearts scrawled on the lime-green plywood wall behind her. Juliebeth, sitting beside Elizabeth, has had her hair cut just like her mum's. Erika, the toddler who hasn't quite yet learned to toddle, has her hair in a tiny top-knot. She is smiling. Her aunt keeps an attentive eye on her as Elizabeth talks. There are few possessions in this scrupulously clean, tidy family home. A school satchel hangs on a hook, there is a kettle, a rice-cooker, a calendar, and, on the wall, an Angry Birds clock, which has stopped. On a shelf to my left sits an old television and a broken DVD player.

Elizabeth speaks some English, but a Filipino journalist friend has come with me to translate from Tagalog. We talk for a bit about her husband, Domingo. It turns out he had spent four years in jail for robbery in the past. Local newspapers had reported that he had been a known drugs pusher, citing the district police chief as their source. Elizabeth denies this, although she readily admitted he smoked it.

'Yes, he used *shabu*. If he had to work all night, to earn more, that's when he'd use it. It's a huge problem here. It's like a virus. But killing people isn't the answer. If he hadn't been so honest and surrendered, he would probably still be alive,' she says, looking down at her baby. 'He signed his own death warrant.'

The police had come after the shooting, she tells me, but not one witness came forward. No one has been arrested.

'We are all still afraid,' she continues. 'We're worried that whoever shot my husband might come back. I don't know why they'd want to; I just hope that what happened is enough, that they got what they wanted.'

After the double murder, it was fear that had spread through Santo Niño, like a virus.

'There's nothing I can do about what has happened. It's done. I just try to accept it. It's very hard, but I still have three kids. I focus on them so that I can move on. Our whole family helps each other out. We just try to survive.'

Elizabeth struggles to even find the money for baby formula. She's renting out the room Domingo and Francis were killed in for 2,000 pesos (US$40) a month; it's not bad for what it is; it's what Domingo used to earn in a fortnight.

Elizabeth seemed consciously in control of her emotions and her demeanour when she spoke about her murdered son, Francis. She looked drained, though, and gaunt; still numb from what she had been through. A terrible sadness exuded from her posture and aura. She could talk about what had happened, but she struggled to articulate what she felt about it. Her agony remained unreleased; she had had to be pragmatic and practical, and, remarkably, she had given birth to a healthy baby, having just seen her husband and son murdered in front of her. It's a wonder she hadn't miscarried on the spot. Perhaps Elizabeth was trying to avoid feeling anything. People elsewhere in the world do years of therapy having suffered what she had endured. It was all still so fresh; but for Elizabeth Navarro, there would be no trauma counselling. All she had to look forward to was a world of pain and a future of inescapable poverty. Aged 29, with three children, no husband, and no income, the future must have looked bleak indeed. So, instead, Elizabeth talked of her memories of her naughty five-year-old son.

'Francis was such a happy little boy,' she says.

Rodrigo Duterte made international headlines when he described the deaths of children caught in the crossfire of his war on drugs as 'collateral damage'. He uses the word 'collateral' frequently in his speeches. 'Collateral damage' is a phrase associated with the unfortunate consequences of war, however. It was President Duterte who has called this a 'war'. No one else had ever really seen the need. And, in the slums of Manila, his war is one-sided.

Francis Meñosca was not the first child collateral, and there have been scores of other children killed since on this battlefield. Operation Double Barrel has left innocent bystanders lying in pools of blood; there have been cases of mistaken identity, and the licence to kill provided perfect cover for personal vendettas. But the rising number of dead children began to trigger particular alarm, not least among the children themselves. Parents from all walks of life began to talk of their children's 'irrational' fears that they too could be killed. But these fears weren't so irrational if the children were poor.

Ten days after Francis was shot and killed, 12-year-old Kristine Joy Sailog was shot dead in the car park of her local church, just south of Manila, as she left Christmas Mass with her mother. She was hit in the chest by a single round, allegedly fired by masked men on a passing motorcycle. They'd been aiming at somebody else, who was also killed. The Children's Legal Rights and Development Center reported that, in the first six months of the drugs war, at least 31 children had been shot dead, the youngest a four-year-old girl. Other children, like Juliebeth, have been frontline witnesses to the murder of their friends and family members. Large numbers of children have been orphaned and left without carers or a breadwinner.

In March 2017, the *Philippine Daily Inquirer* reported the particularly savage, cold-hearted killing of Michelle Mergillano, a mother of five, in Manila's eastern outskirts. She took four bullets, in front of her children. The newspaper said neighbours had confirmed that Michelle and her husband, Bernardo, were both known drug-users, and the *barangay* anti-drugs council alleged that he had run a 'drug-den'. Both, like Domingo, were apparently on the local drugs 'watch list', but unlike him, they had not surrendered to police.

With Bernardo reportedly hiding on the roof of the family home, Michelle's eight-year-old daughter, Bea, begged the four hooded intruders, who had 'kicked the door open', not to kill her mother.

'I have many siblings! Nobody will look after us!' she pleaded.

Her mother had been cradling her youngest, a baby, in her arms when the attackers burst in. According to Bea the gunmen 'dropped the baby on the floor' before shooting her mum in the head. The newspaper report stated: 'Her children, who cleaned the crime scene, recovered two of her teeth from the floor.' It also said Bernardo, their father, had fled.

The murders of three teenagers in August and early September 2017 proved to be a benchmark moment, jolting a country that had become inured to killing into taking notice. As opinion began to harden, Duterte was forced to take notice, too. The teenagers were among 96 people killed in Manila in the space of a few days as part of what the police called a 'one-time, big-time' assault on alleged dealers in the capital region. Two of the three were under 18, which brought to at least 54 the number of children killed in the drugs war. The first to die was 17-year-old Kian Loyd delos Santos, in Caloocan City, on the northern fringes of metropolitan Manila. Police claimed he was a meth dealer who had fired at cops during a raid; they had acted in self-defence, they said, after he had opened fire on them. But, for once, CCTV footage emerged which told a very different story. It clearly showed two plain-clothes police officers dragging the teenager away before he was shot dead in a rubbish-strewn alleyway, his body dumped next to a pig-sty. He was found with a hole in his head and another gunshot wound to his torso, grasping a pistol in his left hand. His parents said their son was right-handed. Justice Secretary Vitaliano Aguirre II described the killing as 'an isolated case'. Human Rights Watch said that 'to deliberately target children for execution marks an appalling new level of depravity in this so-called drugs war'.

A few days later, a former student from the University of the Philippines, 19-year-old Carl Angelo Arnaiz, was found in a morgue 10 days after he disappeared in Caloocan, having gone out with 14-year-old Reynaldo de Guzman, reportedly to buy a late-night snack. Police also said Arnaiz was killed in a shootout with officers after trying to rob a taxi, but a government forensics expert determined that he had been handcuffed, tortured, and shot five times. The taxi driver surfaced after a week in hiding, and, in a news conference organised by a network linked to the Catholic Church, confirmed Arnaiz had indeed tried to rob him at gunpoint, but that he had disarmed him when his gun jammed, driven him to the police station, and left him there — alive. An hour later, the teenager was dead, his body dumped on a vacant lot, a gunfight staged. The bloated body of de Guzman, the 14-year-old, was found floating in a river, 30 miles away, his head wrapped in packing tape (a gruesome hallmark of many extra-judicial killings), and his body punctured by 30 stab wounds — although the police contested the body's identity. The parents of these two teenagers filed complaints against two Caloocan policemen, alleging the planting of evidence, torture, and murder. The president described de Guzman's killing as a deliberate act of sabotage aimed at discrediting the police.

The Caloocan funeral of Kian Loyd delos Santos turned into one of the biggest protest marches yet against Duterte's war on drugs, with more than 5000 people, including nuns, priests, the families of 20 other drugs war killings, and hundreds of children, chanting 'Justice for Kian, Justice for all!' The truck that bore his flower-covered coffin from the church to the cemetery was draped with banners reading 'Run, Kian, Run' and 'Stop the Killings'. His distraught parents filed a murder complaint against three anti-narcotics policemen. Swayed by the ferocity of the public reaction, Aguirre's justice department launched an investigation into his killing, and then, in mid-September, the entire 1200-strong Caloocan city police force was fired on the orders of Manila's police chief. It was said they would undergo 45 days of training, after which those not facing charges would be reassigned to other stations. Kian Loyd delos Santos' parents were meanwhile invited to Malacañang to meet the president who told them 'those who had committed wrong would not go unpunished'. This apparently reassured the schoolboy's parents, but was not enough to head off a dramatic slide in Duterte's approval rating and condemnation from the Catholic Church and the UN's Commissioner for Human Rights.

The Catholic Bishop of Caloocan, Pablo Virgilio 'Ambo' David, who had been overtly critical of the president's 'brutal, cruel, and inhuman' war on drugs, offered sanctuary to witnesses to Kian Loyd delos Santos' murder. He said his diocese had been turned into 'a killing field'. Bishop David's San Roque Cathedral already ran a drop-in centre for street children, many of whom had been forced to live rough after a parent was jailed or shot dead.

The public backlash over this teenager's killing resulted, in January 2018, in the filing of murder charges against the three police officers who had lied about how he died. This was hailed by human rights groups as a rare instance in which the Philippine justice system has taken genuine steps to prosecute anyone for murders linked to Duterte's war on drugs.

But the killing spree which Duterte ushered in as president is not the first time Filipino children have been exposed *en masse* to extreme violence. In Davao City, during Duterte's time as mayor, children were directly targeted. More than 130 of them were among 1400 killed by the Davao Death Squad between 1998 and 2015. Many of the murdered children were street-kids; others were petty criminals, some were addicts. Now, a sizeable number of the 'offenders' in the war on drugs are children, too. In the first six months of Duterte's presidency, more than 26,000 under-18s, allegedly involved in using, selling, or transporting drugs, surrendered to police — according to Philippine National Police statistics. On 30 June 2016, immediately after his inauguration as president, Duterte paid a visit to Tondo, the biggest slum in Manila. There, addressing a crowd of around 500 people, he said:

'If you know of any addicts, go ahead and kill them yourself, as getting their parents to do it would be too painful.'

Allegations of drug abuse have, for a couple of decades, surrounded the president's eldest son, Paolo 'Pulong' Duterte. Now in his forties, he became vice-mayor of Davao City in 2013, under the aegis of his father. When dad became president, Paolo's sister, Sara, took the reins as mayor. No firm evidence has ever emerged to support the allegations that Paolo was either a user or dealer of *shabu*. But as long ago as 2001, Carolyn O. Arguillas, editor of Davao's *MindaNews*, put it to the then-mayor that rumours abounded that 'your son, your relatives, are also involved in drugs'.

Duterte responded: 'Just produce a credible and true witness and I'm going to resign as mayor of Davao City and I will shoot my son in front of you.'

No one came forward, just as no witness had ever came forward to testify over the killings of the death squad in Davao. Fifteen years later, in the final televised debate between presidential candidates in April 2016, Duterte again said that if he ever caught one of his own children taking drugs, 'I will kill him.'

The 'your relatives' reference in the editor's question is interesting. There remain to this day persistent, but unconfirmed, reports that another member of the Duterte clan uses *shabu*.

In Davao, those familiar with Paolo, deride him as a *bugoy* — the Bisaya word many apply to his father. Even the president's devotees describe Paolo like this, and share a dislike for him. He is regarded as an arrogant bully and has a thuggish reputation. Duterte's critics suggest this may reflect very real concern, on the part of the president's supporters, that the antics of his own son may yet prove to be his Achilles' heel. But allegations of Paolo's supposed drug dependency have never stuck. One Davao resident noted that *shabu* keeps you awake; Paolo, they said, was forever falling asleep.

A report by the National Bureau of Investigation in 2007 named Paolo and one of his business partners as members of 'a big time syndicate engaged in smuggling' which allegedly included SUVs and high-end cars stolen from as far afield as Japan and the USA. The NBI intelligence report said Paolo was 'using the power and influence of Davao City Mayor Rodrigo Duterte to avoid arrest / apprehension ... They also enjoy the protection of some corrupt Bureau of Customs officials and members of the Philippine National Police'. The report noted that Paolo even had a car showroom in Davao City — which still exists today.

Rodrigo Duterte reportedly has awkward relationships with all three of his adult children, including his tattooed 30-year-old surf-bum son, Sebastian, better known as 'Baste', the youngest. But the father takes attacks on any of them personally, and, as his political enemies will tell you, if Duterte Sr bears a grudge, he will not let it go. Jun Pala, a Davao City shock-jock radio commentator who once laid into Paolo live on air for beating up a hotel security guard, drew Rodrigo Duterte's ire. The feud between the two men escalated over time and, in September 2003, Pala was ambushed and assassinated by unknown assailants. His murder officially remains unsolved, although in

February 2017, the self-confessed former head of the Davao Death Squad, Arturo Lascañas, claimed under oath in the Senate that he had murdered Pala on Duterte's orders and that the then-mayor had given him a 1 million peso (US$20,000) reward for carrying out the hit.

Five authoritative and credible sources spoke to me off-the-record about Paolo's alleged *shabu* habit, but none had personally witnessed his taking drugs; they'd heard about it, they said, from others who had. Two former addicts, who claimed to have regularly smoked *shabu* with Paolo refused, in the end, to meet.

'This is extremely dangerous information,' I was told. It is possible that Paolo's local infamy and loutish reputation have fed the belief, among those set against him, that he is involved in drugs, just as he's alleged to be involved in a local rice-smuggling racket. The accounts, however, have proved enduringly persistent, and have in the past been examined by a state investigator who heard anonymous witness testimony — but was unable to conclusively establish facts beyond doubt. As with Rodrigo Duterte's own direct links to murders, there is an opaqueness to the allegations, key evidence missing, witnesses not forthcoming.

Lascañas and another self-confessed Davao Death Squad hitman testified in the Philippine Senate that they had killed a man, on Paolo Duterte's orders, following an altercation. The other hired killer, Edgar Matobato, who confessed to murdering around 50 people also claimed in the Senate that Paolo smoked *shabu*, which he described as his drug of choice.

'Sometimes,' he testified, 'he would run amok when he's high.'

He went on to claim he had seen Paolo out drinking with known ethnic Chinese drug lords in Davao City, who, he alleged, were his friends. But Matobato offered no corroborating evidence, and his accounts were dismissed widely as hearsay.

Matobato's boss, Lascañas, testified under oath that Paolo

Duterte had protected a suspected Taiwanese drug smuggler by sabotaging a police operation to entrap him. The smuggler had supposedly been attempting to bring *shabu* into Davao City in a shipping container full of furniture which Paolo had purchased in China. Lascañas claimed Paolo had rung him and told him that he 'would take care of it', and so the police were called off the case. Lascañas admitted he had never seen inside the container and so had no evidence that it contained drugs. Lascañas' testimony was also dismissed by Duterte's supporters because, they said, his broader claims — alleging that Mayor Duterte had ordered executions and paid him for hits — contradicted those he'd made, also under oath, in an earlier Senate hearing, when he was still a serving police officer. In his first brief appearance, Lascañas had rubbished Matobato's claim that the Davao Death Squad had even existed; in his second, he said he had been in charge of it.

After giving his testimony, Lascañas fled into exile, joining his family in Singapore, before moving to another country. I remained in contact with him and questioned him in detail about many of the matters he had raised, but which the senators had not bothered probing. On the question of Paolo's drug habit, he cited conversations he had had with Paolo's former security officer, Steve dela Cruz, another senior Davao policeman. According to dela Cruz, cocaine was actually Paolo's drug of choice, Lascañas said, although he alleged he used other drugs, too. Although cocaine is widely used among Manila's young glitterati, it is less commonly found outside the capital as it is a much more expensive drug than *shabu*. In March 2014, though, a large haul of high-grade cocaine was discovered strapped into the false ceiling of a Maersk shipping container at the wharf in Davao City. More than half the haul of 77 bricks — each weighing just over one kilogram — originally went missing, but most were returned to police custody after the mayor of Davao issued a shoot-to-kill order. A smaller haul of 19 bricks of cocaine had been seized in 2009. International narcotics investigators concluded that Davao City was — and probably remains — a drugs transhipment centre.

In November 2016, after opposition senator Antonio 'Sonny' Trillanes IV had repeated the drug allegations about Paolo and challenged the president's son to undergo a comprehensive drugs test, Paolo, to widespread surprise, agreed to do so.

'I have accepted his challenge, not to dignify him,' Paolo said, 'but to clear my name and the name of my family. His imputations that I was a drug addict were based entirely on a fabricated story by a man whose imagination is as twisted as the senator's' — referring to Matobato. He later challenged the senator to 'take a psychiatric test'.

The results of hair-follicle diagnosis, analysed by a Manila laboratory, showed the vice-mayor of Davao to be clean. He tested negative for seven classes of drugs, including methamphetamine (*shabu*), cocaine, and heroin. There was apparently no need for the president to shoot his son after all.

But Senator Trillanes was on a mission, and, within months, had succeeded in hauling Paolo Duterte in front of a Senate inquiry, where he was grilled about his links to a US$125-million *shabu* smuggling operation, shipping drugs into the Philippines. A shipping broker had alleged that more than 600kg of methamphetamines had been fast-tracked through customs in May 2017 in a shipment from China and that the transactions had been facilitated by Davao-based individuals linked to Paolo Duterte and his brother-in-law, Manases Carpio, who is married to Sara Duterte, mayor of Davao. The shipping agent would later retract his testimony — but only after his protective custody was withdrawn.

According to Trillanes, Paolo was 'the boy with the dragon tattoo', complete with secret coded digits, which the senator insisted was proof that Paolo was a member of a Chinese Triad crime syndicate. In front of the televised Senate inquiry, Trillanes challenged Paolo to remove his shirt to reveal the dragon and the secret numbers which he claimed the US Drug Enforcement Agency would be able to decode. The nation was captivated.

'No way,' Paolo said, refusing even to describe his body art to his inquisitor and invoking his right to privacy several times. When Trillanes suggested he just show the tattoo to the Senate investigating committee, Paolo's lawyer sneered, 'Is he gay?'

Paolo himself grew indignant and offered a cryptic response: 'When the time comes that he fell to the ground, when his wings were broken because he flew so high, I will show it,' he said, the vice-mayor of Davao City suggesting the senator was getting a little too close to the sun.

The *Philippine Daily Inquirer* quoted sources close to Paolo as saying that his colourful tattoo actually depicted the Taoist deity Lao Tzu, accompanied by a quotation — in Chinese characters — attributed to an Eastern Han dynasty general. The words reportedly translated: 'To stand tall between heaven and earth and live without shame or regret.'

Paolo Duterte dismissed many of Trillanes allegations as baseless and refused to answer some questions on the basis that they were in his view 'irrelevant'. Other questions concerned his refusal to reveal details of bank accounts in which he was accused of stashing millions of pesos. His legal counsel later compared Senator Trillanes to Nazi propagandist Joseph Goebbels, and accused him of trying to use Paolo to destroy the president. The pro-Duterte trolls then got to work, alleging that Trillanes had hidden his ill-gotten wealth in secret bank accounts in Singapore. The senator denied this and declared that Paolo's refusal to reveal his tattoo confirmed his allegation that he was a member of the Triad. It descended into a mud-slinging contest; a complaint was lodged against Trillañes with the Senate ethics committee. President Duterte weighed in, repeating that he would issue an order to kill his own son in the event of Paolo being found guilty of involvement in the drug trade.

A Catholic priest, Father Joselito 'Bong' Sarabia — a member of the new anti-drug war group Rise Up — lamented publicly that, as the president's son, Paolo Duterte had been able to stand in the Senate to defend himself against drug allegations, unlike the thousands of young men who had been murdered on the basis of suspicion alone.

In late 2017, as Elizabeth Navarro prepared to mark the first anniversary of the double murder of Domingo and five-year-old Francis, and as the Philippines looked forward to celebrating the birth of *Santo Niño*, there was a dramatic twist in the saga of the president's first-born. Paolo 'Pulong' Duterte was about to have a very bad Christmas.

It all began, strangely, with a photoshoot for the upcoming eighteenth birthday of his own daughter — and first granddaughter of the Philippines — Isabelle Duterte. In a Malacañang Palace spectacular worthy of Imelda herself, Isabelle posed and pouted in the wood-panelled Heroes' Hall for a celebrity photographer. She was accompanied by a 'hi-so' stylist, two make-up artists, and a retinue of hangers-on. Bella's custom-made, Dubai-designed, Swarovski-studded, blood-red ball gown boasted 'a train worthy of a Disney princess', the news site *Rappler* noted, while other media outlets branded her shameless ostentation 'Imeldific'. Clearly struck by the fairy tale symmetry, and mani-festly sharing her grandpa's admiration for the Marcos clan, Isabelle posted an old black-and-white photograph on her Facebook account of 'Beautiful Imelda', in a wedding dress in

Heroes' Hall, Malacañang Palace, in 1979, as the former first lady celebrated her silver wedding anniversary. Imelda is escorted past applauding dignitaries by her long-haired son Bongbong.

The writer Miguel Syjuco took to Facebook, too, commenting that the Garimon Roferos fashion studio in Dubai had told him that such princess dresses start at 400,000 pesos (US$8000).

'That's about one-and-a-half times the average annual income for a Filipino family,' Syjuco wrote. He speculated that Isabelle's dress would have cost more thanks to the embedded crystals and vast train. His rough tally of the total cost of the shoot: 1 million pesos (US$20,000).

'So where do the Dutertes, who've been on government salaries for more than two decades, get their money?' he asked, his rhetorical question destined to hang in the air, unanswered.

It's not clear whether this palatial photoshoot was directly linked to the Duterte family debacle that began in Davao just days later, but when an all-out war broke out on social media between debutante Isabelle (already firmly in the national head-lines) and her father, Paolo, it seemed the two were not entirely unconnected. What happened next scandalised and mesmerised the nation for the duration of the Christmas period — although some other Filipinos were too immersed in concurrent national tragedies to devote much attention to it. If Rodrigo Duterte's relationships with his children were rumoured to be strained and fractious, the depth of the rift between Paolo and his daughter was aired for all to see on social media, playing out with all the clunkiness of a bad soap opera. First came a seemingly petulant tweet from the teenaged Isabella: 'My dad fucks up my Christmas every year,' she wrote in the Bisaya language. A second tweet followed: 'Just because you have a position in the city doesn't mean you have the right to beat [someone]!!! Just because you have power doesn't mean you can hurt people!! That person whom you exerted your power on is a human being!!! Not just [a] human being, but a child!! ... You cannot act like that just because you have a name!!! Just because you are a Duterte ...'

The identity of Paolo Duterte's alleged victim was not clear, but there was widespread speculation that it may have been a boyfriend of whom Isabelle's father disapproved.

Demonstrating characteristic judgement and restraint, Paolo, vice-mayor of Davao City, posted a tirade on Facebook about how his daughter was being 'pimped' — presumably by this unidentified individual — and berating her mother, Lovelie Sumera (from whom he is divorced). Isabelle had embarrassed herself, he declared, urging her to change her family name. 'You don't know how to [show] respect!' he wrote. 'You are a disgrace!'

'Famous for what, Belle?' Paolo frothed, 'Famous for disparaging a father? Just wait for my death so you will be free from me!' Then, employing block capitals, he launched his final salvo at his 17-year-old daughter: 'FIX YOUR FUCKING LIFE FIRST before I will stop "fucking up" your Christmas every year.'

Isabelle's Twitter account is private, but to ensure the wider Filipino public could share in this family squabble, her father helpfully attached to his Facebook rant screenshots of her tweets, so that all the Philippines could see. He didn't care if the episode humiliated him, he said, this was the only way she would learn. By this time, the first family's unseemly fracas had made the foreign pages of *The New York Times* and other global papers. But as the slanging match reached a crescendo, it battled for the headlines with a fatal fire on Christmas Eve in a Davao City shopping mall: 37 young Filipino call centre workers were burned alive. And, even as the blaze erupted, a tropical storm slammed into eastern Mindanao, leaving more than 230 people dead. Meanwhile, 'night watch' photographers, working on the front line of the drug war chose Christmas Eve to publish the photographs of 31 children killed, and the names of 17 others, along with the message 'lest we forget'.

When Christmas Day dawned, Paolo Duterte, the president's first-born, spoke publicly of the hard times he and his compatriots were going through.

'It is a difficult Christmas Day for many [Davaoeños] including myself,' he wrote, sharing the Filipino people's pain. 'But we are strong and resilient and we will move forward.'

With that, he tendered his resignation as vice-mayor of Davao City and deactivated his Facebook account. By way of explaining his decision to stand down, Paolo cited '*delicadeza*' — a Filipino-Spanish word, which means doing the right thing out of a sense of propriety. He specifically referenced Senator Trillañes' allegation that he was a member of a Davao-based drug-running crime ring, his failed marriage, and what he called the 'very public squabble with my daughter'. While some thought the chickens might be coming home to roost, few Filipinos expected Paolo to be out of the limelight for long, particularly as the decision as to whether to accept his offer lay with his father. Two days after Christmas they were proved right, as Paolo Duterte and his brother-in-law, Manases Carpio, filed a libel suit against Trillañes.

'Secondary trauma' is a term used to describe duress felt by someone who hasn't directly experienced a traumatic event themselves, but who has somehow been exposed to the experience or knowledge of it, often visually. It's no less real in its impact on children's lives in particular, and, although obviously less horrific than the extreme violence that Bea and Juliebeth witnessed first-hand, the war on drugs has turned secondary trauma into a nationwide problem. TV news programmes broadcasting in Tagalog and other local languages have long served up a diet of crime-stories and tales of kidnap and murder. Today, though, these programmes are dominated by images of bloodied bodies sprawled on foot-paths with cardboard signs round their necks, scrawled with words such as 'addict' or 'pusher'.

Daily newspapers print graphic photographs of these crime scenes; dead bicycle-taxi drivers, shot on their sidecars, the aftermaths of a vigilante hit or fatal 'encounters' with police. Photographers who cover the gruesome nightshift in Manila are disturbed by their exposure to such scenes. Some are highly experienced professionals who have been in the business for years; others are new to the game, but most will admit to having been deeply affected by their experience. They have also become acutely aware of the impact their pictures are having on the public. As a result, photographers and cameramen have explored ways of conveying the horror of the war on drugs without having to confront their readers and viewers with relentless gore. Some have been so sickened that they no longer want to work in their profession, having seen too much blood without respite. They say they can't help but feel a sense of guilt or complicity. Others speak of being haunted by ghostly hallucinations, as though stalked by the twisted corpses they photograph.

From early on, mental health workers were warning of the psychological impact of the drugs war, particularly on children. They talked of how prolonged exposure to images of extreme violence could lead to their exhibiting violent behaviour, aggression, and delinquency themselves, and, as they grew older, crime. Child psychologist Dr Joanna Herrera was one of the first to ponder publicly whether the side effects of the drugs war were worse than Duterte's prescribed cure. 'Violence can beget violence,' she told a Philippine national newspaper. 'Overexposure can also lead to desensitisation, especially for children who are more malleable ... It is not just about the violence, but the tacit approval of it.'

With the president himself regularly appearing on television, cursing and issuing ever-more murderous threats, it has had the effect of normalising killing, let alone inuring children to colourful language. Anecdotally, Duterte's expletives and profanities are now being imitated in school playgrounds the length and breadth of the archipelago. There are many who are concerned about the long-term damage such exposure to a growing culture of violence will do to Philippine society. Trust in the Philippine National Police has been seriously undermined. Moral values have been eroded. In Manila, a Catholic priest who has worked at the sharp end of the war on drugs related an anecdote about a family he knew in which a child told his father how angry he was with his teacher.

'I want to kill him,' the boy had said.

The priest talked of how difficult it would be to erase the damage that he says has already been done, saying, 'The seeds of destruction have been planted.'

5

DUTERTE HARVEY

The single-engine Piper J-3 Cub had been circling for a while, whining like a mosquito in the azure Mindanaoan sky. Suddenly, the noise of the small plane's engine changed; as the pitch rose to a crescendo, everyone looked up at once. The students of Holy Cross High School, attending their solemn flag-raising ceremony, cast anxious glances at each other, then at their teachers, the notoriously disciplinarian Benedictine Brothers. Then, as the silhouetted aircraft dived straight at them out of the morning sun, they scattered. Most guessed the identity of the as-yet unqualified young pilot. The son of the governor of Davao was one of their own. The year was 1962. Another Duterte legend had been born.

'I knew it was him,' said Jesus 'Jess' Dureza. 'I knew he was going to the city on weekends to get his pilot's licence. So, one Saturday, I was on the parade ground, playing in the band. Then I just saw this Piper Cub, diving, diving, at the campus. That's when I knew it was him.'

Duterte had been trying to impress a pretty girl called Pilang, Dureza said. She worked in the canteen, and, as others who were in Digos at that time confirmed, was famously well-endowed.

'He was very playful with her,' said Dureza, his face creased by a libidinous smirk, reminiscent of the knowing complicity in the expressions of men formerly in Harvey Weinstein's social orbit. 'Every time he would approach the counter, he would snatch her boobs.'

The cabinet minister jumped up from the table in his office and gleefully acted out the groping scene, to the embarrassed amusement of his young female secretary, who continued to make detailed notes.

'He told Pilang, "If you refuse to be my girlfriend, next Saturday I will crash the plane into the canteen and both of us will die and together we will go to heaven."'

Dureza chortled wistfully, as he sat back down. 'He is a very playful person.'

On this occasion, Duterte did not go through with his death threat. It is not recorded whether Pilang resisted the future president's advances, but Dureza says that to this day, the governor's son fondly reminisces about how he'd 'grabbed her boobs' and muses, out loud, 'Where is Pilang now?'

'He loves women, he's a speed-freak, and a show-off,' is the verdict of Duterte's sister Jocelyn.

She talks of what she calls 'the Piper Cub incident' in the way that only younger sisters can when they recall the fabled antics of their older brothers, rolling her eyes and giggling. But, five decades on, Jocelyn remains distinctly in awe of the sheer mischief of this act of brotherly bravado, which happened soon after Duterte had been 'expelled' from the Jesuit-run Ateneo de Davao High School.

'My mother had already begged the Brothers to take him,' she said, and then, to her disbelief, no sooner had he enrolled in his new school than, 'he went Tora-Tora at the flag-raising! Do you know what I mean?'

Waving her arms around, Jocelyn mimed the diving aircraft and the panicked scramble of the students as the crazed young quasi-kamikaze zeroed in.

'I remember the incident because the priests [at Holy Cross] talked to my mother and said to her: "Would you mind thinking about bringing your son to *another* school?"'

The Tora-Tora dive-bombing incident wasn't Duterte's only aerial acrobatic stunt. Jocelyn says he had also done the same thing at their 'ancestral home', 'showing off' as usual. 'He took the plane really, really close to the windows,' she said. 'I'm not joking! My neighbour almost had a heart attack and fainted. My father had been sleeping in the bedroom.'

The governor, she said, was not best pleased: 'My brother didn't come home for three days after that.'

The Piper Cub had been in the service of Duterte's father. It has long been rumoured that, in addition to the flag-raising incident, the daredevil princeling once overflew his old school Ateneo de Davao and threw a rock at its roof. This proved to be an unverifiable yarn.

Another Davaoeño recalled how the young Duterte used to take the controls of the small twin-seater in his early teens; he could take off and fly the thing, but he couldn't bring it down, he said. He used to crash land all the time.

It's striking how those who recall Duterte's 'playful' teenage capers also pass off the murderous excesses of his later years as mayor of Davao and what a human rights group called the 'national calamity' of his presidency. It's not just his cabinet loyalists and family; it's most people in Davao, most members of Congress and the Senate, and the tens of thousands of online trolls who disseminate poisonous pro-Duterte propaganda on social media. In the imagination of many of these supporters, the president is a knight in shining armour, a crusader waging righteous war against criminality and drugs, heaven-sent to save his benighted nation in its hour of need. This is a conceit that's energetically proselytised by his evangelists in parallel to the Duterte Harry narrative. But it's the persona of the badass *bugoy* that Duterte himself has studiously cultivated. This is the version of his life that has him raised, god-like, in the gutters of Davao, the man of the poor. It is the one that has always worked, the one that has earned him votes, respect — and fear.

In reality, the son of the governor, who felt entitled to use his father's government-issued plane when he felt like it, was little more than an amateur character actor — and he has continued to foist on the world his assumed persona. He didn't just act the part that he took on, he became it, and, as he did so, Duterte began to believe his own mythology. He studied for the role of what would become his lifelong gangster warlord incarnation as he swaggered around Davao accompanied by his bodyguards. He fired their guns, mimicked their street-slang, and observed their leering, misogynistic ways. Today, the former Catholic schoolboy has the unrivalled distinction of being the world's most overtly vulgar head of state. Other presidents, prime ministers, and global leaders who raise even an eyebrow at his despotic governance are invariably subjected to a retaliatory tirade of crude invective by President Duterte Harry.

At home in the Philippines, his fearsome reputation has meant that when he says 'don't fuck with me', it is not deemed to be an idle threat. Several key sources for this book — not counting those on watch lists, who are involved with drugs — claimed to have received warnings that they are on some target list for publicly criticising or questioning the hyper-sensitive strongman with a hair-trigger temper. One told me he'd been informed that a 'hit' on him had been ordered; he didn't want to say from where, or how he knew. He was taking precautions, but added that he never knew if he'd make it home.

Donald Trump lashes out on Twitter. Duterte spews his venom, taunting, threatening and traducing his detractors, just as other contemporary authoritarian leaders (look at Vladimir Putin, Recep Tayyip Erdoğan, Narendra Modi) target their political enemies, journalists, human rights defenders, clerics, and lawyers. As a tactic, it works. Demonising groups of people — such as drug addicts — and directing animus at those who oppose the deployment of hatred plays on people's worst fears, spreads malice, and fosters ever-more extreme views. For the politician, this populist polarisation of society, which sows seeds of chaos, is how they stay in power. And it is how and why killing has become normal in the Philippines under Rodrigo Duterte's rule.

Everybody knows that when it comes to *shabu*, Duterte's threats to kill are real. His promise to 'destroy' his nemesis, the former justice secretary, Leila de Lima, proved real enough, as well; his insults directed at her were considered to have crossed a line, but in her case at least he confined his vengeance to character assassination and incarceration. Others who have dared to oppose Duterte's tactics — all members of the groups listed above — and who have crossed swords with him have been compelled to take threats very seriously indeed, having been warned (sometimes discreetly, sometimes not) that they are deemed legitimate targets. This intimidation has caused extreme levels of stress and anxiety for individuals and their families. Some have taken to lying low and hoping things will just blow over; others have gone so far as to 'make arrangements' for their families — in the event of their untimely demise. But there is little they can actually do.

In one of the most connected, Facebook-friendly countries in the world, those who have openly opposed Duterte have found themselves 'unfriended' by people they've known for years.

Yet for all the noise of the Duterte fan club, there are many Filipinos who have vocally opposed his violent methods, not just on Facebook and other social media, but in personal public statements, too. Because the price of public opposition is so high, many choose to remain anonymous. They describe Duterte as a mass-murderer bent on totalitarian control, and share an Orwellian vision of the society now evolving under his grim aegis.

Some of Duterte's influential allies, among them former President Fidel Ramos, have demonstrated a growing disquiet — or, at best, ambivalence — about President Duterte; they despair of his unstatesmanlike behaviour in Malacañang, saying he's failed to conduct himself with the decorum expected of his office. Concern has also grown that Duterte has brought not just the presidency into disrepute, but now threatens to turn the country he claims to love into an international pariah. Gary Alejano, an opposition congressman who filed a failed impeachment complaint against Duterte in March 2017, described him simply as 'unfit to hold the highest office of the land'.

Aside from the rising number of fatalities in the war on drugs, it's the contentious rhetoric emanating from what the president himself concedes is his 'big mouth' that has garnered most attention. His foul language first offended sensibilities at home and then went global.

'We are all the creations of God,' Duterte said in response to clerical condemnation of his papal 'son of a whore' slur. 'We have God-given talents. The talent that God gave me is cussing. Instead of blaming me,' he said, 'blame God, because He created me.'

But in the Philippines, where people have grown inured to his cursing, it's the manner in which he issues his threats that has drawn an even greater level of concern. Duterte's trick is to never make it clear whether they are real or just rumbustious rhetoric. His habit is to shake the devil's hand, then say he's only joking.

Often, during his presidential campaign, and later, as president, journalists who reported on his threats to kill, or his boastful claims of having killed people himself, would be berated by Duterte for taking him too seriously. On other occasions, he has ordered his hapless presidential spokesmen to play down or re-spin whatever he'd said to offend. This has involved point-blank denials that things everyone had heard him say were ever said at all — as with his communications secretary's repudiation of all the press reports that he'd threatened martial law.

On the international stage, his spinner, re-interpreter, and apologist-in-chief for the first nine months of his presidency was his foreign secretary and former roommate, Perfecto Yasay. Even back when they were students, Yasay said, Duterte's cursing, ribald humour, and flashes of temper were well known: 'We were not spared the cusses that came out of his mouth. Oh yes, he was quick to anger sometimes. I have seen that.'

Duterte was nocturnal and always out visiting women, and, 'being the son of a governor, was the only [person] I knew with a car, an Opel Kadett.'

Yasay described Duterte as a natural leader, and dismissed his tough-guy image as 'a façade, to help him overcome his shyness'. Although Duterte does not exactly come across as a shrinking violet, many of those who've known him through the years commented on his apparently diffident nature.

Yasay's appointment as foreign secretary proved a poisoned chalice. He clunkily attempted to resolve crisis after crisis triggered by Duterte's outbursts, and was the one who also had to explain away the spiralling death toll in the war on drugs. He did so loyally and shamelessly, just as the late Tariq Aziz did for Saddam Hussein. When I challenged him on the president's egregious disregard for human rights, Yasay, a lawyer like Duterte, looked me in the eye and said due process was 'the cornerstone' of the president's policies. Duterte, he assured me, was protecting the lives and human rights of innocent people against the murderous drug lords, who were all set on killing each other.

In February 2017, the president helpfully asserted that of every five things he said: 'only two are true. The other three are just wisecracks'. It wasn't clear which of the two categories this comment fell into. He cited, by way of an example, the time he claimed he had promised God that he'd stop swearing — a preposterous yarn that caused much amusement. In a news conference, Duterte said God had spoken to him on a flight back from Japan, threatening to bring the plane down unless he cleaned up his act. He said he had solemnly promised the Almighty he would stop using expletives. These remarks were seized upon and sardonically reported, but, inevitably, within days Duterte was back on form, swearing like a professional.

'The media,' he lamented 'are not really attuned to [my] character.' More apposite examples of possible wacky wisecracks that he could have cited were the occasions he had threatened to declare martial law or pull out of the United Nations or the International Criminal Court — or, indeed, his claims to have planted evidence as a public prosecutor, shot three people dead, and thrown a criminal suspect from a chopper. True? Or just wisecracks? No one's sure.

'I know when he's joking,' said Jess Dureza, laughing heartily. 'You have to know him a long time.'

Dureza's known Duterte for more than 50 years, and shares

his political master's exasperation over the way the media and international community had, in his view, completely misread and over-egged Duterte's statements.

'When he says something, they take it as gospel truth!' he laughed, this time indignantly.

On one occasion, when Duterte's patience snapped after being criticised by the United Nations over his drugs war, he threatened to burn down the UN building if ever he went to New York. Dureza, ever his apologist, had been wheeled out to explain that this threat, like so many others, should be taken with a pinch of salt.

'Don't take him at his word,' he'd said. 'He's a very colourful person. He exaggerates … he never smiles, even though he jokes.'

'When he says a joke,' he told me, 'he puts on a poker face so that you don't know if he's just pulling your leg.'

I pointed out that, given the deadly nature of many of his threats, misreading him could literally prove fatal.

'He sends a strong message,' Dureza agreed. 'I call it dog-whistle politics,' he added, as though he had just invented the term. 'When you sound the whistle for the dog, it's ultrasonic, so only the dog hears it, right? Only the dog. He's very good at that.'

This made sense, coming from a president who has said that drug addict 'sniff-dogs' are not human. The strong statements Duterte makes, Dureza reasoned, are intended only for those he feels should get the warning.

'So when he says "I will kill you", if you're not involved in drugs, why should you worry? Why should you feel threatened? But if you are, you'd better watch out.'

The trouble is that ordinary people not involved in drugs do worry — a lot, as opinion polls have shown. And with so much collateral damage, their concern is not unwarranted.

Many of the threats are overt and direct, but Duterte is adept at sending subliminal orders, too — of the dog-whistle variety, which can be interpreted creatively by those who seek to please him. International criminal lawyers have marvelled at the brazenness of the president's support for those he has licenced to kill. These lawyers go so far as to describe his disregard for the concept of 'command responsibility' as 'highly unusual for a leader under the jurisdiction of the International Criminal Court — a prosecutor's dream'. Duterte's orders are, they say, more explicit than those of other leaders who have been prosecuted for crimes against humanity. It normally takes years for legal teams to sift through the statements of the likes of Slobodan Milošević, Sudan's Omar al-Bashir, or Syria's Bashar al-Assad, in order to establish a direct chain of command. Yet, despite Duterte's murderous threats on live TV and his public declarations of not giving 'a shit' about human rights, his orders can have a Mafiosi subtlety about them. When it was announced in February 2018 that the ICC would start a preliminary investigation into Duterte's war on drugs, his immediate response was to deny he had ever ordered police to kill drug suspects.

As I sat listening to Dureza defend the president's convivial incitements to kill, I was reminded of a conversation in Davao with someone who had probably studied Duterte more closely and for longer than anyone else I had met. Prospero Nograles was a former speaker of the Philippine house of representatives, and, for decades, Duterte's arch-political rival in Davao. Now retired, Prospero's efforts at political sorcery had failed. He had stepped back from the political fray; his rival had won; and, now in his seventies himself, he said he was content simply to have fought him and survived. We had been speaking about exactly what Dureza called the president's 'dog-whistle politics'. Nograles regarded his manner of communicating what he wanted to happen through a more filmic prism.

'This is the way he gives his orders,' Nograles said. 'Godfather-style. "I've got a stone in my shoe" — it means, "Kill the son of a bitch!"'

Yet the president's apologists do just what his sister Jocelyn does: they roll their eyes at what they see as the misinterpretation of their beloved leader. Stella Estremera is editor of the *SunStar* newspaper in Davao and knows Duterte well. She has reported on him, not particularly impartially, for 27 years. She is an acolyte and an expert in what she calls 'decoding Digong-speak'. Estremera insisted that Davaoeños feel lucky to have had him in charge. 'You can never second-guess him,' she told me very earnestly. 'It takes a lifetime to get to know this guy. When he does something, he already knows what the outcome will be and then, when it happens, you just go "Oh, WOW! Okay!"'

I was struck by the startling resemblance between Estremera's adulation of Duterte, who she cast as though he was some poet-warrior, and that of the young Russian in Joseph Conrad's *Heart of Darkness*, who idolised Mr Kurtz, the upriver ivory trader in the jungles of the Belgian Congo whose methods were deemed unsound: '"You don't talk with that man — you listen to him," he exclaimed with severe exaltation. He nodded with a nod full of mystery and wisdom. "I tell you," he cried, "this man has enlarged my mind."'

I recovered from my reverie in time to hear the high point of her Conrad-esque eulogy: 'If only I could have a quarter of his brain, I would be the most intelligent person in the world.'

He's just 'an old-fashioned guy', she said, 'who wants the world to be a safer place'.

As a Mindanaoan, the *SunStar* editor has taken delight in

mocking the failure of her Luzon counterparts to get the joke. 'He speaks the language of criminals. They understand when he's joking and when he's not. Sometimes his threats are made in jest, but they would know exactly when they're not.'

On the day of Duterte's inauguration, Estremera's tabloid ran a cheerleading, but insightful, article by the editor herself, offering five lessons to Filipinos unfamiliar with Mindanao's Bisaya language and the nuances of Bisayan social culture. In her view, the rest of the country needed to consider her points before they rushed to judgement. (The word Bisaya — or Visayan — is used to refer to the people of the Visayas islands and of Mindanao, who speak the 25 variations of the Bisaya language, which is also commonly called Visayan or Cebuano.)

Like all good Bisayans, Duterte does not take himself too seriously, she wrote; they have a 'penchant to make fun of, ridicule or belittle themselves and each other'. Understand that, she said, and you would get the drift 'of when to take Duterte seriously and when to let things pass'. Indeed, for all his narcissism, Duterte does charm his audiences with his disarmingly self-deprecating style. Once his prepared speech has been discarded, his off-the-cuff remarks will often belittle his patchy academic record, for example — and people warm to this; it's part of his *bugoy* allure. (Although Duterte earned a degree in political science and another in law, he was, by his own admission, not an A-stream student; his secondary school records show blank pages where exam results should have been recorded, according to the Holy Cross High School alumni officer.) But he also likes to point out that he is now the boss of those, like Jess Dureza, who had once bested him at school. Popularity in politics is the art of being able to poke fun at oneself. Duterte is a past-master of this technique; it's just that things get tricky when the joke is on him.

Bisaya has a slang term for this cultural quirk that does not readily translate into Tagalog, the Philippine lingua franca, or into English. They call it *yaga-yaga*. It doubles as a verb and a noun, and is probably best summed up as the character attributes of a blackguard. An individual manifesting *yaga-yaga* does not suffer fools gladly, lacks politeness, mocks pretension, treats others contemptuously, wounds their feelings, and humiliates. But because it's done in good humour, it's all okay. Applied to Duterte, this definition of *yaga-yaga* is almost identical to what the psychologist's assessment concluded about his personality on the annulment of his marriage.

Stella Estremera's guide to Digong-speak went on to explain the president's notorious loquaciousness: 'Talk is important and he can talk for several hours.' He resents protocol, she noted, but understands why it's necessary. 'He talks dirty but he knows GMRC (good manners and right conduct).' One thing close associates and those who have covered him for a long time will agree on, she continued, is that 'what he said ten years ago will still be what he will be saying today ... The predicate for "shoot-to-kill" is if the criminal endangers the lives of the policemen.' Estremera's final lesson for fellow Filipinos who remained baffled by Duterte's outbursts was more of an observation and was particularly astute: 'He enjoys bantering with his audience and this is what gets him into trouble; when his typically Visayan banter offends the Tagalog poise and pride.' She finished with a stirring enjoinder to her compatriots to watch and learn: 'It's time to observe the President and be awed by how he will bring his brand of leadership to the national level.'

In bringing his Bisayan brand of leadership to the national — and international — level, the Philippines' lost-in-translation president has, simply, in the view of Davaoeños, been the victim of a culture-clash train-crash. A professor I met at the Jesuit university, Ateneo de Davao, also cast Duterte as a prime exemplar of the Bisayan stereotype, caught in the headlights of an uncomprehending, culturally ignorant, and unforgiving world.

Ramon Beleno, chair of political science, put it like this: 'Bisayan people are happy people. Jokes are very important. They're creative in the way they describe things and this is a problem for our president. He never follows scripts. He inserts jokes in serious matters, even in matters of national security, and people just do not understand that. But it's his way of delivery … We live in hope that he will change, but you can't teach an old dog new tricks. The problem is, it gets him into trouble because people take him seriously.' Professor Ramon paused for thought. 'He's just a playful old guy,' he said. 'And flirty.'

The Bisayan playful flirtiness, which the *bugoy* prince had employed in attempting to woo Pilang all those years ago, turned out not to translate very well either. One evening, over drinks, I asked Stella Estremera what her favourite joke was that he'd told.

'Well,' she said, 'the most repeated ones over the years are his sexy jokes about women. You'd be sitting talking to him,' she reminisced, 'and then he'd break off when he sees a beautiful woman and he'll get distracted and say "Whoooaaarrrrrr! Look at that!" Then he'll come back to the conversation and everyone would roll their eyes.' Estremera giggled.

It wasn't quite what I'd meant when I'd asked about a Duterte 'joke', but I had put the same question to another Duterte-loyalist earlier that day and received an even more bizarre response.

Leo Villareal, a former radio journalist, had worked for the mayor of Davao for many years. His chosen example of Duterte's personal brand of humour left me unsure of how best to react.

'Oh, yes, the Mayor is very fond of jokes,' he sniggered. 'He used to say things like "I love gays because I used to be one!

Hahahahahaha!"' Leo Villareal began heaving with laughter, drawing the amused attention of the table next to us.

Duterte has never made a secret of his hot-blooded heterosexuality. While looking around his 'ancestral home' in Davao with his older sister, Eleanor, as my personal guide, she told me that their mother had built him what she called 'a small apartment', which he allowed 'no one' from the family to enter. Once, trespassing in the hope that she could urge the young Rodrigo to clean the apartment, his mother stumbled across a large stash of *Playboy* magazines strewn around the room. Challenging him on how much money he must have spent on them — and remember, Davao was, in the 1960s, in a remote corner of the deeply conservative Catholic Philippines, where *Playboy* magazine would have feared to tread — Duterte told his pious mother that he'd been given them by friends. He was, by then, too old for her to sentence him to the mung-bean-crucifix penance. The Duterte family *Playboy*-gate scandal left an indelible impression on Eleanor, who all these years on, was, like Jocelyn, amused by her brother's impishness. And yes, she rolled her eyes.

Duterte's teenage roguishness evolved into a Weinstein-esque hands-on approach to women. He became the pastiche of a Hollywood tough-guy, who loved girls and guns and Harleys, and his stash of *Playboy*s would become flesh and turn into his personal harem. Women, his old associates all said, seemed drawn to him. A leading journalist in Davao, who followed Duterte closely throughout his time as mayor, said 'he would always have five or six girlfriends on the go at any one time — and that's not counting one-night stands'.

In October 2017, at exactly the moment the Harvey Weinstein scandal erupted in global headlines, President Duterte was entertaining the Hollywood actor Steven Seagal, the erstwhile blockbuster tough-guy, at Malacañang Palace. He was in the

Philippines to check on locations for his next film, which will be 'about illegal drugs and other crimes', a palace statement said. The two tough-guys were photographed posing together by the presidential media unit, their clenched fists punching towards the camera in Duterte's signature salute. The president reiterated his favourite line to the actor – that movies are a reflection of life — and he offered a hard-sell on his drugs war. Seagal endorsed him, in exchange, confiding that he had made close to a hundred visits to the Philippines over the years — although he didn't say why. What he did say was that he was a big fan of the president, who 'has been instrumental in making the Philippines a safer place'. The previous day, *The Washington Post* had run a searing exposé on Seagal, citing a 'long and sordid' catalogue of allegations against him, from 'too many women to count', that bore a striking resemblance to those against Weinstein. It was headlined 'Steven Seagal: Drug warrior, honorary cop, alleged sex-abuser'. In Manila, the film star had met his match.

The president, whose first marriage was dissolved, rather oddly asked his daughter Sara to be his nominal first lady — an invitation she declined. Duterte has hinted that he would like her to follow him into Malacañang. But his long-term girlfriend, Cielito 'Honeylet' Avanceña, 24 years younger than him, a beauty queen-turned-nurse-turned-businesswoman, is his consort. They have a teenaged daughter, Veronica, known as Kitty. Honeylet helped bankroll Duterte's campaign for re-election as mayor of Davao in 2001 by selling her house in the US — an act of commitment Duterte never forgot. Another ex-paramour, in Davao, Girlie Balaba, is a former anchor of 'TV Patrol', the most watched news-magazine programme in Davao. His ex-wife, Elizabeth, with whom he has three children, had testified to Duterte's womanising and his string of extra-marital affairs. Chief among these was Honeylet, although she lived in California, where she worked as a nurse for six years. Duterte was a frequent visitor — until he was refused a US visa.

As an election candidate, Duterte was happy to boast of his conquests, and laughed off his reputation as a legendary philanderer. He did not moderate his alpha male behaviour when he found himself in front of national TV cameras. Quite the opposite: in campaign rallies he was filmed forcibly kissing women on the lips, on stage, in front of thousands of cheering supporters. When these embarrassed women tried to pull away, he grabbed them by the faces and pressed his into theirs. These lewd displays made news, but in a Duterte Harvey-like way, he always made light of his behaviour, and his fan club tittered at his 'naughty playfulness'. He was often photographed with his arms around good-looking, adoring young women on the campaign trail, sometimes staring smugly at the camera, balancing a pouting beauty on his knee. He would flippantly discuss his sex life, admitting to having three girlfriends, and discussing, in full physiological detail, how Viagra had revolutionised his life.

Typically, when I met Jocelyn, she explained the mayor's attitude to women in the context of Mindanaoan culture: 'It's a kind of a macho system. He can be very, very tough on women. A woman is not supposed to speak her mind.' As an afterthought she added: 'The mayor might be a ladies' man, but he is very respectful to women too, you know.'

Duterte's supporters always point out how, as mayor of Davao, Duterte was credited with giving many women 'a leg-up', in local government, most notably a feminist city councillor called Luzviminda 'Luz' Ilagan. She owed Duterte a debt of gratitude for past legal assistance, and they developed a close working relationship.

Ilagan was a member of the national women's party, GABRIELA, which she went on to represent in Congress. Hand in glove with the mayor, she worked on anti-discrimination laws, including the Davao City Women's Development Code, a trailblazer in the Philippines. In the months before the presidential election, when GABRIELA condemned Duterte's womanising as 'an affront to women's rights', Ilagan defended him. 'Womanising, kissing — most of that is media hype,' she said. 'Even if he says "I am a womaniser" — he has girlfriends — remember that the mayor has separated ... Look beyond the words. Look beyond the actions. Focus on what he has done, what he can do, and what he is still doing that will benefit our people.'

Her party slapped her down.

There's no indication that, as president, Duterte has changed his ways; in news conferences, he continues to flirt shamelessly with young female reporters. A western diplomat noted how, at the Palace, the president had surrounded himself with 'laddery', and a highly respected Filipina journalist advised me that if I wanted a one-to-one interview (which I requested relentlessly over the course of a year) I should hire 'a really pretty Filipina fixer' to help me lobby the president. Otherwise, she said, I wouldn't stand a hope.

'I hate to say that,' she admitted, 'but I'm afraid it's true. That's just the way it works.'

Addressing graduates at his former law school, Duterte said that he 'playfully spanked the bottoms of his female security staff in Malacañang' and that 'too many prohibitions in modern times spoil the fun.' The president, clearly unconstrained by puritanical prohibitions, professed his fidelity to Filipina women, announcing in February 2018, in a speech to the National Economic and Development Authority, that foreign women don't attract him because they have a 'queer' odour. He added: 'I'm faithful to the Filipina. There are many of them, but I'm faithful. It doesn't have to be just one woman. I'm faithful to the Filipina because they're fragrant.' On occasion, during foreign forays, Duterte boasts wistfully about his archipelago of fragrant Filipinas. Also in February 2018, he told a business forum in India that, just as jihadists can look forward to their 72 virgins in heaven, if they die as martyrs, similar — but living — pleasures await visitors to the Philippines.

In May 2017, the president appointed the celebrity sex-blogger, pop star, and 'provocative' dancer Margaux 'Mocha' Uson as assistant secretary for social media in his presidential communications team at Malacañang. Mocha has over 5 million Facebook followers and has long been accused of disseminating fake news — pro-Duterte fake news — via her prodigious output on various social media. Duterte's supporters, like Donald Trump's, have taken to the digital realm as a means of bypassing traditional media, which they view as biased. Mocha is the undisputed queen of the president's cyber-cheerleaders. Duterte's sexy-Svengali, and her all-female dance troupe, the Mocha Girls, also appeared at many campaign rallies. The president said her appointment to his team was a reward for loyal service.

Mocha's background as a sex guru — perhaps most memorably involving a graphic online demonstration, with a female accomplice, on how and where to find the G-spot — should not disqualify her from serving the public, Duterte said.

'There is no law which says that if you expose half of your body with shorts and a bra you are disqualified from being the president of the Philippines,' he said. 'She was not dancing naked ... a little bit sexier than the others. But that does not prevent anybody to deprive her of the honours she deserves [sic].'

Although Mocha's appointment caused a stir and raised eyebrows, it is clear from blog posts and comments on newspaper reports that many Filipinos relish their president's machismo and his contempt for political correctness. Playing devil's advocate, some might argue that this particular presidential vice shouldn't necessarily have any bearing on his competence as national leader — there have certainly been no moves to impeach him over this, and Duterte has never denied 'having sexual relations' with anyone. As a what-you-see-is-what-you-get politician who likes to present himself as flawed but transparent, Duterte has always maintained that hypocrisy is the one thing that gets his goat, above all else. He even said in 2017 that he felt such contempt for sanctimonious priests and self-righteous politicians in particular that one day he would write a book about this particular bugbear. Its title, he declared, would simply be *Hypocrisy*.

Yet following Duterte's spanking confession, opposition senator Risa Hontiveros, known for her strong stance on women's rights, took issue with what she called the president's 'slut-shaming' of Senator Leila de Lima, whom he had viciously attacked — for having had 'an affair'. In common with Duterte, de Lima's own marriage had actually been annulled and her subsequent 'affair' had been with a man who was separated from his wife. Duterte professed to have seen a 'sex-tape' of de Lima with her lover, which, he said, caused him to lose his appetite every time he watched it. He didn't explain why he had watched it more than once.

'De Lima is not only screwing her driver,' Duterte proclaimed in a televised speech, 'she is also screwing the nation.' He mocked what he called her 'propensity for sex', ending his tirade in the Tagalog language: 'Whore-mother. If she were my mother, I'd shoot her.'

Analyse that.

At the root of the president's verbal assault was de Lima's outspoken opposition to Duterte's war on drugs and her singular determination to continue probing his past, particularly his links to the Davao Death Squad. He, in parallel with his sexual shaming of her, also accused her of complicity with drug lords. His comments made headlines and sparked outrage, both from those apparently appalled by her 'lasciviousness' and 'sexual misconduct', and from those alarmed by the very public manner of his personal attacks on her. In the pro-Duterte social media, with Mocha acting as cheerleader-in-chief, de Lima was crucified.

A leading human rights commentator, who requested anonymity, put it like this: 'Duterte is a predator, capable of anything. The existence of the video is immaterial. Whether or not it's real, it served its purpose, discrediting Leila de Lima as an immoral, loose woman who couldn't be believed. The misogyny is breathtaking. You've got to hand it to Duterte's people. All they managed to prove is that she had a relationship. Talk about exploitation of the public purse.'

Adding insult to injury, a humiliated Senator de Lima was interrogated on primetime TV about her relationship with her former driver: 'As a human being, as a woman, I have frailties, I have weaknesses,' she said. 'I have always considered my personal life as a private matter; it's a sacred thing to me. I am not the bad and evil woman or slut they are trying to portray.'

Duterte refused to let the issue of the supposed 'sex video' go. In November 2017, de Lima revealed that, having requested a papal blessing (so as to give her the strength to continue the fight against 'injustice'), Pope Francis had sent a rosary to her for her birthday. The gift had been delivered to her cell by the Philippine National Police chaplain. On learning of this, Duterte quipped — during an anti-corruption summit — that if Pope Francis could only see the video, he might change his mind about the senator.

'Could you find me the video? Let the Pope see it! He might be removed from the papacy,' he said. 'Son of a bitch, this is too much.'

Senator Hontiveros, who had condemned Duterte's treatment of de Lima also rounded on what she called the 'nasty and baseless' sexist remarks Duterte had made against his vice president, Leni Robredo, another woman with whom he had a particularly fractious relationship, because she too challenged him. Robredo's reputation had also been besmirched, Hontiveros said, by fake news and memes, circulated by blogs and numerous fake Facebook accounts. She accused Duterte of contributing to a prevalent culture of misogyny.

'This is the kind of climate we Filipino women are contending with right now. We live in a period where the culture of rape, sexual harassment, and male sexual violence is prevalent, made worse by the dishonourable behaviour of some of our elected national leaders who lend their voices to the gross, blatant objectification of all women.'

On one occasion, in the run-up to his election, Duterte poured cold water on his own daughter's claim to have been raped; Sara Duterte was, he said, a 'drama queen'.

Senator Hontiveros has since been ejected as chair of a Senate committee. By September 2017, allies of Duterte in Congress had filed a criminal complaint against her on a broad range of charges.

In the 1980s, Davao City, known then as the 'Nicaragua of Asia', was wracked by violence and chaos. Assassinations were a daily occurrence; gun-fights were common, as were armed hold-ups, kidnaps, rapes, and murders; much of the criminality was blamed on drugs — although crystal meth had yet to make its grim entrance. Two years after the dictator, Marcos, fled the Philippines, Duterte was elected mayor of Davao City on the promise that he'd clean things up, and, one year after that, in mid-August 1989, he faced his first major security challenge

— a hostage crisis, involving a foreign captive. A gang of convicts, who had already once escaped from the Davao Penal Colony, seized a group of missionaries who were proselytising in their prison. The hostage-takers, armed with knives and an Armalite M-16 rifle they'd snatched from a guard, called themselves 'The Wild Boys'. The Protestant evangelists belonged to a group called 'The Joyful Assembly of God'. After two days of fruitless negotiations — led by Duterte's former classmate, Jess Dureza — the military and police stormed the prison. They had learned from five hostages who had escaped that The Wild Boys had already murdered and raped some of their fellow hostages.

What happened next remains disputed, but in the confusion of the rescue operation, five of the 15 hostages were killed, including the only foreigner, a 36-year-old Australian, Jacqueline Hamill, one of the women raped at knife-point and used as a human shield by the leader of the gang while they tried to make a getaway. It seems she was killed by a sniper's bullet. There is a dramatic photograph of Hamill being held at gunpoint, along with other hostages, in the moments before troops and police opened fire.

The Sydney Morning Herald reported that 'Ms Hamill is known to have sung hymns to calm the other hostages.' Another report quoted a survivor saying Hamill had been singing praises and praying as she lay wounded on the ground. All 16 hostage-takers were shot dead, and photographers who covered the assault took pictures of an officer finishing off one of the wounded gang members who was reportedly still moving.

A subsequent investigation, led jointly by a retired general and a senator, exonerated the Regional Special Action Force-Davao and praised its rescue bid. According to contemporaneous national newspaper reports, the Senate's Defense Committee chairman, in his assessment, 'deplored the lack of training and preparedness of the local civilian officials in handling the incident. He expressed surprise at the decision of the civilian officials to give the shoot-to-kill order.' The top civilian official in charge? The recently elected mayor of Davao, although, strangely, there is no mention of Rodrigo Duterte in newspaper reports from the time.

Twenty-seven years later, in Duterte's own recounting of the tragic events that unfolded that day, he was centre-stage. His narrative, particularly surrounding the death of Hamill, contains inconsistencies over what happened and contradicts accounts in newspaper reports and evidence from photographs. In contrast to the investigating senator's excoriating verdict, Duterte's account paints him as the hero. Enraged, he claimed, by the murder of the Australian missionary, he had personally ordered the assault.

'"Kill them all,"' was Duterte's proud recollection of his orders. 'I said, "Shoot to kill." I got my Uzi from my trailer. I emptied the whole magazine ... Brrrrrrrrrrt. There. They were all dead.'

This, at least, does correspond to the findings of the senator who originally investigated the affair. But a columnist for the *Manila Times*, one of the newspapers that originally reported on the crisis, dismissed Duterte's version of events as a 'necrophiliac fantasy'. It is possible that his version falls into the 'three-out-of-five' category of things he claims and later says are not true. Duterte boasted of his 'heroics' in this hostage crisis to impress the crowds at an election rally in April 2016. He even taunted other candidates, saying that if they hadn't killed anyone, as he had, they shouldn't even be standing for the presidency.

'Me? I killed all of them,' he boasted.

But the reason the death of Jackie Hamill in August 1989 hit the headlines again — more than quarter of a century later —

was less to do with how Duterte spun his own 'heroics' and more about the way he told the story, which he thought appropriate to deliver as a joke. At a rally in Manila's Quezon City a month before the presidential polls, a deadpan Duterte dressed in a red Polo shirt and standing spot-lit, centre stage, told the worst-taste joke he'd ever told — and, quite possibly the worst in the history of political oratory anywhere. A video clip of what he said went viral.

'I looked at her [Hamill's] face. Son of a bitch, she looks like a beautiful actress!' he said, grasping the wireless microphone and pausing, with the timing of a stand-up comedian, for applause. 'Son of a bitch. What a waste. What came to my mind was, they raped her, lined up for her. I was angry because she was raped, that's one thing. But she was so beautiful, the mayor should have been first. What a waste.' His words were greeted by raucous laughter inside Amoranto Stadium where the rally was held, but, as jaws dropped in the world outside, the eye-rolling Duterte fan club brushed off the remarks with that knowing snigger; this was just Duterte being Duterte. The campaign front-runner's popularity in opinion polls continued to rise, regardless.

Yet news of his latest ill-judged rhetorical abomination was met with horror as the story hit front pages not just in the Philippines but around the world as well. *The Washington Post* quoted a tweet: 'Wow, Trump wouldn't even say something like that.' Australia's ambassador to Manila, Amanda Gorley, also reacted on Twitter: 'Rape and murder should never be joked about or trivialised. Violence against women and girls is unacceptable anytime, anywhere.' It is understood that this tweet was carefully considered by diplomats at the Australian embassy, responding to an offensive remark about a deceased Australian citizen. Rodrigo Duterte was, pointedly, not mentioned by name, but nevertheless his riposte to the ambassador's tweet was aggressive: 'This is politics. Stay out Australian government. Stay out.'

The American ambassador, Philip Goldberg, got both barrels, too, after he weighed in, remarking in an interview with CNN that he could only agree with his Australian colleague. His choice of words had also been carefully constructed: 'Any statements by anyone, anywhere that either degrade women or trivialise issues so serious as rape or murder are not ones that we condone.'

To the rage-fuelled Duterte, the ambassadors' comments were a red rag: moralising, arrogant, neo-imperialist, and hypocritical. It pushed all his buttons. As a lawyer, he was aware that they were also in possible violation of strict rules, set out in the Philippines' Election Code, which declare 'unlawful' any foreign intervention in elections. As Filipino commentators pointed out, the diplomats' remarks, even if intended as apolitical, were said in a politically charged environment, and were construed by many as the two countries taking sides. A furious Duterte told the ambassadors to 'shut their mouths' and said if he was elected president, he would sever diplomatic ties.

The real fallout with the United States would come months later, with Duterte ensconced in Malacañang Palace. In a televised address, following a meeting with then US secretary of state John Kerry, the president said he resented what he called the ambassador's meddling in the Philippine election. In a Tagalog-language homophobic slur, he expressed his continued animosity, referring to Goldberg as America's 'gay' ambassador.

'The son of a whore,' he said in a speech to the army. 'He really pissed me off'. He used the Tagalog colloquial term *bakla* — best translated as 'pansy'. In the Philippines, certainly among his supporters, this went down pretty well; in America, less so, causing a diplomatic incident, but Duterte dug his heels in, resolutely refusing to apologise. Neither did he ever apologise for his original rape joke. Instead, he perpetuated the Duterte mythology, blaming what he called the 'gutter language', he had picked up in his childhood.

'It wasn't a bad joke,' he repeatedly insisted. 'It wasn't a joke! I said it in the heat of anger. It's my style!' he said, in his typically defiant, garbled English. 'My mouth. Do not control my mouth! God-given. As a matter of apology, I will not. I will never!'

In December 2016, following the departure of Ambassador Goldberg at the end of his diplomatic tour, allegations surfaced in the press, citing unnamed sources, of what was ominously branded 'The Goldberg Blueprint', supposedly a plot to oust Duterte and 'bring him to his knees'. By then, though, Goldberg was gone, and, during Barack Obama's final weeks in office, the president appointed a new emissary to Manila. When Ambassador Sung Kim, an American of Korean ancestry, was sworn in at Malacañang, President Duterte, true to form, gave Kim a personal welcome gift. It was a copy of what was now his favourite book, which he'd also been handing out to his generals: an account by British journalist Ioan Grillo of the bloodthirsty world of Latin America's narco-cartels: *Gangster Warlords*.

As to Duterte's ribald humour, the president outdid himself one year into his term. Addressing soldiers on Mindanao, where he had recently declared military rule, he sought to reassure them that should they be accused of committing abuses under martial law, he would take personal responsibility for their actions. Then he joked: 'If you raped three, I will admit it, that's on me!'

No one laughed.

When social media exploded with outrage, Chelsea Clinton, daughter of the former US president, denounced Duterte's quip, echoing the words of the ambassadors on the previous occasion. He was, she said, 'a murderous thug with no regard for human rights' and a sickening sense of humour.

'Rape is never a joke,' she tweeted. 'Not funny. Ever.'

As the presidential communications team scrambled to excuse the remark and defuse things by saying the president had been speaking with 'heightened bravado' as a tonic for the troops, Duterte jumped headlong back into the fray. In an expletive-rich speech to naval officers at a base in Davao he said (in a mixture of Tagalog and English) he had been wilfully misinterpreted … again. He would like to remind Ms Clinton, he said, of her father's affair with Monica Lewinsky, the White House intern, which had led to his impeachment in 1998.

'These whores, they hear "rape". Like Chelsea. She slammed me. I was not joking. I was being sarcastic … I will tell her when your father, the president of the United States then, was screwing Lewinsky and the girls in the office of the president, on the table … on the sofa, how did you feel? Did you slam your father?' Chelsea Clinton had been a teenager at that time.

Then, after highlighting rapes and murders by US soldiers serving in the Philippines and Japan, Duterte took another stab at the former US president's daughter.

'So you Americans, like Chelsea … you live in a glass house. I repeat, when President Clinton was fucking Lewinsky, what was … your reaction?'

The naval officers in their smart, white uniforms remained po-faced. The speech was streamed live by the Malacañang communications team. When it was replayed later on national news headlines, they had had time to bleep it.

Chelsea Clinton kept her own counsel.

The President of the Philippines reached a new misogynistic nadir in February 2018, when he delivered a speech in Malacañang Palace to more than 200 communist NPA guerrillas who had recently surrendered, a quarter of them women. Speaking in Bisaya, Duterte declared that it was time that Philippine armed forces got even with the NPA, instructing soldiers not to kill female rebel fighters, who he referred to as 'Amazons'.

'Shoot their vagina,' he said, 'because without that they are useless.'

This was his new order, he said. Soldiers should be informed of how to deal with female NPA guerrillas. 'We won't kill you. We will just shoot your vagina,' he repeated, this time addressing the women who had surrendered. 'If there is no vagina, it would be useless [sic].' The official Malacañang transcript of the presidential address censored the word *bisong* (vagina in Bisaya) and its English translation.

For this, the women's party, GABRIELA, branded Duterte a 'macho fascist' and said he had taken 'terrorism against women' to a new level. He was the 'epitome of misogyny and fascism terribly rolled into one', said GABRIELA Congresswoman Emmi de Jesus, accusing him of encouraging violence against women and specifically encouraging the armed forces to commit crimes of sexual violence. Another activist was quoted as saying: 'We have been reduced to our genitalia.'

A few days earlier, Duterte's spokesman, Harry Roque, had said that feminists were what he called 'OA' (over-acting) when reacting to the president's ribald humour and suggesting they should lighten up.

'I mean, that's funny. Just laugh,' he said, adding that Filipinos loved Duterte because they related to his sense of humour. In reality, ever larger numbers of Filipinos were left lost for words when they read of his *bisong* banter. It was always going to be tough to trump Trump's 'grab them by the pussy' remark, and, in the community of world statesmen, there was only ever going to be one member capable of rising to the occasion.

6

TALKING DUTERTE

There's a spicy street lexicon of popular idiom in the Philippines, its etymology layered with expletives — mostly to do with people's mothers — handed down by Spanish colonial clerics after their 300-year occupation. A further half-century of bawdy US G.I. Joes added a linguistic legacy more scatological and sexual in nature. The Philippines was the Americans' first overseas colony, acquired from the Spanish after a short war in 1898 for US$20 million, a history that gave rise to the aphorism that Filipinos had spent 300 years in a convent then 50 years in Hollywood. Taglish, the portmanteau blending Tagalog (the Philippines' lingua franca) and English (its only other official language), is pretty much a dialect in its own right and is spoken in distinctively Filipino-Spanish-accented American English.

Depending on where in the Philippines you are, Taglish slang also borrows from the coarser traditions of 175 living indigenous languages — including Duterte's native Cebuano or Bisaya —

which belong to the vast archipelago's mostly Malayo-Polynesian people. Outside the big cities and in poorer parts within them, English itself is not widely spoken, but wherever you go, the local vernacular is alive with Taglish slang. Filipinos have married their European, American, Arab, and Chinese interlopers for so long that bloodlines — as with cultural and culinary influences — are a seductive, globalised fusion. Dialectical idiosyncrasies are no exception, with Taglish expletives gratuitously enhanced by the sheer thrill derived from irritating priests.

In everyday Filipino English, quaint anachronisms crop up all the time: words like 'prankster' and 'boondocks' — the latter being the only Tagalog word known to have entered the English language. *Bundok* means 'mountain', and was sequestrated by US troops fighting in the Philippines at the turn of the last century. Then there's 'scalawag', with a rather darker connotation than the quaint image of naughty schoolboys. In the Philippines, a 'scalawag' is a corrupt cop or a murderous villain. In this fluid patois new words and phrases are invented, old ones reinvented and redefined: this is a country of kidnappers and 'carnappers', a place where flip-flops are 'slippers' and where 'personalities' aren't showbiz stars, but often refer to the kingpins of the narco-trade.

The meanings of some English-sounding words have been lost altogether, and sometimes reworked as sinister euphemisms. Take the verb 'to salvage'. In the Philippines, this means 'to commit an extra-judicial killing' — and is thought to derive from the Spanish *salvaje*, meaning 'savage' or 'brutal'. When Duterte's killing spree began, the term 'salvage' was resurrected from the era of the Marcos dictatorship. But now, even the acronym 'EJK' has entered common parlance; it's used, without explanation, in newspaper reportage as well as in everyday speech. For most Filipinos, the terms 'EJK' and 'salvaged' will trigger the image of a grotesquely twisted corpse draped over a kerbstone, caught in car headlamps or a police arc-light, as a pool of blood congeals in the gutter.

The word *tokhang* topped the new-entry list in the Filipino dictionary from the start of the Duterte era, and would likely have taken first prize in any 'Neologism of the Year' award for the president's first year in office. The word combines two Bisayan-language terms — *toktok*, the onomatopoeic word for 'knock', and *hangyo*, which means 'plead' — and for Filipinos it has a particularly sinister connotation. Operation Tokhang involved armed police moving house-to-house through slums across the country, their lists of suspected *shabu* users and dealers provided by district leaders.

The first time I ventured out with my Channel 4 News crew to film on the front line of Duterte's drugs war, we joined police on Operation Tokhang in Tondo slum in Manila, reputedly the biggest and most dangerous in the Philippines, where drugs were rife, and murder, rape, and domestic violence endemic. In three decades of reporting from some of the poorest places on the planet, I had rarely seen such depressing poverty as this; a crush of humanity living on top of each other in broken, teetering shanty-shacks above filthy streets laced with tangled wires and strewn with stinking piles of rubbish. The particular area we were in was called 'Happyland'. The name itself derived not from its residents' sense of contentment, but from the Bisaya word for 'dump'. We squeezed down filthy, crowded alleyways so dark that, despite it being mid-afternoon, the police used torches as they scrambled unsteadily up makeshift ladders to knock on plywood doors — and plead.

It was mid-August 2016 and, since the presidential inauguration just six weeks earlier, Tondo police had already shot more than 20 suspected *shabu* dealers or addicts dead in buy-bust operations. Others had been killed by masked riders wielding Colt .45s, which Tondo residents had begun to call 'Duterte pistols'. We followed officers from a small local station, who told me their unit alone had been responsible for 11 of those deaths in Happyland, the very neighbourhood that we were squelching through.

The cops were on best behaviour for the camera and so was everyone who lived there. We filmed as suspected *shabu* smokers were warned by police to surrender or face arrest. Across the Philippines, more than a million had already done so, but thousands had been killed regardless, the majority shot dead by unknown assailants. These killings — widely ascribed to off-duty cops — have been labelled DUIs (deaths under investigation). This term, like EJKs, had also entered the urban dictionary. The 'investigations' have almost never led to successful prosecutions. I asked the officers we were with who they thought the so-called 'vigilante' killers were. They shrugged.

Despite the carnage, a survey found that four out of five Filipinos claimed their neighbourhoods felt 'safer' as a result of Operation Tokhang. But the police knock-and-plead campaign was also responsible for the suspicion and unease that had settled on the squatter settlements where most of the victims lived, due to the spike in the murder rate, as documented by official police statistics, and the brutal manner in which targeted killings were carried out.

The word *tokhang* inspired a dark, explicit thrash-rock track by a band called Hoodlum, and, in a stab at macabre humour, a Manila restaurant had even begun to offer 'Tokhang Sizzlers'. The dishes on this menu were named after the gorier aspects of the chase, arrest, or EJK of suspects. Delicacies included 'Pork Sausage Stuffed into a Sack', 'The Ham that Fought Back', and 'Mistaken Identity Hotdog'. In slang-speak, *tokhang* has already mutated into *tokbang* — a more accurate description of what actually happens.

There is also a term for the masked motorbike-borne assassins whose pillions 'neutralise' the selected target: this is known as 'riding in tandem', a phrase first coined in Davao City during Duterte's rein as mayor. Every Filipino knows it means death. Police have shot dead around a third of those who have been killed in the war on drugs; the remaining two-thirds are the result of these so-called 'vigilante' hits, most by executioners 'riding in tandem'. Although the term is Filipino, the assassination technique was honed by the cocaine cowboys of Colombia in the 1980s, when drugs gangs ambushed their rivals in public with gruesome regularity. In 2012, Griselda Blanco, a Medellín drug lord known as the godmother of cocaine — for whom the hallmark of her particular brand of vengeance was these motorcycle hitmen — was hoist with her own petard, shot to death in downtown Medellín by two gunmen on motorbikes.

By the early months of 2017, with the number of people killed already well over 8000, half the Philippines was paralysed by motorcycle-phobia. In this case, though, it wasn't fear of riding motorbikes, but fear of the very sound of an approaching motorbike. When a motorbike with two men 'riding in tandem' draws level at lights and cast a sideways glance, the occupants of adjacent cars fall silent. Two men on a motorbike, wearing full-face helmets, spells trouble; they are the horsemen of the Duterte apocalypse. These narcos-style assassinations have become so common that a senior politician I met had employed armed outrider-bodyguards on motorbikes to accompany his vehicle. It was, he said, the appropriate, if imperfect, foil.

The narco-world has itself opened up a whole new terminological universe. A dealer or a pusher is a 'player' — and these days, players have among the lowest life expectancies of all. They get their 'garbage', 'candy', or 'Jollibee' (named after the much-loved Filipino multinational fast-food franchise) from 'source' — the distributors, who are supplied by the drug lords. The 'personalities' at the top of the narco-tree refer to the thousands of allegedly corrupt drug-dealing cops, mayors, generals, judges, and politicians, said to feature on the voluminous 'Narco List' Duterte waves in the air during his speeches.

'Source' supplies 'players' via 'runners' who rarely move around with more than one 'bulk' (five grams) at a time. 'Players' sell *taryang* 500s and *taryang* 1000s (sachets of *shabu*, priced in pesos and worth US$10–20) to 'scorers' to feed their habit — known in Philippine street narco-slang as their 'showbiz'. Armed with their 'Jollibees', the 'scorer' will 'iron' their tinfoil, to make sure their molten 'candy' rolls smoothly. Having heated the foil from below with a lighter, they use a glass 'tooter' to chase the dragon and suck up the smoke. The posh way to smoke *shabu* is by shisha — a water pipe. The sticky residue that forms on the water can then be recycled, re-cooked, and inhaled.

Back in normal street-slang land, the Catholicism practised by 80 million Filipinos has no bearing on the liberal use of expletives peppering everyday speech, more often than not as terms of endearment. Clerics lament how the Philippines' moral values have been eroded by the growing acceptability of the use of foul language, particularly in school playgrounds, and you can guess who they blame for that. But such criticism from the clergy reeks of hypocrisy and Duterte knows it. Many Filipino priests have a luxuriant vocabulary themselves. I was having an earnest discussion with one about the president's apparent blood-lust and he said, with not even a sideways glance at a crucifix, 'Yes, psychologically, Duterte is really fucked up.'

But it's Rodrigo Duterte himself who has introduced the language of the common man to the glossary of national statecraft, and brought his own brand of shock-politics and vivid vocabulary to the august precincts of Malacañang Palace — in contrast to his rather more strait-laced predecessors. When it comes to uncouth language, Davao's hoodlum *bugoy*-king never disappoints. In the run-up to the May 2016 presidential election, while many priests, prudes, and snobs shook their heads and sat tutting, most of the Philippines' educated middle-class laughed off all the effing and blinding as a spontaneous and entertaining breath of fresh air. Besides, Duterte's promises of rooting out corruption and stopping crime were issues they were far more concerned about. Those close to him dismiss his vocabulary as riddled with 'fireworks' and joke that there's no rule of law in his mouth.

As the new president became world famous, in large part due to his earthy language, he also quickly bequeathed his name to the national dictionary. 'Dutertismo' was born. The term (coined in homage to Venezuela's Chavismo) sums up the populist nationalism he has come to personify, symbolised by the aggressive clenched-fist campaign-motif of Davao's Duterte Harry. Among his detractors, (and yes, this too is politically incorrect), the derogatory term for his supporters and trolls is the 'Dutertards'. A derivative of this is 'Dutertireds' (those who voted for him, but then wished they hadn't).

After that, come the Dutertisms — the President's unique and often incomprehensible mangle of Taglish and Bisaya, which he combines with frequent malapropisms, unfinished sentences, inaudible mumblings, and quirky, rarely used words. Tautology is common: the United Nations, he said, 'is one useless, inutile body'. Duterte casually utters old-fashioned words such as 'tarry', which is what he makes journalists do at his press conferences. In his first State of the Nation address, he employed the word 'perorate'. I had to look it up. It's a verb meaning 'to make very long speeches'. Its use, in this case so post-ironic that the fact that he didn't appear get his own joke made it all the more amusing.

Apart from their insurgent populism, Manglish is another thing that Duterte has in common with Donald Trump. Writing in *The New York Times*, the columnist Charles M. Blow noted that 'Trumpian language is a thing unto itself ... a jumble of incomplete thoughts stitched together with arrogance and ignorance. America is suffering under a tyranny of gibberish'. He referred to Trump's style of rhetoric as 'parataxis', consisting of short, sharp sentences used to emphasise certainty and determination, the hallmark of dictators. I was immediately reminded of Duterte's campaign-style, populist sound-bite rhetoric: 'Kill them! These sons of whores are destroying our country. I really will kill you.' There were similarities, too, in the way Duterte spun his half-truths and alt facts, including his oft-repeated assertions that the Philippines is in the throes of a methamphetamine pandemic so serious that national security is threatened, and his claim that as mayor of Davao he'd transformed the city into an oasis of tranquillity.

'Many people expect a political lie to sound slick, to be delivered by intellectual elites spouting $5 words,' wrote Blow. 'A clumsy, folksy lie delivered by a shyster using broken English reads as truth.'

In the course of researching this book, I have waded through the transcripts of Duterte's rambling speeches, just as Charles M. Blow similarly pored over the transcripts of interviews given to the press by Trump. I was struck by Blow's conclusion: 'Read together, the transcripts paint a terrifying portrait of a man who is simultaneously unintelligible in his delivery, self-assured in his ignorance and consciously bathing in his narcissism.'

What has distinguished Dutertismo from Trumpian oratory is Duterte Harry's juicier turns of phrase; the impulsive remarks which even *The Economist* headlined: 'Shoot from the lip — Fuck diplomacy!' Most famously, this has involved him using his favourite home-spun curse *putang ina* — usually translated into English as 'son of a whore' — on Pope Francis and Barack Obama, among others. In one press conference I attended in Davao, he told the UN to 'fuck off and shut up' and accused it of having failed to stop wars.

'The killing is endless,' he said. 'The amount is splattering [sic].'

In another, brandishing a middle finger salute, he said 'fuck you' to the EU (twice) and condemned the gall of Britain and France for criticising him despite their forebears having killed 'thousands of Arabs'. Unfiltered outbursts are more usually associated with his feeling talked down to, personally reprimanded, or publicly humiliated than they are about foreign interference in domestic affairs.

Abroad, this has resulted in Duterte being cast as the developing world's latest irascible strongman. Privately, Philippine diplomats concede that the vulgar verbal assaults have caused concern. Foreign leaders might feign amusement, but Duterte, and the Philippines, they fear, are in danger of becoming an international joke. Other Asian heads of government tend to conform to traditional cultural requisites of leadership — they are consensus builders, non-confrontational, and often exercise excessive politeness in the company of other presidents and premiers. Individualism is frowned upon, as are overt displays of anger. Duterte's brash, undiplomatic diplomatic style is completely out of kilter with that of his deferential counterparts. His sister Eleanor puts these traits down to his Castilian blood.

Filipinos admit that their president is neither eloquent nor, actually, fluent in English, or for that matter, in Tagalog; he appears unable to improvise in one without recourse to the other, and, in his fluent Taglish, seamlessly flits between them both. His command of English vocabulary, though, is sometimes startlingly impressive. English was his language of instruction all the way through his school and university days. At his old school in Digos, they say his knowledge of archaic words is down to the Benedictine Brothers, who would make him wash his mouth out not with soap, but with vocabulary tests of words they'd select for him to learn from the dictionary. This had the added advantage of keeping the rebellious teenager occupied. A local journalist who covered Duterte for years in Davao said 'he speaks English to make himself sound more intelligent'. Duterte clearly thinks this works, and, with his unique combination of the downright obscene and grandiloquent perorations that salvage the obsolete and arcane, it just might.

Duterte might disparage his own academic achievements and trip over his English, but, unlike Trump, he claims to be an avid reader, allegedly consuming the biographies of Napoleon, Barack Obama, and Singapore's late benevolent dictator, Lee Kuan Yew. He's so big on British journalist Ioan Grillo's books about Latin American drug wars that he invited the author of *El Narco* and *Gangster Warlords* to Malacañang Palace, where Duterte showed him his own dreaded 'Narco List', a document no Filipino journalist had set eyes on. Afterwards, Grillo said he'd been 'cautious' about asking what he called 'challenging questions'.

Among presidential reading recommendations: *Altar of Secrets*, about corruption and scandal in the Philippine Catholic Church, and *Asia's Cauldron*, about the precarious politics of the South China Sea. The Philippine online news site, *Rappler*, says that, in contrast, 'First Girlfriend' Honeylet Avanceña 'is more inclined towards self-help books'. Duterte is versed in Mindanaoan and Philippine history, and has reportedly read widely on economics, food-security, and politics. He also claims to devour airport thrillers by the likes of Robert Ludlum and Sidney Sheldon.

'People underestimate him. I used to, but I have learned my lesson,' said his one-time bitter political rival in Davao, Prospero 'Boy' Nograles, a former speaker of Congress, who, like Duterte, had practised as an attorney in Davao. Nograles is amusing in his analysis of his former foe's oratorical skills, or lack of them: 'He loves to be underestimated. That is his trick.'

It's said that Duterte possesses what they call 'native intelligence' — which basically translates as political nouse.

'He is not articulate, so he says "fuck you" a lot, and everybody listens and laughs and claps their hands! They want to know who he is going to attack next.'

Nograles says Duterte's critics invariably top his hit list. 'He really bears a grudge,' he said, speaking from long experience. 'He hates criticism. He is very thin-skinned. Sensitive. Super-sensitive. And easily driven to tears. He cries, you know.'

But, as someone who's probably driven Duterte to tears more than most, Nograles, while not forgiving, said he reckoned that some of more Duterte's more infamous expletive-laden rants are triggered by the excruciating neck and back pain he suffers.

'He is always cranky, and who wouldn't be if they're in pain? Some of his tirades are because he's in pain.'

Duterte has confessed to taking several times the prescribed dosage of the powerful painkiller Fentanyl, the synthetic opioid on which the musician Prince overdosed and died. When it was reported that Duterte himself was a drug addict, he retracted his claim and said he'd been joking. Side effects of this highly addictive drug include mood swings, cognitive abnormalities, confusion, trouble concentrating, feeling sad or empty, and erectile dysfunction — although this would be countered by his enthusiastic embrace of Viagra, about which he has publicly bragged.

Nograles has been at the receiving end of vicious and very personal verbal attacks from Duterte over several decades, although he usually gave as good as he got. Often these tongue-lashings would be delivered on Duterte's own Sunday morning Davao TV programme, whose title — 'From the Masses, For the Masses' — had a Chavismo ring to it. Duterte used his talk show to offer lengthy soliloquys on things or people that bugged him, and to launch expletive-riddled assaults on those who had found their way into his black book. Davaoeños used to tune in in their tens of thousands before church every Sunday because everyone wanted to know who was going to be in Duterte Harry's sights next, just like Nograles said. He was never one to disappoint.

The show was broadcast live, and the ABS-CBN network couldn't live-bleep Duterte's frequent cursing. Before each broadcast, an unusual TV 'slate' would come up, informing the audience that this particular Sunday morning show was 'Rated PG' — requiring parental guidance. Duterte's favoured exclamation, then, as now, was *putang ina* — 'son of a whore' — and tallying his weekly PI-count became local sport. His record, according to a Davaoeño who was fascinated by this, was 48 PIs in 45 minutes. In that record-breaking programme, he was railing against a priest for 'hypocrisy', chiding him to practise what he preached.

There were reports that 'From the Masses, For the Masses' might be re-launched on national networks, Hugo Chávez-style — and, in 2017, a version was put out on Facebook — but Duterte's got the whole country listening to him now anyway, and his PI-count is as high as it ever was. In Davao, though, the show entertained more people than it ever offended because, like his off-colour jokes, it was all understood in that joshing Bisayan cultural context. For Duterte, the use of his well-practised child-hood police bodyguards' street language came naturally, but it was nonetheless conscious. He knew that it guaranteed listeners' attention and achieved stellar ratings. Perhaps his cursing provides Duterte with cover, compensating for an inability to express himself articulately. Sometimes he swears in anger, his venom directed at individuals; on other occasions, expletives are discharged as an involuntary defence mechanism, like a squid spewing ink. It is as though he derives power from his use of bad language.

President Duterte has turned PI semantics into an issue of national debate. While the words *putang ina* would generally be considered an impolite turn of phrase in educated, middle-class society, as versatile exclamatory remarks go, it's actually common as muck with about as much shock-value as saying 'damn it'. It's what someone might say when they're bitten by a mosquito or they've just missed their jeepney. In large tracts of the Philippines, it's also a fairly standard way to greet your best mate. The English translation 'son of a whore' makes it sound rather worse than intended. Duterte's old friend from law school, Perfecto Yasay said that although he and his friends 'weren't spared the curses that came out of his mouth, they were not intended to discredit, demean or chastise us. It was his affectionate way of expressing himself'.

If Duterte is formal with you, Yasay said, that's when you should worry. 'When you talk to him, intimately, he will refer to a good friend as *putang ina.*'

'It really isn't a big deal', he said.

Jesus Dureza, whom Duterte also appointed to cabinet and who has known the president for even longer than Yasay, agreed. 'PI in our local dialect is [like] "shit" or something like that,' he said. 'It doesn't mean anything. *Putang ina* is just an expression.

Sometimes it expresses jubilation and glee. Sometimes, yes, it really is just to "shit" somebody, but not always. In Mindanao, people are never shocked when he uses "the PI". He uses it in the context we're used to. Unless he will face someone and say "*putang ina mo*", then that is directed at you. When he is angry at you.'

Adding the *mo* turns an off-the-cuff 'son of a whore' into a much more serious insult, literally: 'Your mother is a whore.' That, I reminded Dureza, was what Duterte had directed at me in a press conference, when I'd challenged him on EJKs. Dureza chuckled.

There are worse terms referring to mothers — most inherited from Spanish colonialists. In central Luzon, among the Ilonggos, they commonly use the phrase *yodeputa*, derived from the Spanish for 'motherfucker'. And compared to the Spanish *tu puta madre me la chupa* ('your bitch mother sucks me'), Duterte's favoured *putang ina* is pretty tame.

More than five decades ago, there was a Supreme Court ruling which acquitted a defendant charged with slander for using the even harsher expression *putang ina mo*. The 1960 case concerned a shop employee who was fired and shouted 'son of a whore, I'm going to kill you' at his manager. Interestingly, in relation to President Duterte, the judge, who later served as chief justice under the Marcos regime, upheld a lower court's decision that the 'I'm going to kill you' bit constituted 'a grave threat'. Justice Querube Makalinatal decreed that '*Putang ina mo* is a common enough expression in the dialect that is often employed, not really to slander, but rather to express anger or displeasure. It is seldom, if ever, taken in its literal sense by the hearer, that is, as a reflection on the virtues of a mother.'

The term does still raise eyebrows, though, particularly when uttered by the president himself. The Catholic Church took great offence when he levelled the curse at Pope Francis for causing a traffic jam in Manila's already terminally clogged streets. But, after getting away with it, and then branding the US ambassador a 'gay son of a whore' — something for which he never apologised — he went on to extend the straight version to various UN officials while calling the secretary general a 'fool'. In September 2016, Duterte took it up a notch, employing his favourite phrase in a diatribe against US President, Barack Obama, by then in his last months in office. Still sore about the US ambassador's perceived criticism, and barely two months into the job, Duterte was about to embark on his first foreign trip, a regional summit in Laos, which was to be attended by his American counterpart. What happened there would provide an insight into what could be expected of Duterte Harry-style fuck-you diplomacy.

There is no doubt at all that Duterte was angry, but, to be fair, his use of PI was, in this instance, lost in translation, leaving the Philippine president feeling misreported, misunderstood, and extremely indignant. As a columnist on the *Philippine Daily Inquirer* pointed out at the time, had Duterte really intended to insult the American president, he could have employed a whole spectrum of far more colourful Spanish *madre* expletives that, he suggested, 'would have made Obama nuke us'.

Already stung by Obama's personal criticism of his still nascent war on drugs (Obama had urged him to do it 'the right way'), Duterte entered the ring, gloves-off, and took a swing.

'I am a president of a sovereign state and we have long ceased to be a colony,' the president declared in Davao, before leaving for Laos. 'I do not have any master except the Filipino people, nobody but nobody.' His next sentence was uttered in Tagalog, but if he hadn't expected the international press to pick up on it, Duterte was in for a surprise. '*Putang ina*,' he said, 'I will swear at you in that forum.'

News of this reached Obama while still in China, before he had left for the Laotian capital, Vientiane.

'Clearly he's a colourful guy,' he said, adding that he preferred 'constructive, productive conversations'. The White House summarily cancelled a planned one-to-one between the two leaders.

'*Putang ina*,' muttered Jesus Dureza, who, as a cabinet minister and the president's advisor on peace, had accompanied him to the meeting in Laos. His old friend had just shot himself in the foot again.

'Our foreign affairs people and I said, "Shit, you know there might still be a way to repair all this."' Dureza, more used to negotiating peace with communist rebels and Islamist insurgents in Mindanao, suddenly found himself in the midst of unexpected hostilities with a superpower. In a sulk because he'd felt snubbed by the cancellation of the one-to-one, Duterte boycotted the first morning's meetings. According to Dureza, he actually slept straight through them, which fitted his schedule perfectly as he rarely gets up before noon. He was refusing to attend anyway because Obama would have been there, despite Dureza's efforts to extend an olive branch. The word from the White House, said Dureza, was that if Duterte would just approach Obama and say the 'insult' had not been intended, Obama would immediately 'warm to him' and their meeting might be back on the cards.

The Philippine government's original request for a bilateral meeting between the two presidents on the fringe of the summit had been made by Perfecto Yasay, who was also in Laos. It was he who was contacted by Daniel Russel, the US assistant secretary of state for East Asian and Pacific affairs, and it was Russel who suggested that a quick, informal apology might just iron things out. Yasay came up with a statement, which was duly read out to the press by Duterte's beleaguered communications secretary, Martin Andanar. It wasn't much of an apology.

Andanar said: 'He regrets that his remarks to the press have caused much controversy.'

Yasay continued: 'After that statement came out, they said they were going to create a scenario where there would just be a casual encounter with President Obama so that they could talk, to show that the friendship really was there.'

Yasay assured Duterte that the US president would warm to him. 'Yeah, really?' Duterte said to his foreign secretary. 'Are you sure? I don't think so.'

It took a lot of persuasion for Duterte to agree, said Dureza: 'I was the one who was pressing him. I even gave him a scenario. I said, "You know, when you exit from the holding room, you can walk side by side, so that there will be photographs; people know about the cancellation of the bilateral, and you can send a really positive message to the media that you are walking together and chatting along the way."'

It didn't work as planned.

'Obama emerged ahead. There was an exchange, but they were not able to walk side by side. So I sidled up to the president when he emerged. "What happened?" He did not answer. He just had a frown on his face.'

Finally Duterte replied: 'Shit. Shit. It didn't happen. I approached him. And you know what Obama said? "My people will talk to your people." Those were the exact words. I felt so small,' he said. 'Humiliated.'

Duterte refused point blank to appear at any further meetings.

By this stage, his ministers were growing increasingly alarmed that Philippine foreign policy and their country's relationship with its strongest ally were at the mercy of a monumental presidential sulk. The following morning, Duterte was due to address the entire summit, including all the regional heads of government and President Obama.

'We were able to convince him [Duterte]. He appeared — although he was late. He did not attend the earlier sessions.'

When Duterte got up to speak, he saw Obama and immediately veered off-piste.

'He went on to castigate the Americans for what they did to the Moros of Mindanao. I was worried he was going to deviate from his prepared text. And he did.'

In front of all the other Asian leaders, he determined to embarrass Obama over what he viewed as American hypocrisy over its own human rights record, a century ago. What he did had echoes of Muammar Gadaffi's visit to Italy in 2009, on one of his last state visits before his violent overthrow. Gadaffi, wearing dark glasses and lots of gold braid, descended the steps from his aircraft with a photograph pinned to his chest. It depicted Omar al-Mukhtar, leader of the nationalist resistance movement, in chains; it was the last known photograph of Mukhtar, 'The Lion of the Desert', before he was hanged by the Italians in 1931.

On the podium, Duterte held up horrific photographs of what was known as the Bud Dajo Massacre from March 1906, when 600 Moros, armed with knives and spears, were shot dead by US forces, as part of their 'pacification campaign' on the island of Jolo. Twelve Americans were killed in the 'battle'. One of the photographs shows scores of Moro dead, including women and children, their contorted bodies heaped in a common pit in the caldera of the extinct Bud Dajo volcano, as American troops pose for the camera.

'This is human rights ... Do not tell me this is water under the bridge,' Duterte had railed. Obama sat through the lecture and said nothing. There was no formal US response, and, after Duterte's tirade, there was no bilateral one-to-one on the side. Following the summit, in an outburst directed at a reporter, he said of President Obama: 'Who is he? Who is he to confront me? We are not lapdogs. The Philippines is not a vassal state.'

Philippine-US relations swiftly recovered from this Obama nadir when Donald J. Trump took office. At the 2017 White House Correspondents' Association Dinner, which Trump boycotted in protest over his treatment by the 'very dishonest' media, American comedian Hasan Minhaj pilloried the absent US President: 'It was all fun and games with Obama, right? You were covering an adult who could speak English … Now you've got to take your game to a whole new level.'

That dinner coincided with Trump's first hundred days in office, one week short of the first anniversary of Duterte's election. The two men marked the occasion by speaking on the phone and by extending invitations to each others' countries. Duterte views Trump as a kindred spirit and is clearly relieved by his laissez-faire approach to human rights. In their first phone conversation, Duterte claimed Trump had praised and endorsed his war on drugs and told him he was doing it 'the right way'. After the second — the one which was later leaked — Trump again complimented him on 'the unbelievable job' he was doing on the drug problem, and didn't mention any killings. Duterte described Trump as 'a realistic and pragmatic thinker' and 'profound … Just like me'. He said, 'I am not that bright, but I am very deliberate. I really think it over before I curse you.'

The *putang ina* crisis with Obama, however, had caused much debate in the Philippines. Mindanao was not the only part of the country to applaud the sentiments expressed by Duterte. For all the long-standing links with America, there remains a rich vein of unresolved anti-colonial angst. Duterte's audacious recalcitrance played well at home.

One weekend in December 2016, Duterte made a special trip back to Davao City and sent, via Bong Go, his executive assistant, an unusual request to an old political enemy, Prospero Nograles, whom he'd insulted and berated for years. The two men had already agreed to bury the hatchet; Nograles, also in his early seventies, had retired from frontline politics. His two sons were now congressmen, and, as Davaoeños, they had formed an unlikely alliance with their father's former nemesis.

'I hate what he has done to me politically,' Nograles told me. 'I hate him for all the lies he said about me.' He paused. Then he laughed and continued: 'He hates me for all the lies I said about him. But he loves my two boys and that is enough for me to make peace. We are both less likely to have heart attacks now.'

He had swallowed hard, declared an end to their hostilities, and supported Duterte's bid for the presidency.

When I met him, Nograles was polishing off a late Sunday lunch with his two congressmen sons, Karlo and Jericho, at the family home in suburban Davao. I had called him to ask for directions and he told me to just ask any taxi driver to take me to the Nograles house.

'Everybody knows my place,' he said.

He was right. It was a big place in a tree-lined street, with a swish political meeting house opposite that he'd just had built for Karlo's and Jericho's hustings. Later, he would show me round this building where he had his office — and a meeting room with secret escape routes out the back — 'just in case'.

A security guard ushered me into a downstairs waiting area which had a poster on the wall saying 'Duterte for President!' Next to it was another poster depicting a retro, 1950s-style all-American housewife in a headscarf. It read: 'Sarcasm: now served all day'. I cast my eyes around the room and, adjacent to the posters, stood a shrine containing a porcelain bearded Jesus and the Virgin Mary. Inside a glass box, over a vast refrigerator, stood a two-foot-high archangel with white wings spread. The angel gazed down on three big fish tanks, one of which contained two large grumpy-looking fish which were taking an unusually attentive interest in the comings and goings. I was summoned.

At the head of a grand antique dining table sat Prospero Nograles, the patriarch, sporting a scarlet t-shirt, emblazoned with the word 'UNFAIR' in block capitals.

'I wear this for Duterte,' he said, relishing the moment. 'It's unfair that he is president.'

A photograph of Nograles shaking hands in the White House with Barack Obama was hanging on the wall behind him, one of several documenting his long and illustrious political career. I joined the two generations of Nograles politicians round the table as they decanted an expensive bottle of Pauillac Bordeaux Réserve de la Comtesse, 2009 vintage. Nograles Snr filled my glass. After weeks of San Miguel Pale, the wine was sumptuous.

'He calls me Noggie, you know. And Ilong. That means nose. He says I have a flat nose.'

Indeed he does, but even though Noggie had been speaker of Congress, Duterte had pointedly never acknowledged his political stature, consistently refusing to address him by his formal title.

'I went to the restaurant [where they had arranged to meet] and was standing smoking outside when Bong Go came up and said, "The president is looking for you." Duterte had told everyone to go to hell and to leave him alone so that when I went in, the whole place was empty, except for the president who was eating at the bar.'

Duterte, a reformed smoker who had long ago declared war on smokers in Davao, banishing them to a handful of tiny roped-off outdoor 'sin-bin' enclosures, invited his old rival to light up if he wanted. Nograles sensed something was up.

'He said, "Noggie, sit." I said, "No, I'll stand." It made me feel superior. He said, "*Putang ina*, my problem is the American ambassador." I said, "How can I help you?"'

But Nograles knew in an instant where Duterte was heading with this conversation. He wasn't referring to the ex-US Ambassador Goldberg, the one he'd called a 'gay son of a whore'. What he meant was that, since he'd caused the diplomatic incident in Washington DC over that insult, then made things worse in the Obama *putang ina* debacle, the vacancy for the Philippine Ambassador to the United States of America had proved difficult to fill.

'Well, the way you are treating them, who'd want to be ambassador to America now?' Nograles asked.

No one had wanted the job, so what better posting for your erstwhile bitterest adversary than inviting him to live out his retirement in the well-heeled, leafy suburbia of DC? The catch was that he'd be the president's fall guy in the USA. He'd take all the punches whenever Duterte fired off another of his unguided verbal missiles. Duterte never actually offered the job to Nograles; he just raised it, Godfather-style.

'It might have been a pretty good life,' I ventured, as he drained a second bottle of Bordeaux into my glass.

'*Putang ina*,' he said. 'Not even tempted. I couldn't go around justifying his bullshit forever.'

7

DAVAO: EXHIBIT 'A'

Before Duterte Harry had made a name for himself, the city he later ruled for 22 years was best known for its durian; there's even a big monument featuring the king of fruit that greets visitors arriving at Davao City International Airport. For those unfamiliar with the durian, it's green-yellow in colour, weighs about the same as a well-fed cat, is typically about the size of a rugby ball, and is covered in armoured spikes. And it is potentially lethal — you wouldn't want to be underneath when a ripe one falls from a tree. You find the fruit all over Southeast Asia, but *Durio zibethinus* thrives in southern Mindanao's steamy climate and its rich volcanic soil. There are more than 20 different local varieties. On Magsaysay Street (named after a Philippine president who died in a plane crash), opposite Chinatown gate, there's an arcade of durian stalls, open year round, where Davaoeños converge to gorge at night. In popular mythology, the fruit has aphrodisiacal properties. Rodrigo Duterte is such an addict that he invited Shinzō Abe, the Japanese Prime Minister, down to these stalls when Abe visited Davao, and got him hooked, too. In Davao, you can eat durian fresh or processed into cakes or crisps or 'cookies'; there are durian lollypops and durian ice cream, durian sweets and pies and smoothies. Visitors to the city buy it in vast quantities: fresh and spiky, straight off the tree; vacuum-packed, dried, or frozen. Durians are to Davao what coals are to Newcastle, or ice is to Eskimos.

The durian is what Chinese call a 'heaty' food — it is highly calorific, and, it's said, should not be consumed with alcohol, as this too can apparently prove deadly: double-yang, no yin. Accessing the generous globules of creamy-yellow fruit, arranged in segments around large seeds inside, is a challenge; a durian needs to be skilfully hacked open with a machete. Those who know it love and adore it, and suffer serious cravings. Those who don't say even a whiff makes them want to throw up; to them, eating durian is like dining on sweet garlic-onion custard while sitting in a mortuary. The fruit is banned in hotels, lifts, shopping centres, and on public transport for good reason: it stinks. Durian season carries with it the sweet-edged cloying stench of a rotting corpse. Addicts, however, find its unique smell appealing.

During Duterte's long reign as mayor of Davao, the steady supply of corpses brought notoriety to durian city. A Davaoeño paramedic was horrified by the rising body count ascribed to the Davao Death Squad, which was itself ascribed to the mayor.

'Bodies were dumped everywhere,' the ambulance-attendant said. 'Everywhere. All the time. You wouldn't believe it. Most of the victims wore slippers [flip-flops],' he said. 'They were dark-skinned. The poorest of the poor. But nobody speaks about this. They will never betray him.'

The 'salvaging' and dumping of more than 1400 corpses

was documented by members of a now long-defunct Davao-based human rights group, the Coalition Against Summary Executions. Some in Davao thought 1400 was an underestimate; many killings went unreported. Other bodies were likely dumped and never found. The dead included many children, and there were cases of mistaken identity. But, over the years, Davao's residents, who today number 1.6 million, mostly turned a blind eye. The elimination of undesirable elements — drug addicts, criminals, and street-kids — was deemed acceptable collateral — the trade-off for the transformation that Mayor Duterte engineered in the city.

Those who hate Duterte and those who love him say that what happened in Davao is key to understanding where he's headed now — except their respective understanding of what did happen could not be more starkly different. Few things better illustrate the divisiveness of Duterte than the contradictory interpretations of his governance of Davao. The policies he pursued there were as conflicted as his mercurial personality. These incongruities were not aberrations: this was the way he ruled. To those blessed recipients of his munificence, Duterte was a benevolent dictator, exactly the kind of strongman the chaos in their city called for. To his detractors, malevolent was a far more fitting adjective.

As mayor, Duterte was Janus-faced, capable of breathtaking doublethink: he could initiate a progressive treatment-based policy towards drug addiction, and at the same time sanction death squads to kill addicts in cold blood. He could rail against corruption and utter deadly threats to businessmen or politicians on the make, while turning Davao City Hall into a nepotistic cooperative, using public funds to buy votes and bankroll assassinations. A man with the boorish reputation of a sex-pest enacted enlightened anti-sex-discrimination laws. The capricious mayor would donate generously to children with cancer while his city police contracted hitmen to hunt down and murder street-kids. And, in 2016, in selling his Davao model to a nation of 100 million people, Duterte told them black was white and they believed him. Over 16 million voters bought his promise that replicating what he claimed were his astonishing achievements in Davao countrywide would transform the fortunes of the Philippines. Above all, he promised peace and order.

His vanquished rival and fellow Davaoeño, the former Congress speaker Prospero Nograles, wryly summed up Duterte's time as mayor like this: 'He wasn't known for his infrastructure projects. There was no "liquidation" here in Davao that did not go through Duterte's people.' Nograles was not referring to corporate insolvencies. Davao was Duterte's laboratory for killing. It was where the mayor-turned-president honed his violent, totalitarian tendencies.

'The facts are there. The "Davao Experience" is there,' said Senator Antonio 'Sonny' Trillanes IV, among Duterte's fiercest and most outspoken critics. 'We now have, in Malacañang, as president of this country, a mass-murderer and a monster. The body count is real, just as it was in Davao. So what did you expect of this man? Given what we know of him, who he is, and what his past is, it would take a monumentally blind person not to put it all together.' Trillanes, a former naval officer, was jailed for staging a mutiny. From behind bars, he launched a coup d'état against former president Gloria Arroyo. It failed. He is now the leading opposition voice in the upper house. He and the president do not hide their mutual contempt.

'In Davao, Duterte ruled like a king,' Trillanes said. 'He never gave up power and he will never give up power now. He is a very vindictive person, and he is not used to being investigated. His local government was a rubber stamp. The media were coerced and sometimes killed. He picks his targets to send a message that will have a chilling effect.'

Trillanes, who remains a close ally of Duterte's incarcerated adversary, Senator Leila de Lima, became increasingly animated as he spoke. He was scornful of the Faustian compact between the absolute ruler and his subjects. 'In Davao, hardly a single person will say anything negative ... It is similar to North Korea, where they revere Kim Jong-un despite everything because his father and grandfather were able to suck out that will to fight from the people. In North Korea there is no drug addiction. No crime. But there is no freedom either. In Davao City, they are cowards. They just suck it up.'

Few others in Duterte's Philippines would dare to be so bold as to put their name to comments such as these. And there are many millions of Filipinos who vehemently disagree with Trillanes. In their view, the senator wilfully ignores Duterte's prime accomplishment as mayor: the regeneration of his crime-infested city into a thriving business hub. Davaoeños old enough to remember what it was like before Duterte took over as mayor say that in the 1970s and 1980s it was like a war zone. It was a war zone. Duterte promised to restore peace and order. But, in reality, there was neither peace nor order to restore. The city's name was a byword for chaos, with urban guerrilla warfare on the streets and ultra-violent crime endemic. People did not venture out past dusk. In those days, it was known as the 'Nicaragua of Asia' and was the murder capital of the Philippines. The hit-units of the communist New People's Army — known as 'Sparrow Squads' — assassinated policemen; bombings were common, as were kidnaps and disappearances. By 1986, the year Marcos fled, a feared new vigilante group known as Alsa Masa had been formed to purge the city of communists, and Davao became even more violent.

'In the 80s, we lived in the suburbs,' Stella Estremera, editor of the Davao newspaper the *SunStar*, told me. 'Most homes had fox-holes. We had a concrete bathroom. Whenever we heard gunfire, we would run to the bathroom. Even now, I'm a light sleeper,' she said. 'The gun battles! Brrrrrrrrt. Boom! Tak-tak-tak-tak-tak. Ping. It was a city of rebellion.'

Another journalist at that time, Leo Villareal, who ended up working for Duterte at City Hall, recalled covering NPA summary executions by firing squad in the street. 'There were snatchers, kidnappers, rapists, and druggies,' he said. 'I cannot tell you how ugly it was in those days.'

When Corazon Aquino was swept to power in 1986, she determined to clear out the dead wood. Provincial governors and city mayors from the Marcos dictatorship days were summarily fired. In Davao, the new 'People Power' president asked the leader of the anti-Marcos protest movement to be her new mayor there until fresh elections could be held. Soledad Roa Gonzales was already well into her seventies and turned down the offer, but helpfully suggested that her son, a 42-year-old public prosecutor, might be considered in her stead; thus, in 1987, Rodrigo Roa Duterte was duly appointed vice mayor and officer-in-charge of Davao. The following year, he stood for election promising to usher in peace and order.

Duterte's 'hero', Vladimir Putin, also kick-started his political career as a deputy mayor, in his case in St Petersburg in 1994. Many years later, the two men finally met as presidents, Duterte clearly awed by Putin's political tough-guy act. Duterte said the two were 'similar' because of their shared passion for girls and guns. Mayoralty is something he shares with another authoritarian-populist alter ego — this time, in Turkey. President Recep Tayyip Erdoğan launched his political career as mayor of Istanbul, a post to which he was elected the same year an unemployed former KGB agent found his vocation in St Petersburg. Both Erdoğan and Putin were accused of using their municipal positions to hone their skills in corrupt governance. The mayor of Davao City had a long headstart on both of them.

Shortly after Duterte's election, there was a major celestial event in the skies over southern Mindanao. At four minutes past nine on the morning of 18 March 1988, having carved a cone-shaped track across Sumatra, Borneo, then the Celebes Sea, the shadow of the moon passed straight over Davao City, which found itself in the direct path of a total solar eclipse. In indigenous lore, this astronomical event was of enormous and ominous portent. The Bisaya word for 'eclipse' is *bakunawa*, the name of a fabled giant-fanged sea-serpent, which, mesmerised by the moon's beauty, would rise from the depths of the sea to swallow it. *Bakunawa* was the harbinger of earthquakes and wars. Only the banging of pots and pans could dissuade the monster from eating the moon. But this time they failed. In Davao, Duterte's war was about to start, and a political earth-quake, which would one day shake the whole country, had started to rumble. (The total solar eclipse that traversed the United States in August 2017, did not escape the attention of Filipino *bakunawa* catastrophists either. One national newspaper noted that the darkening skies meant that angry gods were about to punish an erring humanity.)

In his *bakunawa* eclipse election in 1988, Duterte was up against one of the leaders of the Alsa Masa vigilante group, Jun Pala, a man whose name would come to haunt him. He would later be accused of ordering Pala's assassination. But the no-nonsense prosecutor — who liked to pose in cowboy boots and had a penchant for wearing his 1970s-style aviator shades indoors — easily beat his rivals with his simple message that he would restore peace and order. He continued to win the mayoral contests for a decade, but after three consecutive terms, the maximum allowed under the new post-People Power Philippine constitution, Duterte had to think of something else to do. So he stood for Congress against his own brother, Emanuel 'Bong' Duterte. Again, he won — but he found the life of a congressman boring. He was frequently absent from sessions, and, just as in his school days, he preferred to spend his time at the cinema, by his own admission. During his time as a congressman in Manila, the killings in Davao dropped off, then picked up dramatically again in the run-up to the next mayoral election he contested, in 2001. On that occasion, he ran against his own younger sister, Jocelyn, beginning another nine straight years before term limits again forced him to stand down. His solution this time was to keep things in the family. He ran as deputy mayor to his daughter, Sara, who trounced her rival, none other than her father's former foe, Prospero Nograles, who alleged a 'conspiracy' against him. Duterte was re-elected mayor for his seventh and final time in 2013, and, when he became president, Sara stood and won again in Davao.

From 1988, the still relatively young attorney-turned-mayor launched an ambitious programme to transform Davao City's fortunes. Over the years that followed, Duterte's achievements were ostensibly impressive. Later, in his run for the presidency, they would enable him to claim that Davao was his 'Exhibit A'. By then, a 'Learn from Davao' movement had gained political momentum, energised by his promise that 'if I make it to the presidential palace, I will do just what I did as mayor'. His threats to kill bad guys, as he had in his Davao days, were accompanied by the whitewashing of what had actually gone on down there. These eulogies, delivered on the campaign trail — and ever since

— have echoes of Maoist China. An electorate thirsty for change bought Team Duterte's airbrushed, alt-fact history. But for all the lacunae in the re-spun version, there were also some seductive truths. Filipinos, convinced by Duterte that their country had been subsumed by a nationwide contagion of drugs and violent crime, learned, for example, that within a short time of his becoming mayor, Davaoeños could walk the streets without fear after dark, wear jewellery in public without it being snatched, and catch jeepneys home at night without fear of being murdered. Taxi drivers no longer risked being robbed at gun-point. The criminals were scared to death — he told them if they didn't leave his city vertically, he'd make sure they left it horizontally. And this was exactly the kind of tough talk Filipinos now wanted from their president.

When I met Duterte's younger sister, Jocelyn, at a chic tapas restaurant called Las Flores in the well-heeled Fort Bonifacio district of Manila, she strode onto the outdoor terrace with her retinue of ravenous sidekicks who promptly devoured plate-loads of pricey dishes then vapourised, leaving me with the bill. Jocelyn knows a thing or two about re-spinning stories. Confidants from Davao allege she dabbled in drugs herself and lived in fear of her elder brother, whose praises she now sings. She admitted to both charges during our evening of surprisingly candid conversation, but said she and the mayor had had their 'closure' and that 'whatever was between us is now history'.

Slight, with short, fashionably coiffured hair, and dressed in a classy business suit, she had arrived at Las Flores sporting chunky diamonds on her finger, in her ears and around her neck.

'His credibility rests on Davao City,' Jocelyn told me. 'It's why he's credible. Look at Davao!'

She said she'd lived in Cebu and Manila for many years and when she'd come back home to Davao she was startled.

'My God! You can walk with your diamonds!' she laughed, glancing at her sparkling ring. 'It's clean! Manila was the worst city. You walk around and you get "snatched". Pretty dangerous. And dirty.'

Most proud Davaoeños share this contemptuous opinion of the capital and thank their lucky stars for mayor Duterte Harry.

The business community in Davao loved Duterte from the start. At a Davao City Chamber of Commerce event I attended in 2017, Duterte was feted with sycophancy so extreme that he looked genuinely embarrassed. His friends say he really doesn't like obsequiousness, but in Davao the corporate sector's excruciating homage was worth suffering for. According to authoritative sources in the city, businesses helped bankroll the mayor's peace and order project; it may not have involved extortion, but it was a protection racket in all but name.

'I protect your business; business pays the bills,' was the way it was explained to me, and, to local business, the mayor's assets definitely outweighed any liabilities.

Davao Crocodile Park is listed in tourist guidebooks as one of Davao City's top two attractions, along with the beaches on nearby Samal Island. It's owned by a prosperous second-generation Davaoeño planter-turned-tycoon called Philip Dizon, chair of the American Chamber of Commerce in Davao and long-time friend of Rodrigo Duterte and his younger brother Bong. When I spoke to Dizon — who also owns a ranch in California — he had recently turned into a missionary for medical marijuana, declaring he wanted to turn Davao into 'the cannabis capital of Asia'. I told him I thought this unlikely in the circum-stances, but Dizon, having confided he had just had a bong himself, said he had raised his idea with the president. He had obviously survived this meeting. It had taken a bit of persuading to get Dizon to agree to meet me again, as he had taken against one of my earlier TV reports which had featured him. In the report, he had been showing me his crocodiles and telling me that, as a species, they had earned an unfairly bad press. Crocodiles had been demonised, he said, but what they actually did was get rid of all the bad stuff.

'And who does that remind you off?' I'd asked. He had laughed at this.

'The president!' he said.

I continued: 'Is he a violent man? He doesn't seem to have a problem killing people he considers pests.'

'Well, not pests. Criminals. People who hurt other people must be hurt first before they hurt other people ... this is simply cleaning up the house. That's it.'

The rules of engagement for our second meeting were set: no human rights. No drugs war — but Dizon was too stoned to keep a rational conversation going anyway. What was it like for business in the bad old days, I asked, before his great friend Rody took the helm?

'How could you have economic development when all that fucking crime was going on? He changed all that. He cleaned up. He wakes up late. Crime happens at night.'

Duterte looked after the business community and they looked after him. When Davaoeño business moguls were kidnapped by gangs and held to ransom (which was not that uncommon), Rody and his boys would sort things out. Dizon meandered off again, showing me text messages he had received from Honeylet, and dropping in that he was a business consultant to Rody's daughter, Sara, mayor of Davao. Back in the old days, he and Rody belonged to a shooting club, and he told me how the mayor would turn up in his green VW Beetle with his son Paolo, then aged 10 or so.

'His mindset was always to defend against the enemy. He's a good shot.' he said, before getting side-tracked again talking about how reformed sinners make the best saints, and calling out to his staff, asking how many crocodile-skin belts they were sending to Malacañang.

'Only belly for the president. Not hornback,' he shouted, before turning and striking a confidential tone. 'Did you know crocodile oil is a very good lubricant?' he asked.

No, I said, that was new to me and suggested that it might make a better present for Rody than a belt.

'I gave him some already,' Dizon said, corpsing helplessly. 'You know, when I'm with the president, we laugh like shit, man.'

By the time Duterte finally stood down as mayor of Davao, the local economy was growing at more than 9 per cent a year — as he liked to point out in his presidential campaign. Some say Davao City blossomed despite him, not because of him, but today there's a construction boom, the city is an international tele-marketing hub, hotels are crammed full, and there are 20 flights a day to and from Manila. The mayor's peace and order campaign turned Davao into what its residents call a 'city of respite'. Warring insurgent groups elsewhere on the rebellion-wracked island, sought him out. He invited the NPA and Moro liberation factions — both nationalist and Islamist — into his city on the condition that warlords behaved themselves and left their guns behind. The children of various rebel leaders even attended schools in Davao. Such grandiose gestures remain typical of Duterte. On the face of it, his broad appeal to a diverse range of people would seem a positive quality — and healing, if it can usher in the peace he's always promised. But, as mayor, and now as president, Duterte was and remains both scheming and manipulative. Ever since those Davao days, he sold himself as everybody's friend so that he would have no enemies, but in the end he has had no hesitation turning on them and spitting them out when they've outrun their usefulness.

One notable exception was Leoncio 'Jun' Evasco, a former communist rebel and liberation theologian, who joined the insurgent New People's Army, the communists' armed wing, when he was a newly ordained priest. He was said to have risen to a senior rank within the NPA, but was captured at a convent in Mindanao in 1983 by Ferdinand Marcos' troops. Four of those arrested with him were executed on the spot, while Evasco himself was tortured in Davao City before being charged with armed rebellion and sent for trial. The public prosecutor assigned to his case was a tough-talking lawyer called Rodrigo Duterte, who saw to it that Evasco was jailed for five years — but interestingly, during this time, he was visited in his Davao City prison cell by ... Duterte. Two years into Evasco's sentence, Marcos was ousted, and the progressive priest was released on the orders of Cory Aquino.

As a defendant, Evasco must have made an impression on the public prosecutor, who has always claimed to have socialist leanings. Perhaps, even then, it was apparent that the quiet, self-effacing priest was a man who knew how to mobilise the masses, organise, and make things happen. And that, thought the would-be mayor of Davao, was exactly what he needed.

In 1988, Duterte plucked Evasco from an ex-political prisoners' association and asked him to manage his first campaign for the mayoralty. The triumphant Duterte then rewarded him with a senior post in City Hall, and Evasco quickly rose to become chief of staff. Often dubbed 'Duterte's Rasputin', Evasco — who left the priesthood and is today married with children and grandchildren — remained a back-room strategist for nearly two decades. He then spent three terms as a city mayor himself, in his hometown of Maribojoc in the central region of Visayas. For those first 18 years in Davao, though, Evasco would likely have known everything. One trusted and authoritative Davao source, who watched, aghast, as the body count climbed ever higher through Duterte's years as mayor, said simply: 'Evasco is the brains behind the death squad.'

Few others knew much about him; like Duterte, he was a Machiavellian schemer, but Evasco was the behind-the-scenes man, with a reputation for exceptional skills in management. In 2016, President Duterte brought his old friend and trusted aide to work with him in Malacañang. Foreign diplomats in Manila today say Evasco wields real power, just as he did for two decades in Davao. Duterte's first presidential executive order put Evasco in charge of supervising 12 separate government agencies, with a vast remit, to the point that he was reportedly run off his feet, an ageing Jared Kushner of the new administration. He also became involved in a ferocious power struggle in the palace with Duterte's special assistant and gatekeeper, Bong Go.

Evasco very rarely gives interviews, but one his oldest friends told the news site *Rappler* that he'd confided that the corridors of power in Manila were like 'a snake-pit'. He was still mistrusted by many in the military, who suspected he retained an extreme left-wing agenda: his communist background alarmed some in the armed forces.

As Duterte and Evasco settled in to running City Hall in the late 1980s, Davao City enjoyed a financial windfall. After 21 years of Marcos — 14 of them under martial law — new president Cory Aquino pledged to devolve power to the provinces, which had been ignored. Davao was a major beneficiary.

The city administration's operating budget increased by 150 per cent overnight, enabling the mayor to order a massive recruitment of staff. Most of the posts were short-term contract jobs, but even three or six months' well-paid work was enough to buy loyalty. But, over the years, questions were raised over who did what at City Hall — and who got paid for it.

In 2015, the Philippine Commission on Audit's report for Davao City during Duterte's final term as mayor questioned his spending the equivalent of more than US$14 million on 11,000 contract workers for the previous year. Based on this report, Senator Antonio 'Sonny' Trillañes filed a plunder case against Duterte, days before the presidential election. The audit report said fewer than a quarter of 14,499 employees on the payroll held verifiable positions. The hiring of 'ghost employees' was also one of the charges in the failed impeachment complaint against the president in the Philippine congress in March 2017. A self-confessed hitman who claimed to be a leader of the Davao Death Squad said that his off-the-books monthly salary was pooled from the combined wage-bills of between 10 and 12 'ghost employees', providing him with a pay cheque of the equivalent of US$1,400 a month, over and above his official salary as a senior police officer and bonuses he claimed to have received for high-profile assassinations.

An informed source in Davao, intimately familiar with Duterte's style of local governance — and who, for obvious reasons, must remain anonymous — said that, from the late 1980s, the city's freshly replenished coffers afforded manifold opportunities for corruption, which the overtly anti-graft Duterte allegedly used to great effect. New multi-million peso contracts were awarded for everything, from public transport to waste disposal. It's alleged that when the standard 20 per cent of the value of these contracts was skimmed off the top, the contractor would be asked to distribute the kickback equally between city council members.

Duterte himself stayed clean; no contractor could ever testify against the mayor. He, in turn, was now aware that his councillors had accepted kickbacks, and so when he asked them to approve his billion peso peace and order programme, they did so without question. This programme was defined with a wide latitude, and, for example, could cover the cost of hiring and rewarding hitmen without a paper trail. Only the council chairman was ever authorised to inspect the audit of how the Peace and Order Fund was spent, but he was forbidden from examining individual documents. Ten per cent of the peace and order tranche of the city budget was devoted to the mayor's Intelligence Fund. Disbursements from this were at his discretion and required no auditing at all.

In other words, it was a massive slush fund, topped up by willing contributions from the business sector. By the time he reached the presidency, the former mayor was well practised in this dark financial art and, predictably enough, in late 2016, he requested — and was awarded — a five-fold increase in the presidential Intelligence Fund for 2017. As in Davao, disbursements from this fund were kept completely confidential, unaudited on the grounds that they contain 'military secrets'. Justifying the phenomenal increase from the previous administration's 500 million pesos (US$10 million) to 2.5 billion pesos (US$50 million), Duterte's budget secretary said it would be used in the war against drugs.

The people of Davao basked in their mayor's munificence. He appeared to be very generous, although it wasn't his money. When Philip Dizon mentioned to the mayor that he needed a road built to his remote hilltop Vista View restaurant, overlooking an overgrown former quarry, 'It happened!' he said. 'A new

Mayor Rodrigo Duterte poses with Uzi sub-machine gun in mid-1990s on the outskirts of Davao City. He allegedly used an Uzi to kill National Bureau of Investigation agent Vicente Amisola in 1994, in a case of mistaken identity. **Photograph by Rene Lumawag**

Duterte photographed for *Esquire Philippines* in Davao, 2015, a year before he was elected president. The boys were students in a nearby school. The photographer said they idolised the mayor, who joked and bantered with them. **Photograph by Jason Quibilan**

The Trump-Duterte bromance blossomed at a summit in Manila in November 2017. Duterte crooned his favourite ballad: 'You are the light in my world. You are the love I've been waiting for.' Photograph: Reuters

Duterte Harley, 2004; the mayor-turned-president loves guns and girls and motorbikes. He suffered a neck injury in a crash, for which he takes Fentanyl, a powerful synthetic opioid. Photograph courtesy Davao City Information Office

ABOVE: Duterte with his mother, Soledad Roa Gonzales, during his rebellious teens. His father, Vicente Duterte, became Governor of Davao in 1959; two years later, Rodrigo was expelled from high school for playing truant and attacking priests. Photograph courtesy Davao City Government

RIGHT: Duterte, aged five. The portrait hangs in the 'ancestral home' in Davao City. His expression as hard to read then as it is now. Some see defiance, others the sneer of cold command. Photograph courtesy Duterte family collection

President Ferdinand Marcos (left) swearing Vicente Duterte into his cabinet in 1965. Soledad, Vincente's wife, stands by his side. Vicente Duterte died in office in 1968, four years before Marcos declared martial law. **Photograph courtesy Duterte family collection**

Rodrigo Duterte weeping in the family mausoleum at 3am on the night he was elected president. Here, he slumped and sobbed on the tomb of his father who had called him a '*bugoy*' — or hoodlum. **Photograph courtesy of Edith Ging Z. Caduaya**

A victorious Rodrigo Duterte with his 'first mistress', Cielito 'Honeylet' Avanceña, a former beauty queen, and their daughter Veronica, better known as 'Kitty', arriving at Malacañang Palace for oath-taking ceremony and inauguration, 30 June 2016. Malacañang Pool Photo

Sara Duterte-Carpio, mayor of Davao City, and her brother, Paolo, former vice-mayor of Davao City, attend the birthday party of a grandson of Rodrigo Duterte, former mayor of Davao City, himself son of the late governor of Davao. Photograph courtesy of Edith Ging Z. Caduaya

Presidential candidate Rodrigo Duterte kisses a supporter during a Mad for Change campaign rally, November 2015. 'Duterte Harvey' is known for his 'naughty playfulness'. Inquirer Photo / Grig C. Montegrande

Hollywood tough-guy Steven Seagal endorses Duterte at Malacañang Palace with a clenched fist salute, October 2017. A day earlier, Seagal had been accused by *The Washington Post* of a catalogue of 'sordid' assaults on 'too many women to count'. Malacañang Pool Photo

The commander-in-chief of the Armed Forces of the Philippines, Rodrigo Duterte, together with Eduardo Año, his chief-of-staff, inspects firearms captured from Islamist rebels during a visit to Marawi City, July 2017. **Photograph: Reuters**

President Duterte arrives in Mindanao for a visit to Marawi City, July 2017. Having recently extended Martial Law in the south, this is thought to be his first outing dressed in military fatigues, albeit in unorthodox fashion. **Malacañang Pool Photo / Ace Morandante**

An overcrowded holding cell in a Manila jail, after hundreds of thousands of drug addicts surrendered to police to escape assassination by the roving death squads. AFP / Noel Celis

A .38 homemade pistol next to the body of an alleged dealer as Duterte's drugs war began in July 2016. Revolvers were often allegedly planted on bodies, shells did not match the calibre, and guns were found in the right hands of left-handed people. Mark R. Cristino / Epa / REX / Shutterstock

Leila de Lima, former justice secretary and Duterte's nemesis, speaking to the author in the Philippine Senate in February 2017, just before her arrest on drug charges which were condemned as 'pure fiction'. Photograph courtesy of author

Alleged top drug dealer, Jessie Hudas, killed in a police buy-bust shoot-out in Quezon City, Manila, October 2016. By then, less than four months into Duterte's presidency, the death-toll was already nearly twice what Marcos managed in a decade. Inquirer Photo / Raffy Lerma

Pietà: the photograph which shocked the nation and flashed across the world, depicting Jennelyn Olaires holding her dead partner, Michael Siaron, a pedi-cab driver. It evoked Michelangelo's *Pietà* sculpture and was mocked by Duterte. Inquirer Photo / Raffy Lerma

Elizabeth Navarro, heavily pregnant, holds a lonely vigil in a Pasay City funeral parlour with coffins containing her husband, Domingo, a pedi-cab driver, and her five-year-old son, Francis, both shot dead by an unknown gunman inside their slum home, December 2016. James Nachtwey Archive, Hood Museum, Dartmouth College

The murder in Manila of another pedi-cab driver, by two masked men on a motorbike, photographed by Luis Liwanag, as I reported for Channel 4 News. 'People are being killed like insects,' Luis said. **Photograph by Luis Liwanag**

The author's testy encounter with Duterte in November 2016, in which he conferred on me the 'Order of Son of a Whore' was my second such run-in. The president does not like to be questioned on matters relating to human rights. Screen-grab from DZMM TV

The author with self-confessed former Davao Death Squad hitman Edgar Matobato, who confessed to murdering more than 50 people and participating in the killing of 300 more. He claimed he had witnessed Mayor Duterte personally executing victims. Photography courtesy of author

Arturo Lascañas, self-confessed former head of the DDS, testifying to a Senate inquiry while still a serving policeman. Within months, he retired and turned whistle-blower, alleging that Mayor Duterte had been the godfather of the death squad. AFP / Ted Aljibe

ABOVE: Scene from the aftermath of the Bud Dajo massacre on the island of Jolo, Mindanao, 1906, with a trench piled high with more than 600 'Moro' bodies as US forces look on. In 2016, Duterte railed against this at a summit as Barack Obama listened. Photograph courtesy of US National Archive

LEFT: Australian missionary Jacqueline Hamill and other hostages used as human shields by armed prison inmates in Davao City, 1989. Minutes later, she was fatally shot. Duterte, then mayor, later 'joked' that he wished he had had the chance to rape her. Inquirer File Photo / Boy Cabrido

The funeral of teenager Kian Loyd delos Santos, shot point-blank by plain-clothes police in August 2017, and whose murder was caught on CCTV. It triggered public revulsion and began to galvanise opposition to Duterte's drugs war. Photograph: Reuters

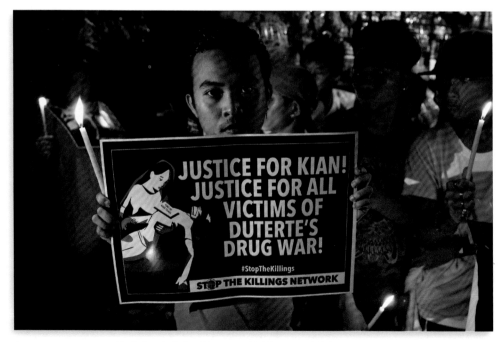

A protestor at a candle-light vigil for 17-year-old Kian Loyd delos Santos. In January 2018, a court filed murder charges against three police officers. As this book goes to press, not one person has been convicted of any killing connected to the drugs war. Photograph: Reuters

concrete road! He came up to have coffee.' Duterte would have known the view well. The disused quarry directly below Dizon's restaurant was the execution ground for the Davao Death Squad.

Duterte lodged the love of grateful Davaoeños in his ever-growing vote bank. He was famed locally for his support of a children's cancer charity — his supporters like to cite this as evidence of Duterte Harry's tender side — with local newspapers regularly printing photographs of the mayor with children ill from cancer. He splashed out on assisting the poor and needy whenever possible: vote buying disguised as altruism. Because his pockets were so deep, his political opponents couldn't compete. One of the mayor's more bizarre habits was to prowl around the city late at night visiting funeral parlours (he has always been a creature of the night). He would arrive with flowers and dish out thousand-peso bills to bereaved families. This too increased his popularity.

In speeches and on his TV programme, Duterte railed against corruption, and would hand local police gifts of groceries for their families to discourage them from accepting petty bribes. In 2002, *Time* magazine ran a feature on the mayor of Davao, which noted that despite his zero-tolerance, 'part of the fascination with his personality' was that he had 'an incongruously soft and liberal streak'. The article, headlined 'The Punisher', went on to recount how he sent food to Muslim communities during Ramadan and to Catholics at Christmas. 'In one 10-minute span, he gives a mother the bus fare to her home village, counsels a woman seeking a job and tenderly tells a young, badly scarred burn victim that he will pay for her operation and follow-up treatment.' A gold-framed copy of this article hangs proudly in the family hall of fame in the wood-panelled living room of the Duterte 'ancestral' home. It's odd that it should be so honoured, for the article doesn't pull its punches in describing 'the swaggering new-sheriff-in-town' who had created an atmosphere where death squads were free to operate with impunity. 'The DDS is commonly referred to as the "Duterte Death Squad" — even, jokingly, by Duterte himself,' the reporter, Phil Zabriskie, wrote. Duterte told him: 'If I'm going out, I'm going out with my guns blazing.' *Plus ça change.*

Duterte's elder sister, Eleanor, who still lives in the family home, preferred to focus on the touchy-feeliness of her brother's magnanimity. 'He uplifted people socially,' she told me. 'When they didn't have food to eat, when they couldn't pay their hospital bills. He was everything to them: priest, father, confessor, and protector.' To frame his mayorship in any other light, she said, is to fall under the spell of Senators de Lima and Trillañes.

Despite having raised their names herself, Eleanor Duterte became extremely agitated. 'They are sons of Lucifer,' she shouted at me. 'They are the psychopathic killers and liars, these two people who are doing the "human rights".'

The last two words, she spat out, complementing her younger brother's own derisive rhetoric.

As 'a vehicle of the Holy Spirit', she told me, Duterte possesses a righteous anger. 'It takes a person who is determined to open the gates to prosperity,' she said. 'It can never happen under a cloud of drugs, graft, and corruption. He was never defeated in an election.'

As time passed, the prospect of him losing lessened because the attentive mayor's benevolence put his loyal subjects for-ever in his debt. As with the city councillors, Duterte bought their complicity and silence. The murders committed by the roving killers of the Davao Death Squad — the dark side of the peace and order project — increasingly became the elephant in the room.

———

As mayor, Duterte cultivated his tough *bugoy* persona; he liked to pose with guns for the camera, and, with Evasco at his right hand, he pledged to get things done. He delivered. He was credited with slashing red tape, just as he has as president; civil servants were required to process business applications within three days — this, it's understood, on Evasco's orders. Those accused of inefficiency or, worse, corruption, were publicly shamed on the mayor's Sunday TV programme. He himself lived frugally, in a modest wooden house owned by his girlfriend, Honeylet. It backed onto a golf course (where he would later park the helicopter he 'borrowed' from a millionaire pastor) in a suburban backstreet. He had no interest in the flashy four-wheel-drives seen everywhere in Davao. Duterte Harry owned a second-hand Harley Davidson, later changed for a low-slung, high handle-barred Yamaha Virago. Flor de Lisa Mercade Sepe, who has worked as his cook, babysitter, and seamstress, paints a picture of a man with simple local tastes in food; he preferred to get old clothes stitched and mended than to throw them away.

I ate out in a couple of the restaurants frequented by Duterte in both Davao and Manila, wondering if it might help me get the measure of the man. As a public prosecutor, he would often lunch with fellow lawyers in a simple place on Piapi Boulevard called Sana's Carinderia, owned and run by Proferia 'Sana' Valles — 'Sana' being an affectionate nickname for a married woman in a local language, which is what Duterte called her. Sana is four years older than Duterte, but looks 10 years younger, and she adores the man. She insisted on serving up all 'the mayor's' old Bisaya favourites, including her signature dish — Duterte's number one — which she's been making for more than 40 years: *tapang kabaw*, trimmings of lean *carabao* (water buffalo), fried and dried and cured with salt. It's crisp and served up with fish sauce, chilli, salt, and lime; Sana guards her recipe with the ferocity of Colonel Saunders. Her carnivorous feast is eaten with plain rice and set off by a spicy *carabao* (on the bone) and cabbage soup. Compared with the ubiquitous and awful mall-food that's become standard Filipino-fare, this is unusually good. So taken was Duterte with Sana and her *tapang kabaw* that he and the entire Duterte tribe became her regulars. One wall of Sana's restaurant is plastered with memorabilia, with Sana and her family grinning proudly, draped around the prosecutor-mayor-president. In one fading colour print, Duterte is sitting in his cowboy boots and stone-washed jeans: the Godfather of Davao City, with his godson (one of Sana's) standing at his shoulder. In another, he's at a table in her restaurant, in his trademark gold-rimmed aviator sunglasses, being Duterte Harry. Sara and Paolo, Davao City's mayor and vice mayor, also figure in these pictures, as does Elizabeth Zimmerman, their mother. Sana's place is a no-frills, what-you-see-is-what-you-get place — completely without ostentation.

In the Philippines Rodrigo Roa Duterte's zero-tolerance of official malfeasance is as renowned as his zero-tolerance of drugs.

'The cry of the people is "corruption"', Duterte said at presidential election rallies, amid promises that, if he made it to Malacañang, he would fire high-ranking bureaucrats, even ministers, at the 'first whiff' — as he had done in Davao. He has threatened to kill corrupt government officials, corrupt business-men, corrupt police, and corrupt journalists.

'If you are corrupt, I will fetch you using a helicopter to Manila and I will throw you out. I have done this before, why would I not do it again?' he said — oddly, while addressing victims of a typhoon in December 2016. The same month, President Duterte made a great show of his dismissal of three senior immigration officials accused of involvement in an extortion and bribery scandal. Two of them were former classmates from San Beda law school. 'You're fired,' he said, in Trumpian style.

In April the following year, he abruptly sacked his interior minister, a close ally, amid accusations of questionable wealth. By then, he had ordered the removal of dozens of bureaucrats and a senior campaign spokesman suspected of corruption. In March 2017, Duterte told a group of businessmen he had refused the gift of a gold Rolex watch and told them to refrain from offering bribes.

'My birthday's coming up,' he said. 'Do not give me the gifts ... Who would believe me if I talk about corruption then I wear a Rolex?' Earlier the same month, he said he'd refused the gift of a Mercedes Benz 'to maintain my moral ascendancy [sic]'.

But Duterte's critics allege there's long been a whiff of corruption around him. They question how, in a democracy, a local mayor was able to hold on to power for 22 years and maintain popularity ratings of 96 per cent in the local polls. A resident of Davao — who requested anonymity — and who had lived through Duterte's reign told me, 'When you fight corruption, it makes you very popular. But when your daughter and your son become mayor and vice mayor, don't tell me you are not corrupt.'

Among Duterte's biggest donors in his presidential election campaign were Davaoeño businessmen, but, as cash ran dry, he received a donation from a government contractor, whose tycoon-chairman is a former president of the senate, Manuel 'Manny' Villar Jr. Once elected, Duterte appointed Villar's son, Mark, to his cabinet as his public works and highways secretary. He also appointed a little-known television host, Martin Andanar, as his communications secretary. Andanar is related by marriage to the Villars. When challenged on this, Andanar denied any connection, insisting that Duterte had no idea he was related to the Villars.

'Honestly,' he said.

He'd got the job, he added, because his TV programme had been 'very consistent in promoting and saying that Mayor Duterte was the solution to the crime in our country ...' and that the president-elect had been very grateful.

Other campaign donors were likewise rewarded with government posts, the most prominent being Carlos Dominguez, another of Duterte's former classmates from Davao, whom he made finance secretary. Such appointments are legal under Philippine law. Nevertheless, Duterte's statement on election contributions and expenses failed to list one particular donor, which he later admitted to: Imee Marcos, provincial governor of Ilocos Norte and daughter of the former dictator. Failure to disclose contributions is illegal. Imee Marcos denied she had helped finance Duterte's campaign. The president was 'only joking', she said.

Under Duterte, the city administration in Davao was long accused of bribing reporters in the Philippine tradition of 'envelopmental journalism' — referring to the contents of little brown envelopes — or simply by extending timely financial assistance for matters such as hospital treatment or family funerals. In addition, self-confessed former hitmen from the DDS claim that large sums of money — in the form of rewards and bonuses, as well as hefty payouts for high-profile assassinations — were used by Duterte as an incentive to kill. The self-confessed head of the DDS claimed under oath that he and his fellow killers were motivated by a reward system — although the Philippine government has dismissed his testimony as a fabrication.

'Is Duterte corrupt? There's your answer,' the anonymous Davao resident said. 'He was morally corrupt to the core. Corruption comes in different guises.'

Whenever Duterte has been directly accused of financial corruption, he has always denied it robustly, but, as with Trump's tax returns, he has not produced evidence to lay doubts to rest. One of his fiercest critics, Senator Antonio 'Sonny' Trillanes IV, has repeatedly alleged that Duterte has more than 2 billion pesos (US$40 million) stashed — undeclared and unexplained — in hidden deposit accounts belonging to him and his family members. If it were proved that Duterte had concealed ill-gotten wealth, it would be very damaging. In 2012, a Philippine Supreme Court judge was impeached for a fraction of this sum, in undeclared accounts. The impeachment complaint filed against Duterte in March 2017 cited his allegedly undeclared bank accounts as one of several accusations against him. The complaint was thrown out two months later by a committee stuffed with Duterte loyalists.

At a Senate news conference televised live on all channels in February 2017, Trillanes challenged Duterte to reveal the source of these alleged funds. 'Don't be fooled by his simple lifestyle,' the senator told the packed press conference. 'It's time to unmask this guy,' he went on, promising to resign if Duterte proved his allegations wrong. 'I know he will not release [the account details] and he will not accept my challenge because it will be proven that he is really a corrupt official.'

The president's spokesman batted away the allegations as 'grandstanding', and Duterte then said he too would resign immediately if the senator — whom he called a 'brigand' — could prove he had even a quarter of the amount alleged. With no hint of irony he suggested that Trillanes 'stop opening his mouth when he has nothing to say'. He later said 'I destroy him or he destroys me'. Honeylet Avanceña was quoted as saying that the fact that the senator remained alive proved the president was not a murderer.

At the end of his first six months as president, Duterte's declared net worth stood at 27.4 million pesos, just over US$500,000. This included several houses, and plots of both residential and agricultural land, all in Davao City. According to the Philippine Center for Investigative Journalism, his net worth grew exponentially during his time as mayor, but Duterte maintains this was the product of inheritances and investments.

But, with Tillañes continuing to claim the president had billions stashed in foreign bank accounts, the Philippine Ombudsman launched an inquiry into the Duterte family's finances. Duterte responded by promising to file an impeachment case against the Ombudsman and the Chief Justice. He also countered Trillañes' claim about his owning secret bank accounts by alleging that the senator had some too, in Singapore. The president even cited an account number — which he was later forced to concede he had invented. Trillañes revelled in making a trip to Singapore where he produced evidence that his supposed accounts were non-existent. The senator signed bank secrecy waivers to allow scrutiny of his finances and challenged Duterte to reciprocate. He didn't.

As mayor of Davao, the man who never followed rules himself made everyone else obey his. He made up lots of them; some petty, some draconian, some hailed as progressive. All rigorously policed and enforced. In Davao City today, these local laws remain: jaywalkers are fined US$4; miscreants are also often sentenced to community service; it is illegal for school children to be out on the streets alone after 10 pm lest their parents be fined; licensing hours cease at 1 am; and Duterte imposed a 9 pm ban on boisterous karaoke on the grounds of noise pollution. (The Philippines is a nation hopelessly addicted to crooning to music videos. This did not stop Duterte from continuing to croon — quietly — in his own favourite Davao karaoke joint, After

Dark.) Firecrackers — which injure up to 800 people in the Philippines every year — are outlawed altogether. Speed limits were reduced to 30kph (19mph) within city limits and 60kph on highways. This reportedly lowered the accident rate by an estimated 40 per cent. Those caught breaking the speed limits — as the president's son and vice mayor, Paolo Duterte, was in 2016 — are fined the equivalent of US$200 — in a country where 13 million live on less than US$2 a day. Two years earlier, Duterte's daughter, Sara, was caught speeding at 57kph in a 40kph area. Stopped by nervous traffic cops, she reportedly insisted that they fine her and confiscate her licence. There are countless stories of how, as mayor, Duterte would patrol the streets either on his Harley or incognito in a taxi, checking that traffic was flowing smoothly and that his rules were being observed. There are photographs of him directing traffic and admonishing lawbreakers.

'It happened to me,' his sister, Jocelyn, admitted. 'One time I took a taxi; the traffic was really bad and the driver did not stay in line. Then I saw the mayor on the street manning the traffic!' Duterte pulled her over, gave her driver a dressing down, and issued an on-the-spot fine.

Prostitution is still allowed in Davao; registered sex workers are required to undergo regular health checks to make sure the services they offer are risk-free for the Russian and Chinese sailors whose warships periodically dock in Davao City. The mayor even threw parties for prostitutes every Christmas. Duterte, notorious for his philandering, enacted enlightened gender codes, in support of women's demands for equality. A radical reproductive health and birth-control programme was introduced, despite protests from the Catholic Church. He offered cash to those who opted for vasectomy and other forms of contraception. The Church was also opposed to Duterte's support of same-sex relationships and LGBT rights. His anti-discrimination legislation formally recognised the rights of the indigenous Lumad tribes and the Mindanao population. Before this, Lumads were often turned away from cinemas and shopping centres. He re-invigorated the annual Kadayawan Festival, celebrating the cultures of Davao's indigenous tribes, which, depending on who you ask, number between 11 and 14 different ethnic groups.

Another of his progressive laws was the ban on smoking in public places — a law which, as president, he enacted nationwide in May 2017. In the Philippines, nearly one third of the adult population smokes. A former smoker himself, the mayor introduced a fine of the equivalent of US$100 or four months in prison. This ban is enforced by Davao's Anti-Smoking Task Force. Smokers were — and are — confined to small roped-off 'leper-colony' enclosures, well-away from buildings, where sinners inhale under big signs detailing all the ways they are destined to die painfully if they refuse to quit. The public smoking ban in Davao followed a similar ban in Singapore, which had begun to prohibit smoking in public places as early as 1970. For this, and a slew of other petty regulations such as the banning of chewing gum and jaywalking, it was derided as a nanny-state. Some say Singapore's late leader, Lee Kuan Yew, was an inspiration for the regulation-obsessed Duterte.

But it was draconian legislation in Lee's law-bound city-state — in the form of capital punishment — that provided the pretext for Duterte to indulge in an act of political populism that won him proper national attention for the first time. It concerned the tragic case of Flor Contemplacion, a Filipina maid executed in Singapore in 1995. Then, as now, many tens of thousands of Filipinas worked there, most as child-minders, cooks, and cleaners. Contemplacion was convicted of the double murder of another Filipina maid and a three-year-old Singaporean boy. When evidence emerged that suggested she had been framed by her employer, President Fidel Ramos appealed for mercy. The hanging in Changi Prison went ahead regardless, and roused great anger in the Philippines. As protests spread across the country, an estimated 1000 municipal employees demonstrated in Davao's Rizal Park (named after Jose Rizal, the Filipino martyr executed by the Spanish for his outspoken demands for independence), outside City Hall. The mayor ordered that a Singapore flag be set ablaze. If this had happened today, the video would have gone viral; then, TV pictures of Duterte shouting 'Fuck you, Singapore' as the flag was torched elevated him to the status of national hero. During his presidential election campaign, he repeatedly claimed he'd set fire to the flag himself. He hadn't — Davaoeño journalists who covered the event saw someone else put a match to it. Still, his boasts made headlines in Singapore's *The Straits Times*. At one late pre-election rally, Duterte clarified his stance on flag burning in characteristic style: 'A flag symbolises a nation,' he said. 'If someone were to burn a Philippine flag in front of me, I would kill him.'

The enforcement of Duterte's laws was iron-fisted, personal, and unconstrained by any sense of political correctness. As he grabbed more and more media attention at his presidential-election rallies, reports also began to emerge of the mayor of Davao's authoritarian tendencies. The outgoing president, Benigno Aquino III — whose father's assassination had triggered the downfall of Marcos — warned fellow-Filipinos that in Duterte he saw another self-styled strongman and 'a dictator-in-waiting'. He compared Duterte's rise to power to that of Adolf Hitler, which Duterte appeared to revel in, later making the same comparison himself.

One of these reports concerned a tourist who Mayor Duterte

had forced to eat a cigarette when he refused to stub it out. It came from an authoritative source — Manny Piñol, a former provincial governor in Mindanao and now Duterte's secretary for agriculture — who said the mayor sat down beside the man, 'pulled out a snub-nosed .38 revolver and poked it at the man's crotch'. Duterte Harry told him: 'I'll give you these choices: I'll shoot your balls, send you to jail, or you eat your cigarette butt.' According to Piñol, the unidentified man uttered the words: 'Sorry, Mayor', before swallowing his butt.

Witnesses heard Duterte, as he left the restaurant, tell the tourist: 'Never, ever, challenge the law.'

He was clearly in full character.

When Piñol's account was published, Duterte's spokes-man said the mayor had never pointed a revolver at anyone, 'as far as I know' — only to have Duterte himself pop up on national TV5, confirming everything. In an expletive-laden interview, he boasted that he had told the tourist: 'I will make both your balls explode!' On another occasion, the mayor slapped a South Korean gambler whom he spotted smoking in a casino. And then there is the case of a man who was caught selling fake land titles; Duterte forced him to eat them in front of TV cameras. Reporters remember him instructing the cameramen to zoom in on him chewing.

Yet for all Duterte's iron-fisted policies and zero-tolerance of drugs, he was also a man capable of visionary — even humanitarian — projects, which flew in the face of his deadly reputation. The most astonishing of these is a drugs rehabilitation programme which, although dating from the mid-1980s, was massively expanded and inaugurated by the mayor in 2003. Set in a high-walled, secure compound down a jungly road in Davao City's outer suburbs, the centre caters for around 100 addicts at a time and 1300 have been through since it opened. Its director, Dr

Gene Gulanes, claims a success rate of 80 per cent — very high, but not impossible.

'We have some former addicts working here as staff,' he said to me. 'They were hired by the mayor himself. Since July 2016, we have been getting up to 100 addicts coming every month. We call them "residents". When the president was mayor he was branded by association with the DDS and shoot-to-kill,' Gulanes said. 'But there is no such thing. The mayor is very soft-hearted. He really believes they should be reformed. He keeps in touch with me. I used to speak to him personally.'

I was incredulous. But the very serious director, who speaks in a high tenor, assured me that I'd got the wrong end of the stick. Shortly after launching his national war on drugs, President Duterte declared that 'rehabilitation is no longer a viable option' and said he considered addicts 'beyond redemption', yet here was a facility that afforded *shabu* addicts a second chance.

The Philippines has a tiny fraction of the rehabilitation centres it actually needs, which is why most of the hundreds of thousands of addicts who surrendered when Duterte came to power are crammed into ludicrously overcrowded jails. The Davao rehab centre was as Spartan and regimented as a jail, and, although its 'residents' spent their nights in tightly packed bunks in featureless dormitories, conditions seemed infinitely preferable to those in Davao City jail or other prisons around the country. Soldiers from Task Force Davao, wearing camouflage uniforms and armed with semi-automatic rifles, patrolled the grounds day and night. The military unit, whose primary role in Davao is as a counter-terrorism squad, had a base inside the rehab centre.

'Not much chance of them escaping, then,' I joked with earnest director.

'No, the Task Force is here to protect the centre from attacks by communists,' he said. 'They raided a nearby compound and stole their rice.'

I was given a tour of the facility, which began in a separate area for the 17 female inmates who were laughing and chatting with their supervisor. I was accompanied by the centre's director and James, a vocational instructor. He told me they used an 'alternative learning system' to help push recovering addicts through their unfinished primary or secondary education, and that the centre could even boast some college graduates.

'This place was assigned by our beloved mayor who is now our beloved President Duterte.'

In those days, James said, the centre was ahead of its time. The mayor would even permit admissions of addicts from elsewhere in Mindanao, even from Luzon. My tour took in the dorms and classrooms, and ended under a tree at a spiritual guidance session for the 24 boys aged under 17.

'This is the character-building programme,' Dr Gulanes said. 'They study the advantages of obedience over disobedience.'

As one boy started strumming a guitar, the others began to sing some Christian choruses.

'We have spiritual activities for one-and-a-half hours every day except Fridays,' Gulanes said proudly. 'Friday is sports day. We have Zumba on Thursday and Friday afternoons and every day we pay respect to the flag at 5 pm.'

Flag-raising ceremonies are taken very seriously in the Philippines, and early one Monday morning I attended one at City Hall, Davao, an imposing monolith with Doric columns painted cream and terracotta, bathed in sunshine as municipal employees and hundreds of local police arrived to pledge allegiance. Dramatic instrumental music played on a Tannoy and dignitaries sat down on plastic chairs under gazebos erected in the square. The flagpole was surrounded by four large concrete eagles, wings spread in flight, and four fountains with durians spouting jets of water from their spikes. Security men in white Polo shirts, jeans, and dark glasses kept a close eye on proceedings. On San Pedro Street, jeepneys disgorged locals at a bus stop, over which a rooftop sign read 'JESUS CHRIST IS LORD' in capital letters four feet high. As I made may way to the square, I passed a car with one of the ubiquitous Duterte stickers in the back window, the kind that featured his clenched-fist campaign logo, though unusually it featured another sticker saying: 'I love you but promise me you will never kill me'.

The ceremony opened with a prayer for the president's health and supplication that he should be able to carry on with the tasks he had set for himself. This was followed by the national anthem, at which all present stood to attention, each with one hand across their chest. It had the feel of Havana in 1961, except for a rap performance by local college students, whose lyrics extolled the virtues of solid-waste management and quitting smoking. This didn't prompt a single smile from the ranks of over-heating city police who listened, clearly bored, to a succession of announcements from the podium. I was attending the ceremony in part aiming to talk to the elusive mayor and vice mayor, Sara and Paolo Duterte, but neither had turned up.

I was there also to meet three former *shabu* addicts employed by City Hall. Ronaldo, Kenneth, and John, now working for the Davao City Anti-Drug Abuse Council. All three had been through the rehab programme — one of them twice — and none could contain their gratitude.

'If we hadn't had the help of President Duterte in our rehabilitation, we wouldn't be sitting here talking to you now,' Ronaldo said.

Over his shoulder stood City Hall, through whose doors the

former mayor and members of the death squad had trudged for more than 20 years.

'We all wanted to thank him for what he's done for us,' John said. 'We always wrote him thank-you letters. But he doesn't like that sort of thing.'

The three men, all now in their twenties, agreed that the *shabu* problem in Davao was very serious.

'Twelve thousand have surrendered from the *barangays* [districts],' they said, but there are probably 12,000 more who haven't. It's not as big a problem here as it is in other cities thanks to Mayor Duterte.'

'But he killed people like you!' I said. 'Or at least the death squad did.'

The former addicts insisted that it couldn't have been the mayor.

'It's the syndicates,' Ronaldo said. 'They're the ones doing the killing. They're the ones trying to put the blame on the president.'

This was the standard response of Duterte supporters when challenged on the ever-rising body count in the drugs war.

'Mayor Duterte established the rehab centre! It's cheaper than buying bullets and guns!' Ronaldo continued. 'Even if the success rate is only one in ten, it's worth it. As long as you can get the tools for change.'

With the zealotry of apostates, they went on to enthuse about the Tarana Project — in Tagalog it means 'let's go' — a community-based rehab-aftercare programme involving local churches and schools. Pupils call ex-addicts 'friends' and take meals to them; priests offer soul food. I would later meet one of the priests involved in the Saving Lives, Saving Souls programme. The three former addicts told me the mayor's office was the lead agency, and that the mayor and vice mayor were directly involved — as was Paolo's wife, January Duterte, president of

Davao Barangay Kapitans. For a moment, it seemed that the citizens of Davao really had seen the light. But only for a moment.

Duterte also won national praise for his city's achievements in local governance, welfare, education, and health, and is particularly famed for setting up an integrated, round-the-clock emergency response centre: Central-911, said to be the first of its kind — not only in the Philippines but in all of Southeast Asia. The Central-911 squad was also able to clear up the mess left by the Davao Death Squad, some of whose killings were caught on the CCTV cameras Duterte installed throughout the city. This civic surveillance system was known as the Intelligent Operations Centre. Cameras are hidden everywhere; miscreants are caught before they can flee. In 2012, the US hi-tech multinational IBM announced an agreement with the Davao City government to 'scale-up' its existing Public Safety and Security Command Center by integrating city operations into a single system. An IBM press release from the time trumpets the city's 'tremendous transformation' and says the new plan would 'enhance the management of Davao's four pillars of public safety: crime prevention and suppression; emergency response; threat prevention and response; and traffic management'. This 'collaboration' — as the company put it — played into Duterte's promotion of his myth. IBM said its advanced 'smart-city' system would make 'Davao a model city in terms of livability and safety'.

One evening over dinner, the editor of the pro-Duterte *SunStar* newspaper, Stella Estremera, told me: 'He said, "I have this city covered. Even if you fart, I will know you've farted."'

I looked at her, across the table. 'Seriously? He said that? What's the Bisaya word for fart?'

Estremera laughed. '*Utot*! He used to say this on TV every time a criminal got caught. It's very Big Brother. It's not just CCTV,' she went on. 'He has his network of moles, supporters, friends, and agents in the communities, and they move fast. That's how he ran it. And now he will replicate it.'

By 2010, in a *Reader's Digest* poll, Duterte was ranked fifth among all Filipino politicians for 'trustworthiness'. In April 2014, as he entered his final year as mayor, the man who once told a national newspaper that 'I never thought I'd be a mayor; never in my wildest dreams' was nominated, by a Japanese investor, for the international World Mayor Award, which celebrates outstanding community leadership. In his apparently self-effacing way, he turned down the nomination.

'I did it not for my own glory,' he said, 'but because that was what the people expected me to do.'

He had previously also declined international awards for his anti-smoking campaign.

Successive Filipino presidents bought into the good publicity, apparently wowed by Duterte's no-nonsense reputation for delivering on his promises. He claimed to have turned down the offer of a cabinet post as interior minister under all four of his predecessors in Malacañang. This despite repeated allegations of links to the Davao Death Squad by national and international human rights investigators over many years. None of the presidents ever seemed to question the accuracy of Davao police statistics, or whether the mayor's boasts were a figment of his own imagination.

Today, Duterte's thought police operate not only within communities but online too, trolling, hounding, and threatening deviants and doubters who fail to toe the line. Fifteen years after his first appearance in *Time*, President Duterte was placed number one in the magazine's 2017 readers' poll for the world's 100 most influential people, receiving a total of five per cent of all votes cast. He consistently led voting in the survey, and trounced Putin, the Pope, Canadian prime minister Justin Trudeau, Mark

Zuckerberg, and Bill Gates, who each received three per cent of votes. Clearly alarmed that their poll had been hijacked by Duterte trolls, *Time* reported, two weeks before the result was announced that: 'Duterte has been known to use social media to promote his agenda and has reportedly paid people to push him to popularity online.'

Those who have supported Duterte through the years say that, above all else, he delivers on his promises, which is why, they say, he's never lost an election. His loyal followers talk of his *palabra de honor* — Spanish-Tagalog for 'word of honour' — as being the Duterte watchword for integrity in governance.

For Duterte, the end has always justified the means. This is how, as he campaigned to be president, he sold the Davao prototype to the nation. But Davao City is not the garden of peace he would have Filipinos believe; the president suffers from selective amnesia, and data that do not fit the narrative are ignored. Duterte's detractors point to Davao City police statistics showing that, contrary to his claims, the crime rate in the city actually rose — by no less than 248 per cent — in the decade 1999–2008, the latter seven years of which coincided with his second stint as mayor. Worse, Davao, rather than being the safe city Duterte boasted of at his election rallies, remains the 'murder capital' of the Philippines today, first among fifteen cities, with more than 1000 recorded murders committed between 2010 and 2015. It ranked second for rape. According to a presentation by the city police force in 2016, there were 363 murders in Davao in the first six months of the previous year — Duterte's last as Davao mayor. There were an additional 252 'unlawful killings'. More people were murdered in Davao between January and June 2015 than were murdered in the whole of New York City —

which has more than five times the population of Davao — during the entire year.

Neither did Duterte's iron-fist approach to solvent-sniffers, *shabu*-dealers, and others cast as sub-human low-lifes have any notable beneficial effect on drug addiction rates in Davao. This claim was demolished by the late Davao City judge, Adoracion Avisado, who knew Duterte and whose husband, Wendel Avisado, now advises Duterte in Malacañang. Judge Avisado, who died suddenly of cancer in late 2016, wrote just before her death that despite the boast of Davao being drugs-free, 'statistics show otherwise. The number of drug cases pending before the two drug courts are close to 4000 as of the end of 2015.' She said that, on average, 70 drugs cases were scheduled to be heard every day in the two special drugs courts in the city, despite the fact that they could only realistically handle five each. Meanwhile, the Davao City jail had more than three times the number of inmates than the 800 it was built to handle, meaning prisoners had to sleep in shifts. While some of the pending court cases could reflect the serious backlog of old cases, the 17,211 drug users who surrendered to police in the Davao region during the first 10 days of Duterte's presidency attested to a serious and unsolved problem.

'It's a nonsense we're drugs-free in Davao,' one resident of the city, and a known authority on this subject, told me. 'If you go into the slums, it's there, like candy. It's a myth that Duterte banished drugs when he was mayor. It's just a myth.'

I became further convinced of Duterte's Davao delusion that *shabu* had been banished, along with murder and violent street crime, on a visit, early one morning, to the beach. In a friend's pick-up, we navigated the potholes along the rather grandly named Nograles Avenue, after Duterte's now subdued former rival, Prospero, the former Congress speaker. The seaward side

offers a sunny vista of Davao's playground, the Island Garden
City of Samal. The city side is a dense cluster of tightly packed
tin-roofed shanties and shacks that comprise Barangay 76a — a
slum. The beach was busy with fishermen inspecting their nets
and boat builders hammering and chiselling at the skeletal
beginnings of the distinctive brightly painted vessels with their
elegant eagle-winged outriggers that lined the shore. I'd come to
meet Rubylyn Abi-Abi, the widow of a fisherman, who ran a tiny
beach-front fish stall, and who, in the dying days of Duterte's
mayorship, had lost her 21-year-old *shabu*-dealing son to the
Davao Death Squad. The killers were still alive and kicking in
Davao. Rubylyn was standing at her stall when I arrived; she
ushered me into a nearby beachside shack and, unprompted,
began to tell me a story that I'd heard many times before — and
would, many times again, in different guises.

'It was 5.30 pm on 25 January 2016,' she said. 'I was at the
stall. A vehicle drove up. A light blue minivan. About six or eight
men got out. I had no idea who they were. I saw no guns. They
went down to our house, down there, in behind' — she gesticulated
down the alleyway on the other side of Nograles Avenue. 'Seconds
later, I heard three gunshots. Bang! Bang! Bang! Straight afterwards, police cordoned off the area. I was stopped from entering
my house. I saw then that the men had guns: Colt .45s,' she said.

I asked if they'd been uniformed. No, they'd worn plain
clothes. So how did she know they were police? She shrugged.
Everybody knew. Only the police had Colt .45s.

'One of my neighbours had witnessed my son being shot and
falling on the floor. He was hit in the back of the head and
through the heart. The third shot was from the police too, but
they'd fired a .38 revolver in the air and planted the gun on my
son and put his fingerprints on it to make it look like he had
resisted arrest. I know my son did not have a gun. When I was

allowed to go in, he had been put onto a stretcher. He was covered by a cloth. I saw the bullet wounds. The shot that went through the back of his head came out through his eye. As he fell, he was hit in the chest from the front.'

Arvee Jay had been a fisherman, like his late father. His friends, Rubylyn told me, had enticed him into selling *shabu*. Barangay 76a, she said, was infested with the stuff. She'd begged him to stop, she told me, because the previous year her daughter, Chaysser Dawn, had been arrested on drugs charges and was now in the city jail awaiting trial.

'After he was killed, I learned from my neighbours that Arvee Jay was rumoured to have been on the police most-wanted list — and the next morning, the TV news quoted the police as saying this, too. I don't know why he would have been,' she said, 'because he was only a small-time dealer. I pleaded with him not to do this because I was aware of Mayor Duterte's campaign against drugs.'

Rossando, her father, who had joined us, agreed. 'I knew where this would end up,' he said.

When Rubylyn had learned that Arvee Jay's name had been on a police watch list, she'd seen no point in filing a police complaint into his murder. 'Immediately after his death, his case was closed,' she said.

Unlike most other distraught relatives of those killed by Duterte's death squads who I've spoken to, Rubylyn did not betray emotion. Perhaps she was all cried-out, having just been through too much in her 48 years, but her face, while not hard, had the look of a survivor. This was a woman who had known hardship, violence, and bereavement. Like so many of the victims of the Davao Death Squad over so many years, this was a family that was among the poorest of the poor.

'I can't even count how many killings there have been in this *barangay* over the years,' she said. 'At least two or three a month over the past 20 years, during all the time Duterte was mayor. I knew that Duterte was the law and that he could do whatever he wanted. The Duterte guys are the law in Davao City. I don't know how he can sleep at night if it's true that he is the one who orders these killings.'

But Rodrigo Duterte does not sleep well. When, eventually, he does go to bed, he relies on an oxygen concentrator to help him get through what's left of the night. He blames his past smoking, but maybe Rubylyn was right. In public, he has never betrayed any semblance of guilt, though. His economy with truth and outright fabrications were extended to his presidential raison d'etre, the national war on drugs itself.

Duterte's city of peace and order also remains one of the most violent in the Philippines when it comes to terrorist attacks and bombings. On the night of 2 September 2016 an explosion ripped through the crowded night market just down from the Marco Polo hotel on Roxas Avenue, killing 16 people and an unborn baby, and injuring 70. Martin Andanar, the president's spokesman, immediately blamed drug traffickers opposed to Duterte's war on drugs, but added that Islamist militants might have been responsible, as a few days earlier, he had also declared an all-out war on the jihadist group Abu Sayyaf. Word on the street was that it might have been a combination of the two, but in October 2016 three men allegedly belonging to the radical Islamic State-linked Maute group were arrested. (It was the Maute group, in conjunction with the leader of Abu Sayyaf and foreign jihadists who were to occupy the Mindanao City of Marawi a few months later.) The bombing prompted Duterte to declare a 'state of lawless violence' throughout the Philippines, which many at the time thought a prelude to martial law. Sure enough, in May 2017, he declared what was christened 'partial martial' across the whole of Mindanao in response to the crisis in Marawi. Throughout Duterte's mayorship, there had been periodic bombings in Davao, with targets including the cathedral, a hotel, the airport, a wharf, and a cinema. Communist NPA rebels have also attacked targets in the city and ambushed police.

Through all of this, the Duterte clan has toughed it out and has established itself as the uncontested ruling dynasty in Davao. Together, Grandpa, Dad, and Sara have notched up a total of three-and-a-half decades in power. As Duterte's sister, Jocelyn, puts it (and her son, too, is employed by City Hall): 'Being a Duterte in Davao is like a brand, like Calvin Klein.' Dynastic politics is the norm in one of Asia's oldest democracies — at the local, provincial, and national level. Three-quarters of elected members of the Philippine Congress come from established political families scattered throughout the archipelago's 80 provinces. Theirs is a political world where your name matters more than anything you might claim to have achieved, and the Dutertes have now climbed the ladder from the provincial to national level.

Although in Davao they haven't reigned continuously for decades, like the three Kims of North Korea, they too are in their third generation of leadership. Sara Duterte, mayor of Davao (and, as First Daughter, the Ivanka Trump of the Philippines) still has some way to go to match the cult of personality her father enjoys, but she has hitched her star firmly to her father's bold dynastic ambition. In late October 2017, at an event in Manila attended by Marcos' daughter, Imee (governor of her home province), and former president Joseph 'Erap' Estrada (now mayor of Manila), Sara launched a new alliance supporting her dad's administration — and attacking his critics, with Senator Trillanes singled out as the number one enemy of the people.

'This is not a part of any campaign to run for any position,' she said in her speech. 'It is not about me. It's not about my political plans.' Few in attendance were in any doubt that that was exactly what it was all about. Presidential communications assistant — the queen of the trolls — Mocha Uson, had earlier posed for a selfie with Sara, during the 2017 State of the Nation address. She posted the picture on social media accompanied by the caption 'Our Next President'.

At Malacañang, Duterte retains the thuggish traits that he brought from Davao. For now, the Duterte branding is still that of a provincial oligarch, and, although he promised the Philippines that he would change the political landscape, the Duterte political dynasty has moved into the space previously occupied by the better established big families with names like Marcos and Aquino. Unlike the past elites of 'imperial Manila', which lost touch with the people they governed, Duterte presented himself as a man of the people and pulled the wool over their eyes. Before long, Sara 'Inday' Duterte will have helped soften her father's uncouth *bugoy* image — although he jokes that she's more iron-fisted than he is. In a TV interview, the president (ever the narcissist) said he had heard people say that when he was gone they would need 'somebody like me to replace me'. He had someone in mind, he said: a woman who kicks, punches and slaps.

'You want someone like that? It's Inday,' he said.

Exhibit 'A', Plan 'A'.

8

CHRONICLE OF DEATHS FORETOLD

There's a narrow road that runs along a razor-ridgeline just northwest of Davao which, on a clear morning, offers a sweeping view over the city and beyond, across the Gulf of Davao and Samal Island. One Sunday, I set out early for the hill, but hit the evangelical rush hour: huge crowds of God-fearing Davaoeños —Protestant and Catholic—clogged the streets as they converged on churches, while the less devout headed off to cock-fights, many with their prized birds tucked under one arm. By the time I reached Langub Hill, the morning sun was blazing and the temperature was climbing fast. The dazzling intensity of the light injected a tropical vividity into the already vibrant palate of the distant cobalt sea and the lush low-rise cityscape below, with its red-tiled roofs, shade trees, and coconut palms. It didn't look like the murder capital of the Philippines, where liquidation squads run wild; a city that still comes under periodically violent attacks from communist and Islamist insurgents. Down there, at a resort on the beach-fringed Samal Island, 10 minutes' boat ride from Davao City, two Canadians and a Norwegian had been kidnapped in late 2015; the Canadians later beheaded by the jihadist group Abu Sayyaf, the Norwegian eventually released to Duterte's old friend Jesus Dureza, who had negotiated a ransom of more than US$600,000.

Davao City lies to the east of the ridge on Langub Hill. Turning to face southwest, you can trace the jungled outline of Mount Apo, a magnificent slumbering volcano; at nearly 10,000 feet, it is the archipelago's highest mountain, and home to the critically endangered Philippine Eagle, the country's national bird. Looking the other way (as people in Davao are sometimes prone to do) from a picnic shelter at a restaurant called Vista View, you can face north and gaze down into an expanse of secondary forest in an abandoned limestone quarry. From its depths, a rhythmic cacophony of cicada percussion rises up the scarp in hypnotic soundwaves.

Laud Quarry, in the Davao district of Ma-a, is named after its former owner, a retired senior Davao policeman called Bienvenido Laud. This was the execution ground of the Davao Death Squad (DDS), and, according to the sworn testimonies of some of the killers themselves, it's where the bodies are buried — or some of them, at least. According to these executioners — and local residents I spoke to, who knew the mayor's black Honda Civic sedan — Duterte Harry was a regular visitor. The disused quarry was a known dumping ground for bodies long before the DDS began its reign of terror; from when the Sparrow Squads of the New People's Army terrorised the streets in the 1970s and 1980s, and after that when the Alsa Masa vigilantes engaged in bloody battles in the dirty wars that preceded the People Power revolution of 1986. The quarry later became a firing range for police, but at night it would revert once again to local killing field. Today, the quarry's rusting iron gate is chained, padlocked, and overgrown, and Laud has sold his land to the owner of a local hardware franchise who, it is said, plans to develop a holiday home from an existing building on the site. You can see these buildings on satellite images of the site on Google Maps. An adventure centre has rigged up a zip-wire where daredevils can skim at speed across the lake and above Laud Quarry's haunted treetops, to an outcrop on the far side where there are several caves.

The quarry has been at the heart of a legal battle for more than a decade. In 2009, a man called Edgar Avasola, who claimed to have helped bury the bodies of six men there, testified before a court in Manila in support of the Philippine National Police (PNP). The head of the PNP's Criminal Investigation and Detection Group (CIDG) had sought to search the quarry compound, together with a team from the Philippine Commission on Human Rights (CHR), a statutory body, after reports that human skeletal remains had been discovered. Very little is known about Avasola, other than the fact that he used to run errands for his boss, the former cop, Bienvenido Laud, whom he called 'Tatay' — or 'father' — Laud.

Avasola told the judge that one night in December 2005 he was summoned to the quarry where, he claimed, he had heard Laud himself call out the names Pedro and Mario, the only two victims who, he claimed, were still alive. Like the other four, the two men were killed, and Laud ordered him, together with the six killers, to bury the bodies in three caves on the north side of the quarry compound. Avasola claimed he did not know who the men were or why they were being summarily executed.

The search warrant was duly issued, but Laud's lawyers appealed the ruling and, just days after the search began, the warrant was set aside. The PNP took its application to the Court of Appeal, which reaffirmed the warrant — but Laud's lawyers again challenged the ruling and took their appeal to the Supreme Court. Tatay Laud was determined that the PNP should not gain access to the property, further increasing suspicions about skeletons in his quarry. Finally, in November 2014, the Supreme Court affirmed the validity of the search warrant. In stating the facts of the case, the judge said the police were seeking 'a warrant to search three caves located inside the Laud Compound ... where the alleged remains of the victims summarily executed by the so-called Davao Death Squad may be found'. This was the first formal confirmation of the existence of the DDS by a Philippine court. The Supreme Court judge also deemed credible the eyewitness account given by Edgar Avasola five years earlier. The PNP was 'commanded to make an immediate search ... and forthwith seize and take possession of the remains ...'

But the CIDG is extremely unlikely ever to do so. On becoming president in 2016, Duterte appointed as justice secretary Vitaliano 'Vit' Aguirre II, one of Laud's two lawyers who had battled for years to prevent the police from gaining access to the quarry. Previously, in Davao, the humourless, bespectacled Aguirre had represented a close friend and former classmate from San Beda College of Law in Manila, one Mayor Duterte. He defended the mayor in cases filed by the Commission on Human Rights, in which Duterte was accused of links to the Death Squad. At the time, Aguirre rubbished these charges as 'baseless'.

In his new role, Secretary Aguirre has continued to rigorously defend his former clients' interests — both those of Duterte and Bienvenido Laud. Secretary Aguirre — accused by his critics of 'lawyering for the DDS' — has specialised in obstructing all efforts to investigate Duterte Harry, past and present. In February 2017, Aguirre ordered the indefinite suspension of the National Bureau of Investigation's remit to investigate cases relating to drugs — meaning the NBI (the Philippine equivalent of the US FBI) was barred from looking into any killings arising from Duterte's war on drugs. That same month, Aguirre denounced as 'false' a forensic report on extra-judicial executions by the human rights group, Amnesty International, declaring that drug lords and pushers were not human.

'Do you consider them humanity?' he asked. 'No! Believe me.'

Over the years, Aguirre has loyally protected his San Beda 'batchmate' from the swirl of allegations surrounding Duterte's links to vigilante assassins, whose murderous ways have now come to define his presidency, just as they did his mayorship. In March 2009, the then head of the Commission on Human Rights, an independent body under the Philippine constitution, initiated an investigation into the Davao City mayor's involvement with the DDS, which by then was accused of carrying out more than 1000 extra-judicial killings.

The chair of the CHR was another ex-San Beda lawyer, Leila de Lima, who had been appointed to the post by President Gloria Arroyo. In a series of public hearings in Davao City, de Lima summoned nearly 50 people to give evidence into 206 deaths determined by the CHR to be attributable to the DDS. On the first day of the hearing, Mayor Duterte asserted under oath that there were no state-sanctioned killings in the city and swore that he would resign as mayor 'if there is an iota of evidence' that he or the city police were behind them. Nevertheless, testimony from other witnesses again pointed to Laud Quarry as the site where victims of the DDS were summarily killed and buried. Others who weren't taken to the quarry to be killed, the inquiry learned, 'were either shot or stabbed by motorcycle-riding assailants'.

Given what is now known about what happened in Davao City under Mayor Duterte, it seems incredible that he had ruled

Davao for 21 years before the CHR finally launched an invest-igation into the killing spree. The evidence that has come to light about Duterte's direction of the DDS will be as central to any future prosecution as his incitement of killings in the drugs war. In the early days, national and foreign press coverage of the DDS was scant. Local Mindanaoan papers and broadcasters did report the killings, but the scale of what was happening there did not reverberate much beyond Davao until Duterte won his fourth and fifth terms in the early-to-mid 2000s. Internationally, the Philippines remained a country best known for having inspired the world by toppling a corrupt dictator whose wife had a legendary shoe fetish. Few seemed interested in the antics of a small-town mayor from distant Mindanao. Slowly, however, the mayor of Davao City began to get himself noticed.

In November 2001, when Duterte returned from his stint in Congress, the Davao City newspaper, *MindaNews*, ran an interview with him. It's a remarkable read because, if there is one thing you can say about Duterte, it is that he has never wavered in style or substance. By way of introduction, the paper's editor, Carolyn O. Arguillas, wrote:

> Many in Davao City were 'shocked,' to say the least, to see their controversial mayor on national television late Tuesday night last week, talking tough (his expletives unedited), toting a gun and kicking the corpse of a suspected drug pusher, reportedly killed by the vigilante group, the 'Davao Death Squad.'

Arguillas had covered Duterte from the start, and, in journal-istic circles, remains one of the dwindling and distinguished few who have managed to retain impartiality and independence in their reportage. In the 2001 interview, she challenged Duterte repeatedly over his alleged direction of the DDS, at one point even asking him if he was bothered about being referred to as 'the godfather of the DDS'. Duterte said he wasn't because it wasn't true, and that he didn't 'give a shit' what people thought or said. There was no such thing as government-sponsored killings in the city, he insisted. 'That is utterly false. I swear to God.' The mayor claimed to have no idea as to who the 'vigilantes' were. And then, as ever, he started muddying the waters, making statements that were tantamount to admissions that he was indeed the godfather: 'I was elected by the people after I promised them I would go after kidnappers, druglords, drug pushers, holduppers and rapists,' he blustered. 'I don't give a damn. I don't give a shit. What I should do now is to honour my commitment ... To be really truthful and honest about it,' he confided, 'I would rather see criminals dead than innocent victims die, being killed senselessly.'

At the time, Duterte had recently read out on his TV programme the names of 500 people who were on his 'watch list'. When Arguillas interviewed him, four of them had already been killed, and at least another 17 would be murdered by the time the interview was published. They were reportedly suspected drug pushers and mobile phone snatchers; four of them were minors.

By 2005, the year Avasola testified that he had been summoned by his boss to bury bodies in the quarry, news of the killings had spread far and wide, even attracting the concern of US Congress and prompting visits from a UN rapporteur and other international human rights investigators. On 20 January 2005, a confidential US Embassy cable to the State Department, later published online by WikiLeaks, noted 26 reported killings in Davao City 'since the new year began'. Looking back now, the observations of the embassy's then political officer, Andrew McClearn, are startling in their prescience; US Embassy cables about President Duterte may read similarly today. McClearn noted that the 'Davao Death Squad, a vigilante group linked with Davao Mayor Rodrigo Duterte' had been implicated in the killings. The mayor, he said, clearly 'condoned' these killings, which 'seemed very popular' and had given him 'some bounce' politically. The cable continued:

> The latest killings in Davao serve to add to the lethal image that Mayor Duterte has carefully cultivated since coming to office ... Mayor Duterte all but acknowledged his active support of the DDS group.

It quoted a classic Duterte statement from the previous week: 'Drug lords are garbage and we will dispose of them like garbage.' It also says he offered cash rewards to citizens for information on drug traffickers or labs so they can be 'punished and destroyed'. Even then, his 'past patterns' of behaviour were cited as reason for concern. The US cable identified the 26 victims killed in less than three weeks as including 'marketplace vendors, construction workers, a housewife, and two members of a leftist political party'. The cable concluded that Duterte's 'clear support for and public encouragement of extra-judicial killings has only added to his popularity — he won his last two races for mayor by landslides'.

The Davao Death Squad proved an inspiration to the mayors of other cities in Mindanao, and even in Visayas, to the north. Death squads began conducting similar campaigns of targeted killings in General Santos City and Digos City, southwest of Davao, and in Tagum City, a couple of hours' drive northeast. In 2008, a local radio journalist in General Santos City reported that: 'There is a clear pattern, including the profile of victims, the choice of weapons, the use of motorcycles without license plates, and police failure in investigating the cases.'

A decade later, whistle-blowers would admit to collusion between the Davao killers and their 'colleagues' in nearby Tagum City. In January 2005, another US embassy cable — also published subsequently by WikiLeaks — noted that copycat DDS vigilante-style killings had spread beyond Mindanao, to the central Philippine island of Cebu. The then-mayor of Cebu City, Tommy Osmeña, had been implicated in a spate of recent killings following his decision to create a special police squad to hunt down criminals for bounties. 'In pressing his anti-crime fight in such extra-judicial directions,' the classified cable said, 'Osmeña seems to be modelling himself after Rodrigo Duterte, the notorious mayor of Davao City.' Osmeña even couched his response to accusations that he was behind the killings in a manner identical to Duterte: 'I am not behind it,' he said. 'But I will say I inspired it. I don't deny that.'

Mayor Duterte's own cavalier willingness to condone the killings proved to be another recurring pattern. Many then, as now, have thought him inexplicably incautious for a former lawyer. The first international investigation was led by Philip Alston, then the United Nations' special rapporteur on extrajudicial, summary, or arbitrary executions. His report was presented to the UN General Assembly in April 2008 and examined targeted killings throughout the Philippine archipelago, and the failures of the justice system to prosecute or convict the killers. Alston devoted a section to the increasingly alarming situation in Davao under Mayor Duterte. His introductory summary stated baldly:

> A death squad operates in Davao City with men routinely
> killing street children and others in broad daylight ... It has
> become a polite euphemism to refer vaguely to 'vigilante
> groups' when accounting for the shocking predictability

with which criminals, gang members, and street children are extrajudicially executed.

He noted that, in popular perception, the mayor had insulated his city from armed conflicts raging elsewhere in Mindanao, and limited criminal activity. These apparent accomplishments, he said, 'appear to have bought acquiescence in the measures he takes, and the public remains relatively ignorant of the human cost of death squad "justice".'

Alston interviewed in detail witnesses or family members of seven of the victims. In one of these cases, Duterte had actually said on a local radio show 'that he doubted the victim would live through the week given the (petty) theft that he had just committed'. Almost all the victims had received warnings, most were killed in public places; some were stabbed, some shot. The UN report stated that *barangay* — or district — officials appeared to be involved in the selection of targets.

Alston described the Davao City mayor as an 'authoritarian populist' and judged his position to be 'frankly untenable'. He too challenged Duterte face-to-face on the existence of the Davao Death Squad.

'When we spoke,' Alston wrote candidly in his report, 'he insisted that he controls the army and the police, saying, "The buck stops here." But he added, more than once, "I accept no criminal liability." While repeatedly acknowledging that it was his "full responsibility" that hundreds of murders committed on his watch remained unsolved, he would perfunctorily deny the existence of a death squad and return to the theme that there are no drug laboratories in Davao.'

This, like many of Duterte's assertions, was not true. There had been a *shabu* lab operating out of a three-storey warehouse in Davao City as recently as 2005, and its existence has come back to haunt Duterte as president. When the lab was raided, Davao police shot six suspects — who succumbed to their wounds — and seized more than 100kg of high-grade crystal methamphetamine with a street value of 300 million pesos, along with equipment and precursor chemicals for its manufacture. Ten Chinese nationals were arrested, according to newspaper reports from the time, but then, bizarrely, eight were released without charge by Duterte six weeks later 'in the spirit of the Chinese New Year and for humanitarian reasons'. Duterte, then in his fifteenth year as mayor, declared that the eight had been cleared of any involvement in narcotics manufacturing, without them ever having appeared in court. Duterte has never offered further explanation of this incident, but the existence of the laboratory prompted persistent allegations from Senator Antonio 'Sonny' Trillañes that Duterte was himself involved in an illegal drugs protection racket. In September 2017, he suggested in a Senate hearing that the former mayor was the Pablo Escobar of Davao, and alleged that the city was used as a drugs trans-shipment centre for Chinese triads, and that Duterte's son, Paolo, then the vice mayor, was a member of a trafficking cartel known as 'the Davao Group'.

Following his investigation, the UN rapporteur recommended that the national police should terminate Duterte's powers of supervision of the local PNP units, and should hold the officers commanding those units responsible for shutting down the DDS. They never did. Watch lists should be abolished, he said. They never were. And an independent inquiry should be conducted to identify those directing the hit men. Of his three recommendations pertaining to Davao City, only the last one was eventually acted on.

At around the same time, the DDS began to receive the odd mention in international press coverage — both print and broadcast — in part triggered by interest in Alston's report. Most of the reporting was orientated towards the general problem of vigilante killings in the Philippines, though, rather than what was going on in Davao specifically. After 9/11, through the invasions of Afghanistan and Iraq, and later the conflicts and revolutions spurred by the Arab Spring, foreign affairs coverage by western media had been skewed towards incessant war news. Working out of London, where, prior to returning to Southeast Asia, I worked as foreign affairs correspondent for 15 years, I was acutely aware of this, as were my colleagues. From time to time, earthquakes or tsunamis, wars in Lebanon, Libya, Gaza, or Congo, or occasional political crises elsewhere would spark sufficient global interest for news teams to be deployed, but small wars in far-flung parts of the developing world rarely received much coverage. The excesses of nasty regimes went virtually unreported, as did what was happening in a remote and little-known city in the deep south of the Philippines. *Time* magazine's feature 'The Punisher' was published in 2002, as Duterte began his fourth term as mayor. Five years later, a team from my company, ITN, reported from Davao on the murders of street children, petty criminals, and drug addicts. A couple of years later, Al Jazeera also reported on the Davao Death Squad. This wasn't the only international coverage of Duterte's reign of terror, but he largely waged his war out of the media limelight.

In 2009, Human Rights Watch (HRW) published a report entitled 'You Can Die Any Time', which investigated summary executions in Mindanao, Davao in particular. The report was highly critical of the Commission on Human Rights' sluggish response to the targeted killings in Davao, just as the UN special rapporteur had been. The new report provided what HRW called 'an anatomy of death squad operations'. It makes for grim reading. It too concluded that police officers and local *barangay* officials were either involved or complicit in DDS killings, and called on the mayor of Davao City to 'cease all support, verbal or otherwise' for the targeted executions. Duterte's name features prominently. The report quotes the Davao City official website, which claimed that crime rates were so low that Davao was an 'almost Utopian environment'. HRW said: 'These descriptions attempt to conceal a rampant crime wave — namely, the murder of hundreds of alleged drug dealers, petty criminals, and street children.' Again, it painted a picture of Davaoeños being seduced into ignoring the DDS and imagining their city was virtually crime-free — just as Filipinos will today tell you they feel safer thanks to Duterte's war on drugs, as the homicide rate spirals off the scale.

Few Davaoeños suffered bereavement inflicted by the DDS more intensely than Clarita Alia, a widow whose four sons were murdered one after the other between July 2001 and April 2007. Her story was highlighted in the HRW report. The first to die was 18-year-old Richard, a known member of the local Notoryus gang, who had previously been arrested on charges of petty theft. When, two weeks before he was fatally stabbed, police had arrived at the family home in a shanty district called Bankerohan, Clarita had refused to let them in without a warrant. Richard was accused of rape. His mother told HRW that a senior police officer told her: 'Ok, you don't want to give your child to me, then watch out because your sons will be killed, one by one.' Richard's 17-year-old brother, Christopher, was stabbed in the market three months later. Two years went by before Bobby, her 14-year-old, was stabbed in the same local market, and finally, four years after that, Fernando, then 15, was stabbed to death on a bridge nearby. He had been arrested a few months earlier on charges of sniffing a solvent known locally as 'rugby'. After Christopher's killing, his mother filed a case with the Commission on Human Rights, but nothing ever came of this. Nothing ever came of police investigations either, and not one person was arrested. Clarita told HRW she was too scared to share information she had with the police, and witnesses were too afraid to testify. Davao City police said the killings were probably down to gangland feuds. She claimed her boys were the victims of a local hitman, a known close associate of Davao City policemen.

In August 2016, I went to meet Clarita Alia while working on a Channel 4 News report in Davao. Fifteen years had elapsed since the first of her sons was killed, but sitting with her at the stall she still runs in Bankerohan market, Clarita remained raw with a mother's grief. She went into the lean-to shack behind the stall and came back clutching photographs. Tearfully, she recounted her tragic story, just as she had for the HRW investigators, years before. She conceded that her sons had indeed been local terrors; anywhere else, they might have run the gauntlet of the police, but not been stabbed through the heart by a municipal assassin. The last picture showed 14-year-old Fernando, the year before he died. She had sent him off to school on nearby Samal Island to keep him out of trouble. He's standing, smiling, in a stripy navy shirt, leaning on a red Honda motorbike with his school satchel on his back. He scarcely looked his age. I asked her who she blamed for all that had befallen her. She answered with one word: 'Duterte'. Again, she broke down in tears. 'It really hurts because it started with my sons,' she sobbed. 'It saddens me that they are doing this everywhere now. I saw this coming. I warned them he would do this everywhere.'

Leila de Lima's team from the national Commission on Human Rights finally began its long-called-for investigation in March 2009. But it was never properly completed because she was appointed justice secretary the following year, and it wasn't until 2012 that the commission, under a new chair, published its recommendations. Mayor Duterte, the CHR said, should be further investigated for possible criminal liability over 'his inaction in the face of evidence of numerous killings committed in Davao City and his toleration of the commission of those offenses'. Inevitably, nothing happened.

At the beginning, it had all looked promising; de Lima's investigation had got off to a flying start. In July 2009, a joint task-force from the CHR and PNP, led by de Lima in person, had entered Laud Quarry with a warrant to search the three caves on the basis of Edgar Avasola's court testimony. This search was explicitly restricted to the caves: two small, one big. During the few days they spent there, the investigators exhumed thigh bones, forearm bones, a complete skull, other skull fragments — one of them with a 'gunshot mark' — and more than 4000 other bones, including vertebrae, ribs, pelvic, and collar bones. (Former DDS hitmen say they often used to chop up the bodies before burying the remains.) The PNP's Scene of the Crime Office (SOCO) — whose officers can be seen today carrying away the corpses of victims killed by police or hitmen in Duterte's drugs war — confirmed at the time that the bones were human remains. They were discovered at all three sites specified by Avasola. The exhumations were featured daily in the national press, and the CHR released a statement saying the team in Davao were 'very optimistic that more remnants of summary executions are about to be unearthed'. The multi-agency task-force, the statement said, 'assured the public that this no-nonsense effort will continue without leaving any stone unturned to carry out its mandate'.

It was not to be. Even as they searched, Vitaliano 'Vit' Aguirre II — who would eventually succeed de Lima as justice secretary — was scrambling to protect his client, Bienvenido Laud. He argued before the judge who had granted the search warrant that, as no criminal complaint had been filed against his client, any application for a warrant should have been filed with a court within whose territorial jurisdiction the alleged crime had been committed. The police had in fact filed an application for a warrant to a Davao City judge, who had denied it, which is why they'd reverted to a court in the capital. The denial of the application had infuriated de Lima and prompted her to label the Davao courts 'uncooperative, obstructionist and accessories to the culture of impunity'. Laud immediately filed a contempt case against de Lima in Davao. In Manila, Aguirre dug up an obscure law — the Sanitation Code — which required the supervision, by local health officials, of exhumations. Six hundred miles away, in Davao, local heath officials had not participated in the search. The judge who'd granted the warrant accepted Aguirre's argument and revoked the warrant. But in doing so, he may inadvertently have saved de Lima's life.

In September 2016, a few months into Duterte's presidency, a self-confessed former hitman in the DDS emerged from the shadows to testify as the star witness in a Senate inquiry into the extra-judicial killings in Davao City when Duterte was mayor. The inquiry was chaired by de Lima, who by then had been reincarnated as the head of the Senate committee on justice and human rights. The former DDS hitman, who went by the name Edgar Matobato, said he had 'found the Lord' and could no longer live with his conscience. He confessed to having personally murdered more than 50 people and participated in the killing and disposal of around 300 more. Matobato's estimates are thought to be on the low side, considering he had been working for the DDS for 24 years. In the Senate hearing, broadcast live on several national TV stations, Matobato claimed that back in 2009 he had been assigned to assassinate Leila de Lima at Laud Quarry.

'When you dug up the quarry at Ma-a,' he told the senator, 'we waited for you. You went inside. We were in an ambush position.' Matobato said the ambush failed because de Lima hadn't reached the area where he and the other gunmen were lying in wait. The startled senator asked the hitman who had ordered her assassination.

Matobato responded matter-of-factly: 'It was Mayor Duterte, Ma'am.'

Matobato's testimony was dynamite, but his claims to have taken orders from Duterte, and to have witnessed the mayor himself shooting people dead, were deemed to have been riddled with inconsistencies, and were ridiculed by the president's irate and belligerent supporters, chief among them Justice Secretary Aguirre, who branded Matobato 'a liar' and 'a stooge' of Senator de Lima. Referring to the human remains that had been found buried in the quarry during de Lima's search, Aguirre said: 'The bodies did not prove anything. In fact there were statements that they were the bodies of people who were executed during the Japanese occupation.' Some of the skeletons, he added, were probably those of animals.

Leila de Lima's decision to initiate a Senate inquiry into Duterte's links to the DDS was the political equivalent of kicking a nest of hornets. After she summoned Matobato to testify, the angry hornets attacked, unceremoniously ousting her from chairmanship of her committee and replacing her with a Duterte ally and former PNP chief, who disparaged Matobato as 'damaged goods' and promptly closed down the inquiry.

The removal of de Lima was engineered by world champion boxer Senator Emmanuel 'Manny' Pacquiao, one of the president's men in the upper house. In December 2017, at his 39th birthday bash, Duterte anointed Pacquiao, who is also popularly known as 'Pacman', his chosen successor ... although by then the president had already said he wanted his daughter Sara to take over — 'a woman who kicks, punches and slaps'. To his opponents, Pacquiao's punches have proved even more lethal though and he is regarded as being as dangerous outside the ring as he is in it. In his long career, he won 11 world titles across five different weight classes and was nicknamed The Destroyer. He gained immense popularity in the Philippines and was a source of great national pride. This helped launch his congressional career at the age of 32. He served two terms before running for senator. Like Duterte, Pacquiao is from southern Mindanao, a city called General Santos, and, like Duterte, he won the votes of more than 16 million citizens in the senatorial election in 2016. He was hailed as 'the people's champion'; having grown up in poverty, Pacquiao is worth US$500 million, according to *Forbes* magazine. Like Duterte, he claims to have had a vision and heard the voice of the Almighty. In his first year as a congressman, and still an unassailable force in the ring, Pacquaio said he had a dream in which he saw two angels ('with white, long, big wings') in a beautiful forest and he had heard God speak in a voice 'ten times louder than thunder'. He told the US Christian TV network CBN: 'I was kneeling and praying with my face on the ground and then I saw a light, a very white light and I heard the voice.' Amazingly, the senator claims to have then forgotten about this dream until, one day he picked up a Bible again. 'I realised, wow, my dream was real,' he told the network. 'I have found the right way.'

Senator Pacquiao saw no conflict between his strident born-again evangelical beliefs and his wholehearted support of President Duterte's murderous war on drugs. He claimed to have tried all kinds of drugs himself before becoming a champion boxer and then finding the Lord. He said he backed the drugs war and that he believed God had put 'The Punisher' in power so that he could discipline the people. As an attack-dog for Duterte in the Senate, Pacquiao has poured scorn on the religious conversion of former DDS members who claimed their penitence stemmed from their own spiritual renewal.

One day, on the fifth floor corridor in the Senate building, where de Lima still has her office in Room 526, I bumped into 'The Destroyer' as he waited for a lift. Like many of the leading players in this clunky political soap opera, his office was also on the fifth floor. I asked him what he made of the rumours — circulating wildly at the time — that Senator de Lima faced imminent arrest. He crossed his boxer's arms and stood defiantly, knees locked, legs astride and scowling. 'No comment. She has to be investigated,' he said, as though trying to mimic the manner in which politicians bark at journalists in films. His posture made it very clear that he did not want to engage.

I continued: 'Is what's happening to her part and parcel of President Duterte's war on drugs?'

The lift doors opened and Pacquiao bolted. Once inside, he turned and, for a moment, we briefly stood there staring at each other. Images of those scowling boxers' weighing-in shots came instantly to mind. Except I lacked his lean, ripped abs, and, anyway, he was surrounded by other senators heading off for lunch. Then, just as the silver doors slid shut, he said, still glaring at me, 'He's doing it right.'

The following day, 17 February 2017, Justice Secretary Aguirre announced that drugs-trafficking charges had been filed against Senator de Lima; if convicted she could face between 12 and 20 years in jail. On becoming president, Duterte had repeatedly spoken of his indignation over how a female lawyer from 'imperial Manila' had sought to humiliate him in his own city, in front of his own people. Now it was payback time.

In the days leading up to her arrest, de Lima's office was

swarming with advisors. As she consulted in her inner sanctum, her large staff — I counted more than 20 of them — were furiously tapping away on keyboards, as other senators and, to my surprise, another government minister, bustled in and out of her office. The atmosphere was edgy with what turned out to be an accurate sense of foreboding. On the wall facing the small sofa where I was waiting in her ante-chamber, there was a large oil painting of a cock-fight, with two birds whirling and writhing in a colourful, all-action flurry of feathers, beaks, and blades.

'I know it's not a good moment,' I started.

The senator grimaced and agreed.

De Lima is in her mid-fifties; her auburn-tinged hair styled in a short, business-like cut; her dark-rimmed glasses and her black suit were brightened by plum-hued lipstick. Although she was dignified and remained composed, anxiety was etched on her face.

'I've been expecting the worst,' she said. 'They are capable of the very worst things.'

Over previous months, Duterte had bombarded her publicly with insults loaded with sexual innuendo after her 'affair' with her driver was revealed. They were both accused of being in cahoots with the drug lords.

'She was not only screwing her driver,' the president had quipped, 'she was screwing the nation.'

'This doesn't come out of nowhere though, does it?' I suggested.

De Lima seemed resigned to her fate. She nodded. 'I have been the object of persecution and the most vicious forms of vilification and character assassination ever since I called for a Senate inquiry into the EJKs,' she said. 'And then we have some history, the two of us. It goes way back to 2009 when I investigated the Davao Death Squad phenomenon. This is just a part of his personal vendetta.' De Lima paused and her forehead became furrowed. 'He's very dangerous,' she said, almost confidentially. 'He is a very dangerous person and a very dangerous president. But I refuse to be silenced. I refuse to be intimidated.'

I asked her if what lay at the heart of all this was her concern that Duterte now wanted to emulate what he'd done in Davao on a national scale.

'Oh yes,' she said. 'Because that is what's happening. That's exactly what is happening now. Almost 8000 deaths already — and also attributed to policemen. It is just like the DDS.'

I accompanied her down the corridor as one of her senator-enemies strolled purposefully past, pretending everything was normal.

A few days later, amid a surge of international outrage, Senator Leila de Lima was detained at national police headquarters in Manila's Camp Crame on 24 February 2017.

It hadn't soothed Duterte's ire that, by this time, another veteran senior Davao cop had entered the fray: an earnest, balding, 56-year-old super-grass who was busy spilling secrets. Arturo 'Arthur' Lascañas, who had recently retired after 34 years in the Davao City Police, first appeared at a dramatic news conference at the Senate in Manila to corroborate many of the claims of his former henchman, Matobato — who himself had named Lascañas as the leader of the DDS. Breaking down in tears, he claimed to have killed 200 people as its chief. Following that appearance, Lascañas was called to testify before the Senate committee on public order and dangerous drugs in March 2017. Like Matobato, Lascañas said he had experienced a 'spiritual renewal' and that his love of country and new-found fear of God meant that his 'blind obedience and loyalty to Mayor Rodrigo Roa Duterte will now end'.

He said he was aware that he was about to self-incriminate,

but that he wanted people to know the truth of what had happened in Davao: 'The killings in the Philippines have to stop.'

A detailed 12-page sworn affidavit, signed by Lascañas, had been leaked to a whistle-blowers' website a few days earlier. It was full of extraordinarily precise recollections about individual killings, and how ambushes and assassinations were executed; detail of the sort it is hard to invent.

Lascañas declared that he had been among those who had started the DDS, and confessed to — literally — calling the shots. He said he had personally killed 300 people in total, among them his own two brothers, who had been involved in drugs. Lascañas had served in the aptly named Davao City Police Heinous Crimes division, and claimed — as Matobato had before him — that Duterte had personally ordered 'numerous' liquidations, including the notorious assassination of local radio commentator Jun 'Porras' Pala, who had once run against Duterte for the mayorship. For this hit he said he had earned a reward of 1 million pesos from the mayor.

Pala had been a larger-than-life character, and, though he and Duterte had once been friends, the city was not big enough for two such figures. Pala liked to swagger around strapped with bandoliers of bullets and armed with an M-16. His leather jacket concealed a Magnum revolver; a hand grenade would dangle from his belt. The year before Duterte was appointed acting mayor, Pala had become the mouthpiece of the violent anti-communist Alsa Masa vigilante group, which was responsible for many civilian deaths. An article about him in the *SunStar* noted that, 'Pala liked saying his idol was Joseph Goebbels, Hitler's chief propagandist' and that he had styled himself as a fearless anti-communist crusader. His radio show earned this self-styled Filipino Contra a lot of money, popularity, and power, but he was less a journalist than a corrupt and violent shock-jock. In

1999, Pala — by then an elected councillor — berated Duterte's thuggish son, Paolo, live on air for beating up a lowly hotel security guard on Vicente Duterte Street, named after Paolo's grandfather. The incident had made national news. Paolo was reported to have been armed and accompanied by two body-guards, and was restrained as he was 'threatening [to] finish off his victim'.

Rodrigo Duterte, it seems, never forgave Pala. Over the next few years, their feud escalated, with Pala relentlessly attacking Duterte on his radio programme — he used to bill himself as 'the voice of democracy in Duterte's reign of terror' — and Duterte firing back on his Sunday morning TV talk show. At around 8 pm on 6 September 2003, on the third attempt to kill him, Pala was gunned down in the street, a few hundred yards from his home, with an M-16, his own weapon of choice. The murder went unsolved. Duterte denied involvement, but claimed he knew who was behind it. 'He was a rotten son of a bitch,' he said. 'He deserved it.'

In his affidavit, Lascañas revealed how the killing had been commissioned on the mayor's instructions. Another senior police-man, Samson 'Sonny' Buenaventura, who doubled as Duterte's long-serving bodyguard, had, he claimed, offered him the equiv-alent of US$60,000 to organise Pala's liquidation. This is five times the average national annual salary in the Philippines, and more than 60 times as much as a chief superintendent could expect to earn in a month. Lascañas claims he divvied out the reward money and that a month after the murder Duterte had personally given him a 1 million peso cash bonus (US$20,000).

While the mayor had a generous slush fund — his Intelligence Fund — to bankroll such off-budget projects, Lascañas claimed that remuneration for this and other killings had been drawn from the pooled salaries of 'ghost workers' at City Hall. He said Duterte paid DDS members between 20,000 and 100,000 pesos (US$400–US$2,000) per execution, 'depending on the status of the target'. He also claimed he had received a 100,000 peso monthly allowance from Duterte, on top of his police salary, an allowance handed over by Sonny Buenaventura, the bodyguard. Duterte's office supplied everything, Lascañas said: cars, guns, ammo, food, and money. Ronald 'Bato' dela Rosa, later chief of the PNP, had known about some of the DDS killings when he was the police chief in Davao. Both super-grasses also told their lawyers that dela Rosa had taken part in DDS operations while Duterte was mayor of Davao City.

Lascañas named all the 'triggermen', many cross-corroborated by Matobato's evidence. Most were policemen; others were contract killers like Matobato. Lascañas claimed that Bienvenido Laud, the quarry owner, had been the police handler for a group of hired henchmen who were turncoat former Sparrow Squad assassins. The former NPA killers targeted glue-sniffers and alleged petty thieves, while the police and their contractors went after bigger fish — kidnappers and drug lords. Lascañas also confirmed the use of Laud Quarry as the execution ground, and, when questioned, said he could point to burial sites. These included those of an entire family killed with a silenced .22 calibre pistol: a suspected kidnapper, his Muslim-convert wife (who was seven months pregnant), their four-year-old son, her 70-year-old father, an elderly male relative, and the family maid. Having abducted them from a neighbouring town, the DDS had held them for hours in a building inside the quarry before their executions. The personal belongings were removed and burned, including the wife's Koran, he said, adding that the bodies were then stripped and buried by three of Bienvenido Laud's trusted men.

'Here, evil prevailed,' Lascañas said. Mayor Duterte, he claimed, had personally instructed them to 'erase' the entire family, ordering him in the Bisayan language, over dinner with other Davao senior policemen: 'Just go clean up.'

In his affidavit, Lascañas said that Duterte's DDS codename was 'Superman'.

Innocent people had been killed, Lascañas said, adding that he and his fellow policemen had failed in their sworn duty 'to serve and protect'. He wrote:

> I do not expect forgiveness from the families and relatives of the people we killed. I do hope that they would at least find comfort in knowing what really happened to them and who was truly responsible for their disappearance and murder. I know it is not enough to say sorry, but I am truly sorry for what I have done and I am ready to face the consequences of my actions.

He said the incidents he had recounted were 'just some of the many' of which he had personal knowledge, killings carried out 'with the prior knowledge, direct orders, consent, tolerance, or acquiescence of then-mayor Rodrigo Roa Duterte of Davao City.

During the Senate inquisition of Lascañas, Senator Manny Pacquiao asked him whether he'd been paid to testify. Other senators questioned his credibility, and, with Pacquiao, mocked his 'spiritual awakening', which, Lascañas said, had followed a near-death experience during kidney transplant surgery the previous year.

Lascañas retracted what he had said at Matobato's hearing, where he had denied the very existence of the DDS, claiming it was a figment of the media's imagination. The hostile, sceptical senators pointed out that he'd already found God by the time of that inquiry, to which he had been summoned alongside all the other alleged members of the DDS named by Matobato. The senators asked the 'born-again' Lascañas why he had lied under oath.

Lascañas maintained that at that time he was still a serving policeman, surrounded by Duterte loyalists, and that he was under instruction about what to say. He said he had feared for the safety of his family, who at that time weren't protected. After his retirement in December 2016, Lascañas said he had entered the protection of the Catholic Church. Due to his act of perjury, however, his gruelling six hours of testimony was dismissed by Senator Panfilo Lacson, chairman of the committee, as having 'no probative value'. The hearing was wound up after a day, with Lacson saying that the Senate committee on public order and dangerous drugs would recommend the filing of a perjury case against Lascañas.

Martin Andanar, Duterte's communications secretary, described Lascañas' testimony as 'a demolition job' and, fittingly, 'a character assassination' of the president. But it is not easy to be a whistle-blower in the Philippines, particularly when you are blowing the whistle on the president himself. To do that credibly requires extremely detailed inside knowledge of things that happened, and, on that score, Lascañas delivered. The Commission for Human Rights issued a statement saying the testimony was 'too compelling and too detailed to ignore' and that, on the basis of Lascañas and Matobato's evidence, the CHR would now relaunch its abandoned DDS investigation.

From her cell inside police headquarters, the former head of the CHR and ex-justice secretary, Leila de Lima, described Lascañas' revelations as 'hair-raising', and said that, following his and Matobato's testimony, the country could not afford to become 'bewitched' as the city of Davao had been, having fallen 'under the spell of its ruthless king'. She believed she and other investigators had been regarded as enemies and intruders in a 'kingdom engulfed by a false sense of peace and order'. After months of living in hiding at a safe house in the capital, Lascañas — who had fully expected to be jailed or killed — fled the Philippines for Singapore in April 2017, assisted by the Catholic Church. His family had left for Singapore before he testified in the Senate. The city-state was a bit too close to home, though; more than 140,000 Filipinos work on the island — and overseas Filipino workers are known to strongly support Duterte. Trade relations between the two countries are strong and Duterte paid a visit to the city-state in December 2016. Perhaps Singapore derived a secret satisfaction from hosting this turncoat former killer as it still smarted from Duterte's first outburst of nationalist populist sentiment at Singapore's expense, following the execution of the Filipina maid Flor Contemplacion there in 1995, when he had participated in the burning of the Singapore flag.

In mid-2017, Lascañas and his family were granted political asylum in an undisclosed country and completely disappeared from view. I managed to remain in contact with the former leader of the DDS through a trusted intermediary. Via the Signal messaging app, whose encryption is considered the most secure, I continued to ply him with questions that he answered willingly and in detail. He confirmed that Matobato's testimony had been accurate and that apparent inconsistencies were readily explained by the fact that he had run what he called 'a compartmentalised system of operation' on the orders of Mayor Duterte, so that 'force-multiplier players' — i.e. hitmen like Matobato — were not told everything, and were, on occasion, fed misleading information on the identities of those they were ordered to kill. The same compartmentalisation affected Lascañas, too: there were gaps in his own knowledge, he admitted, because he did not oversee every operation. When I asked questions concerning individuals or events about which he had no personal knowledge, he said so. But what he did know about the DDS over the period 2001–2016, when he ran it, was not far off encyclopaedic. I did seek precise clarification of the command structure of the death squad. This was his response:

> Mayor Rodrigo Duterte was the one who created and organised the Davao Death Squad. Therefore he is the real leader of the DDS. I am just the one who implements and enforces his orders.

Given the truncated nature of his testimony in the Senate and the necessarily limited scope of the handful of press interviews he granted, many questions had remained unasked. What he had revealed so far was, he had said while giving evidence to the committee, 'just the tip of a bloody iceberg'. Perhaps it was the policeman in him, but Lascañas needed to be asked specific questions in order to prompt him to volunteer information. When asked such questions, though, his answers were authoritative and detailed.

Lascañas confirmed that an assassination plot had been hatched by Duterte in which a hit-team had been deployed to kill Leila de Lima at Laud Quarry. The orders, he told me, had been given by Sonny Buenaventura. When I questioned Lascañas about individual members of the DDS, he told me of how one police officer under his command, Enrique 'Jun' Ayao — a member of his heinous crime division — was known for confiscating *shabu* from dealers whom he had arrested or killed, then 'recycling' the drug, selling it on through other dealers and profiteering from his already lucrative sideline as a paid killer. I had heard that this practice was common in Davao and in other cities, where the police themselves were deeply involved in, and sometimes key suppliers in, the trade in methamphetamines. No action was taken against Ayao, although Lascañas claims that he had unsuccessfully recommended his transfer from the unit because of his recycling.

His most startling revelation concerned a former very senior Davao City policeman, Chief Inspector Jacy 'Jay' Francia, who Lascañas knew well, and who was named by Matobato as a member of the DDS. I asked Lascañas whether he could confirm rumours that, after Duterte won the election, Francia had been reassigned to the Presidential Security Group (PSG) at Malacañang Palace, which is tasked with providing close protection to the president and his family.

'Jacy Francia was a member of a Death Squad within the heinous crime group, a special unit under the direct supervision of the mayor,' Lascañas confirmed. 'Francia was reassigned to the PSG when Duterte became president, along with another senior police superintendent, the former director of Davao City police, Vicente Danao.' Their reassignment orders, he said, had come directly from the president through his special assistant Christopher 'Bong' Go.

This meant that not only were two key members of the DDS now at the heart of security in the presidential palace but, Lasacañas continued, employing a euphemism, 'play', to mean that, with Duterte in Malacañang, other DDS-men had joined the new death squads in the capital:

> There are several Davao City policemen, all of them my former comrades in the Death Squad, who are now in Metro Manila, playing the game of death of President Duterte in his campaign against illegal drugs. I too was invited by senior superintendent Vicente Danao to play in Manila after I retired from police service in December 2016.

Instead, Lascañas decided to blow the lid clean off. The former

DDS leader said he hoped to be called to give evidence against his former city mayor at the International Criminal Court in the Hague.

'There are several mass graves in the Laud Quarry which I can personally point to if given the opportunity through legal means by the United National Human Rights Council or by the International Criminal Court,' he told me. Lascañas claimed he had been present with Aguirre, Sonny Buenaventura, and Bienvenido Laud when they discussed what to do about the discovery of so many human bones in the caves. It was decided, he said, that it would have been too risky to attempt to remove the skeletal remains now, in case movements at the site were being monitored. Lascañas believes those remains are still there, somewhere beneath the adventure centre's zip-wire. He also promised that more former DDS members would emerge to corroborate his statements.

The failed impeachment case against Duterte, and the complaint against the president lodged in the Senate early in 2017, drew heavily on the testimony of both Matobato and Lascañas. In May 2017, the impeachment complaint was dismissed by a Senate committee dominated by Duterte's allies on the grounds that Senator Gary Alejaño, who had filed it, had no personal knowledge of the allegations he had made in his complaint. Forty-two of the 49-member House Committee voted to declare them 'insufficient in substance'. Alejaño told reporters the process had been 'railroaded' and said that the House 'is not independent'.

For all Duterte's ambiguous denials of the existence of the Davao Death Squad — and of his being its godfather — he has actually gone much further, by way of his admissions, than he did when he told the UN rapporteur 'the buck stops here'. In May 2015, almost exactly a year before he was elected president, during an interview on his Sunday morning TV talk show, he said: 'They say I am the Death Squad? True, that is true.'

His statement made headlines nationwide. This appearance came at a time when he was floating the possibility of standing for president, and he would often cast himself as a reluctant candidate forced, against his better judgement, to take on the thankless task by insistent Filipinos. But he could not be accused of mis-selling his intentions were the presidency to be thrust upon him.

'I do not want to be the president,' he said. 'I do not want to kill people so do not elect me as president. I will kill all of you who make the lives of Filipinos miserable. I will kill you.' This was also the occasion on which he said that if he won, the fish in Manila Bay would grow fat feasting on the bodies he dumped there: 'If by chance, God will place me there, the thousand will become a hundred thousand.' The 'thousand' was a reference to the conservative estimate of the numbers killed by the DDS while he was mayor — the number cited by Human Rights Watch, which had once again called on the government to investigate his links to the DDS.

President Duterte won a standing ovation at a national business leaders' forum in Manila after he told them how he would patrol Davao City at night on his Harley 'looking for trouble. I was really looking for an encounter so I could kill.' He explained that, 'In Davao, I used to do it personally. Just to show the guys [the police] that if I can do it, why can't you?'

On another occasion, he told reporters that he had killed 1700 people; the next day, he said he had been joking, berating journalists for taking him too literally. Duterte also explained that his 'I am the Death Squad' statement on his talk show had been tongue-in-cheek as well — his way of challenging human rights groups to file charges against him in a court of law. In an interview with the digital news site *Rappler* in October 2015, Duterte was described by its CEO, Maria Ressa, as 'brutally frank' when he said 'I had to act decisively. Let me just say that there were things which I had to do because I had to do them.'

Ressa asked him to clarify: 'Like what?'

'Like the ones that people are crying about until now,' Duterte said. He told her he had no regrets. 'I must admit, I have killed.'

Duterte had already admitted to killing for the first time when he was 17, when he said that 'maybe' he had stabbed someone during a drunken beach brawl. Later he said he had committed this murder when he was 16. Speaking to Filipinos working in Vietnam on the eve of a regional summit, Duterte said: 'When I was a teenager, I would go in and out of jail. I'd have rumbles here, rumbles there. At the age of 16, I already killed someone. A real person, a rumble, a stabbing. I was just 16 years old. It was just over a look. How much more now that I am president?'

On another occasion, he claimed to have shot (but not killed) a bully at law school in Manila. He also boasted that he has thrown a criminal suspect from a helicopter. In December 2016, just hours after his spokesman Martin Andanar denied that the president had personally killed anyone and said that his claims should not be taken literally, Duterte boasted — for the second time — of having shot three men. The president was speaking to a cluster of reporters, with his Chief of Police and Andanar standing behind him: 'I killed about three of them because there were three of them … I don't really know how many bullets from my gun went inside their bodies. It happened. I said I cannot lie about it.'

Down in Davao, I had been told of an incident in the city's western Toril district just after Duterte had been elected mayor, in which he claimed on the local TV evening news to have killed the operators of a *shabu* laboratory. Pictures reportedly showed a number of dead bodies sprawled in front of a warehouse as Duterte stood with local police, all holding guns. His cabinet minister and old schoolmate, Jesus Dureza, related another story to me that he had heard from Duterte personally and, he said, from others who had witnessed what had happened. Duterte — in his Clint Eastwood persona — claimed to have shot dead members of a gang holed up inside a house surrounded by Davao police. According to Dureza, who was laughing as spoke:

> He [Duterte] said 'I personally would like to kill these guys', but he didn't kill these guys just like that. He positioned himself in one place, down by the stairs — and this is a story I got from those who were present — and he was ready to fire, like this.

Dureza adopted a cops-and-robbers pose, arms outstretched as if holding a pistol.

> But he didn't fire ... He ordered the bad guys to surrender ... It was only when they raised their guns to fight back that he shot. He pulled the trigger. In other words, he is a very legal person. He knows exactly when justified killing is allowed. And when unjustified killing should not be done.

Perhaps Duterte was referring to this incident when he encountered the reporters in December 2016. But, on that occasion, he had added a qualifier to his boast: 'If it means killing people, kneeling down with their hands tied at the back,' he said, 'that's all bullshit.'

The self-confessed DDS hitman, Matobato, told a very different story. Three months earlier, he had claimed under oath in the Senate that he had witnessed Duterte kill 'seven or eight' times throughout the 1990s, all but one of these incidents at Laud Quarry in Davao. The other alleged Duterte murder he witnessed was that of a National Bureau of Investigation agent Vicente Amisola, who was shot dead in 1994 in a case of mistaken identity. Amisola had been driver and bodyguard for the NBI chief in Davao, and Matobato accused Duterte of 'finishing him off' with a burst from an Uzi sub-machine gun. But Matobato's detailed testimony was torn apart by senators in de Lima's inquiry, denied point blank by the presidential palace, and disparaged by large sections of the press and by the president's supporters. Matobato is illiterate, and in the inquiry his inquisitors mocked him and sought to undermine his credibility, pointing up the apparent inconsistencies in what he said. They accused Duterte's enemies, senators de Lima and Trillañes, of coaching their star witness; however, independent voices — lawyers, priests, and human rights investigators — were convinced of Matobato's credibility. I wanted to meet this hitman myself, but organising this was to prove no easy task as he was being moved secretly between different safe houses, far from the capital. Finally, a date was set for me to meet him at an undisclosed location.

9

A JEALOUS MISTRESS

Travelling in a sturdy vehicle with a trusted driver and a Filipino colleague, I had agreed to rendezvous with Edgar Matobato's security detail early one wet morning a few hours' drive outside Manila. We had no idea where we would be headed. I was communicating with the ex-hitman's protection team on Signal, the only secure encrypted messaging app they trusted. They instructed us to follow their vehicle, which soon veered off the main road. Our route was complex, clearly designed to reveal or shake off anyone who might have tailed us from the capital. We drove through a torrential downpour for more than an hour, through rain-lashed towns with clusters of dripping tricycle-taxi drivers cloaked in ponchos on the roadside, then down long, straight roads dissecting paddy fields. In the distance, hillsides appeared, steaming after the morning deluge, their forested canopies still veiled in swirling cloud.

The road became more remote; the phone signal more erratic, and then it completely disappeared meaning it was no longer possible to track our position. Matobato had voluntarily left the government's Witness Protection Programme just before Duterte won the 2016 election. He felt he could no longer trust his own government to protect him; those providing security to Matobato now believed him to be an assassination target. It wasn't clear whether their extreme paranoia was entirely justified, but the two men in the lead vehicle were not taking any chances; Matobato was on Duterte's wanted list and was actively being hunted by the National Bureau of Investigation.

When, finally, the security men were satisfied that we had not been tailed, we were taken to our destination: a smallholder's wooden farmhouse situated down a lonely track, hidden in a bamboo grove by a river. The simple house was positioned halfway down a hillside. Two umbrellas and some laundry hung from a clothesline slung between two sturdy bamboo uprights: a pink t-shirt, a faded-green patterned sarong, a small white towel. They did have electricity up here, but it was from a generator out the back — this place was too remote to be on the mains.

At 57, the contrite killer's face was showing signs of wear. He had thick black and steely-silver hair that matched his grey-marl t-shirt, and big, brown eyes which were impossible to read. A chunky wooden crucifix hung on a cheap ball-popper chain which he wore out, over the t-shirt. The cross had been a gift from his priest-protectors. Matobato was stocky, with a prominent flat nose, a deep-etched brow, and, when he smiled (which wasn't often), laughter lines creased around his eyes, although he'd lived a life bereft of much hilarity. He offered me some coffee, which his wife went off to brew in the outdoor kitchen area on the balcony behind where we were sitting. There was a gas cylinder, a cooking ring, a tap, and a metal rack containing a rice cooker and a few well-used plates and aluminium pots and pans. The roof was made of corrugated tin. This presented an immediate problem as I had decided to film my interview with Matobato and the rain on the tin roof made a racket.

The coffee arrived, and I watched as the hitman shovelled creamer and sugar into his. He took a slurp and smiled. He'd only ever made it through grade one at school, he said, and had grown up on the slopes of Mount Apo. His father, a forest ranger, had grown coffee in the rich volcanic soil. When Matobato was in his late teens, NPA insurgents had beheaded his father in front of him, impaling his head on a wooden stake, he claimed, after they had raided the family farm in search of weapons. Afterwards, he signed up with a civilian paramilitary unit to fight the communists and wreak revenge. This was to be the beginning of a long and violent career, which saw him joining the ranks of various vigilante groups including the 'Lambada Boys', forebears of the DDS, which Matobato said was often just referred to as 'The Mayor's Unit'.

At my request, he showed me his documents and Davao ID cards, one bearing the signature of the former mayor. Another referred to him as 'Agent Edgar B. Matobato', and had been issued by the Criminal Investigation and Detection Group of the Philippine National Police, CIDG stamped in big red capital letters above his photograph. Another of the cards, bearing the insignia of the City Government of Davao, described him as an 'Auxiliary Service Worker'. His wife, he told me, had had no idea about what he really did — she'd thought he had a proper job at City Hall. Instead, Matobato had done the bidding of the man he knew by the codename 'Charlie Mike' — C. M., the City Mayor, a certain Rodrigo Duterte.

The inconsistencies in his statements to the NBI and his testimony to the Senate had been ruthlessly exploited and used by pro-Duterte senators to undermine his account, but Matobato had stuck to his guns and maintained that his real job was to carry out hits for 'Charlie Mike', and that he took orders directly from Lascañas.

For more than three hours, I fired a constant stream of detailed questions at Matobato, forensically covering the same ground again and again. The quick-fire questioning did not give him time to think — his responses were immediate, and, when pressed, full of apparently trivial memories: colours, exact locations, strange and precise little details it is unlikely he would have thought of had he not been there. He was patient with my questioning and said he understood why it was necessary. I was certainly not the first to interrogate him — he would have had plenty of rehearsals — but these were not the answers of a man searching the further reaches of his memory to recall what he'd been told to say. He remained composed and confident, and if he didn't know something, he said so, or said he hadn't been there. As we spoke, Matobato's wife mostly remained out of sight, inside the house itself, but sometimes her husband's answers to my questions drew her back out onto the balcony again, where I would suddenly become aware of her listening silently behind me. It was she, when he had finally told her the truth about what he had done all those years, who had helped him tally up his kills.

Among the claims that the NBI and the Senate had discounted was Matobato's assertion that he had helped murder and then dispose of four bodyguards of Prospero Nograles, Duterte's political rival in Davao. When I spoke to Nograles, he denied that this had ever happened. I was later to learn from Matobato's Davao Death Squad boss, Arturo Lascañas, that the four security people killed had indeed been assigned to work with Nograles, and had been murdered on Samal Island, off Davao, allegedly on instructions from Duterte and his bodyguard Sonny Buenaventura.

Matobato had also claimed to have been a member of the team that had killed Jocelyn Duterte's dance instructor, with whom, it was alleged, she'd been having a relationship. She denied both the affair and that her dance instructor had been killed. Reinforcing her denials, a man claiming to be the dance instructor had popped up on Facebook. Lascañas later backed up Matobato's claim; the DDS chief said Jocelyn had been deceived, and that the man in question had been murdered and disposed of at Laud Quarry — whether or not he'd been her dance instructor, as the kill-team had believed.

It seems the apparent inaccuracies in Matobato's rendering of events arose from his either having been misinformed about the true identities of those he had been ordered to kill, or because, over the course of more than two decades as a contract killer, his memory had merged incidents he'd actually witnessed with those he'd learned about from others he'd worked with. If he had made it all up, as most of Davao and half the Philippines continue to believe, it would have involved a phenomenal feat of memory. As merely a contractor, he had an incomplete picture of the operations of the Death Squad. He had, as he had told de Lima, just been following orders. I asked him if he had informed de Lima of the alleged assassination plot against her prior to revealing it during the Senate hearing.

'No,' he said. 'She was shocked when I said that if she'd walked any further we might have killed her.'

'And did you apologise?'

'No. I just said I'd been following orders.'

Sitting on the farmstead balcony, bamboos behind him rustling gently, Matobato related the grisly details of many of the murders he claimed to have personally committed. They included the bombing of a mosque and the kidnap and murder of what he called 'innocent Muslims'. In his deadpan, matter-of-fact delivery,

Matobato told me how others had been stabbed or hacked to death, their bodies subsequently torched or dumped by the roadside, or left to rot in banana plantations outside the city limits. Those shot dead at Laud Quarry were chopped into pieces, he said, before their body parts were scattered and buried.

'Of the 1400 killed by the DDS,' he said, 'I was personally involved in killing and disposing of the bodies of around 330 of them.'

One of Matobato's most extraordinary accounts involved an alleged kidnapper who had himself been abducted in the province of Sarangani on the southern tip of Mindanao in 2007. Matobato told me he had been the only civilian contractor on a joint operation involving the Davao City Police Heinous Crime division and the NBI. One of the NBI agents was a lawyer called Dante Gierran, who would later rise to head of the bureau in Davao. In July 2016, President Duterte appointed Gierran as national director of the NBI. Matobato said he had worked with Gierran over a 15-year period, but when he made this claim during the Senate inquiry Gierran said that, although they had known each other, he had 'never brought him into my operations in Davao' and suggested that Matobato might have had some hidden agenda for implicating him. Weeks later, Gierran stepped up the hunt for Matobato, setting up a taskforce to hunt him down. Agents who raided one of his suspected hideouts (far from where I met him) found nothing.

What happened that day, though, was a truly heinous crime. The alleged kidnapper, whose identity Matobato said he never knew, was taken to Digos, the city in which Duterte had completed his secondary education, 50 miles from Davao. There, at a compound owned by the NBI, Matobato said they had fed their trussed-up victim to a crocodile, 'a pet of the NBI. It could eat at least 50 kilograms. They used to feed it pigs. This man was small.'

'Did you actually witness that?' I asked, incredulously.

'I was the one who pushed him in,' he answered. 'They asked me to do it because they thought I was brave and because I gave everything to the job.'

'Had the man realised what was happening to him?'

'We wrapped masking tape around his eyes and stuffed a "Good Morning" towel into his mouth so that he couldn't shout. Then we wounded him in the chest so that the blood would flow. He didn't know what was going on.'

'How did that feel, for you to do that?' I asked.

His answer floored me.

'Well, when I saw him being eaten I was happy actually, because the crocodile was full.'

His mention of the 'Good Morning' towel was the sort of trivial detail that seemed to lend his story credibility. These cheap white cotton towels — known as GMTs — with their red crest and 'Good Morning' logo embroidered in English and Chinese are a ubiquitous Philippine and Asian icon. A GMT was hanging drying on the farmhouse balcony as we spoke.

Matobato went on to describe countless plain-clothes police operations he had been on, where .38 calibre revolvers were placed next to the bodies of those they had murdered 'so that the police could say [their victims] had shot back', he said, in self-defence. Just as he'd done when he testified in the Senate, he named all his accomplices, most of them serving policemen under the command of Arturo Lascañas. In all, 16 out of the 19 police officers and four civilians that Matobato had accused of belonging to the DDS appeared at the Senate hearing to debunk his claims, including Lascañas, who, at the time, repeatedly dismissed them as 'all lies'.

When I spoke to Matobato, he named one of these policemen, Vivencio 'Jun' Jumawan, who, he alleged, was involved in the murders of all four of Clarita Alia's teenage sons. Jumawan, Matobato claimed, was also among a group of four police who had raped and stabbed to death three girls, aged 17, 18, and 20, whom Matobato had been ordered to abduct from a Davao apartment building on suspicion of their involvement in drugs. He said they had found no evidence in their flat, but had nonetheless blindfolded the girls and driven them in a Toyota HiAce minivan to San Rafael Village in Davao City to hand over to Jumawan and his colleagues. Later, Matobato claimed, he had thrown their bodies on the roadside. He told me tearfully that his involvement in their deaths had had a profound effect on him. Lascañas would later confirm this story; the girls' bodies were recovered from the roadside where Matobato dumped them.

Not long before the three young women were murdered, Matobato had told Lascañas that he'd had enough and wanted out. But his boss insisted that he had seven more 'jobs' he wanted him to do. He did them. They included the abduction of the girls, and the killing, he claimed, of a young man who had irritated Duterte's son, Paolo, in a queue for petrol at a Shell service station.

Matobato also alleges he was framed for the murder of a Cebu billionaire businessman in Davao in 2014. He was, he claimed, picked up and 'tortured' by his colleagues, including Lascañas. They were worried he was going to squeal. Matobato was only released on bail, he said, because his wife made such a fuss about his disappearance, and his uncle, a serving cop, had intervened. He had fled immediately, and tried to bring his story to the attention of the then justice secretary, Leila de Lima. She later admitted to me that she'd palmed him off on the NBI because, at the time, he was only alleging torture at the hands of Davao police, not confessing to having been a member of the DDS. Matobato was placed on the government's Witness

Protection Programme, but when he realised Duterte was poised to become president, he did a runner and approached the Catholic Church for help. This is when he found God.

'I want to give my life to Him and ask for forgiveness for all the killings I have done,' he told me. 'I need to pay for my sins.'

To my surprise, the ageing former hitman began to cry. Unfolding his arms from across his chest, his big hands clumsily wiped away the tears.

'They ordered us to kill many innocent people,' he said. 'Slaughtered. Like chickens. I want people to know that Duterte's ways are wrong. If he is the father of the country, he should love his people. Not kill them.' Matobato clutched a kitsch icon of the Virgin Mary, her hands folded in prayer, which had been glued to clouds of cotton wool and mounted in a recycled turquoise plastic smartphone box. He'd found the statuette, he said, lying in a heap of rubbish at around the time he'd found the Lord. He believed it to be a sign, he told me earnestly, that he should mend his ways. By then, though, Matobato was a hunted man.

We paused for a break. The kettle went back on the gas ring and a box of plain crackers was placed on the table. A priest arrived and Matobato chatted to him in Bisaya. The two security guards who had escorted us to the farm joined in. One caught my eye and nodded, knowingly. Heavy rain once again lashed against the leaky tin roof. We waited for the noise to subside and then started again. Round two.

Matobato told me that when he and his team had abducted 'an important individual' on Lascañas' orders, they would take them to Laud Quarry. There, Lascañas would call the mayor and they would wait for him to arrive. Matobato claimed never to have known the identity of the individual to be killed — 'we weren't allowed to ask,' he said — but when Duterte arrived, he would know, Matobato alleged, and, once satisfied, he'd shoot the person dead himself.

'Did you actually see him kill people with your own eyes?'

'Yes. Duterte would borrow his bodyguard's gun and shoot the person in the head when they were sitting on the ground.'

'So it's like an execution?'

'Yes. Sitting on the ground. The whole face would be wrapped in masking tape.'

'Did he use an Uzi or a revolver?'

'When he went there, he always borrowed his bodyguard's gun. A .45 calibre.'

'But how could he tell it was the right person if his face was wrapped in masking tape?'

'Duterte would check them first, then we put on the masking tape.'

'How many times did you see Duterte do this?'

'I saw him kill eight times.'

'Before, in the Senate, you said 'seven or eight'. Are you sure it was eight?'

'Yes.'

'And then what did he do? Get in his car and head back to the office?'

'Duterte would go back downtown and we would be left to clear up ...' Matobato continued. 'The mayor looks happy when he kills people. That is his habit. I think he thinks he's doing good. My colleagues would say "he's a brave mayor". We were helping the good guys and killing the bad guys.'

But in Davao, he added, discussion of the killings was taboo.

'No one talks because of fear.'

The only occasion Matobato claims to have witnessed Duterte killing someone outside Laud Quarry was the case of the NBI agent Vicente Amisola, on 11 February 1994. Amisola was the bodyguard and driver of the then NBI director in Davao, Eufronio Hernandez, whose children he had just picked up from school before dropping them back home. According to Matobato, Amisola was in his pick-up truck, talking to a woman on the roadside, apparently right outside the director's house, when a Heinous Crimes Division team came racing up the road, led by Major Fulgencio 'Boy' Pabo, on a motorbike. They were responding to a reported nearby kidnap incident. The vehicles carrying Matobato and the police couldn't get past Amisola, whose vehicle had blocked the narrow road — Tulip Drive.

There was an altercation. Pabo and the other police had no idea that Amisola worked with the NBI, and Amisola would have had no idea that plain-clothes Pabo was a cop. On seeing Amisola was armed, Pabo drew his weapon. Amisola was faster on the draw and Pabo, according to Matobato, was shot in both arms and both legs. A Wild West-style shoot-out ensued with the police who were following behind, and, out of ammo, a wounded Amisola rolled under his pick-up truck. Matobato watched as his colleagues dragged the NBI man from under the car just as the mayor arrived in his City Hall pick-up, alerted on the radio that Pabo had been shot.

'Amisola was innocent,' Matobato said. 'Duterte came with an Uzi submachine gun and killed him. He even changed magazines.'

Matobato told me he had watched all this from a distance of just 20 metres; that the mayor had borrowed the weapon from his bodyguard. In his evidence to the Senate hearing, he described Duterte Harry's furious burst of bullets — about 200, he claimed — as 'overkill'. Only hours afterwards did it emerge that the mayor of Davao City had just pumped an NBI man full of holes.

By the time I met Matobato, I had already raised the Amisola killing with journalists in Davao, asking whether they recalled the incident. One of them, Virgilio 'Ver' Bermudez, who was then editor of the *Daily Forum*, did, and very clearly: 'At about 2 pm we were told that a kidnap incident was unfolding in Flores subdivision, so we sent out a reporter.'

His was not the only news outlet to deploy staff to the scene — another sent there was Davao City TV camerawoman, Linda dela Cruz, who worked for the station SBN TV7 and who, I was told, had filmed the mayor's Godfather impersonation.

'At 5 pm we have the local TV news,' Bermudez said, referring to dela Cruz's dramatic footage, 'and I remember seeing a guy slumped on the hood of a car. He was identified as a kidnapper. Duterte's pick-up arrives with another vehicle. The TV footage showed him go up near to the guy slumped on the hood so that he could see his face. He took his Uzi and started pumping bullets into him. I remember all this clearly,' he told me, 'because I was the one who wrote the story. Duterte wanted everyone to see him doing this.'

According to Matobato, there had been around 30 policemen present.

Bermudez said, 'Duterte would have wanted those guys to understand that he can also kill.'

Another vehicle that arrived at the same time as Duterte's contained local official Antonio Llamas, who was gunning to be vice mayor. According to Bermudez, Llamas also shot at Amisola's already bullet-riddled body.

Later, off camera, when it eventually became clear they had killed the wrong guy, a furious Hernandez, the NBI director, threatened to sue the mayor. It was reported that the two men held a meeting to resolve a brewing and unwelcome scandal. A case was filed against the police and against Duterte, but was dismissed for lack of evidence; Linda dela Cruz's video was lost in transit and has never re-appeared. Back in 1994, the digital revolution had yet to dawn. Copying videotapes was a laborious process, and it seems no copy of dela Cruz's rushes or cut news report was ever made.

Duterte, who once openly admitted to me in a Davao news conference how he would 'plant evidence' when he worked as a prosecutor, also knew, it seems, how to make evidence disappear. He discovered, as his sister Eleanor observed, that: 'he could get away with murder'.

In my conversations with Lascañas, using an encrypted app, he said this incident had been before his time, but that he had long heard rumours in police circles that what he called 'monetary considerations' had occurred regarding 'this story about Linda dela Cruz'.

Ms dela Cruz did not respond to my requests to discuss her recollections of the incident.

It's no wonder Matobato's sudden re-emergence in Manila ruffled feathers; imagine the heated discussions behind Malacañang's elegant closed doors about how to close him down. Add to this Matobato's claims that two members of his former cohort of killers, both policemen, had already been killed to silence them.

I had also learned of another known Davao hitman, who went by the name 'Blackie', who was killed by assassins riding in tandem in March 2016, on his way to an interview with the media. A Davao-based journalist claimed he had been contracted by a US TV network to obtain an interview with a member of the DDS. Blackie, the journalist said, had reluctantly agreed to talk, allegedly in exchange for a large financial inducement. Blackie, who allegedly had photographs of himself posing with guns with police officers while on an operation, yet who said he'd never seen Duterte kill, had been shot dead two weeks before the scheduled interview.

The journalist who told me this said he had also received threats and these had clearly spooked him: 'The DDS is a jealous mistress. They don't want their people getting burned. There is a code of honour.'

10

THE DRUGS WAR, PART (I): LISTS

Raphael is on the run. He is a soft-spoken, middle-aged man of wiry build — and he is wired, exuding raw angst; it's infectious. The friend who had put me in contact with him said that Raphael had been in this hyper-adrenalised state for months, ever since he had learned he was on the police 'watch list'. A local councillor had casually asked him to pop down to the police station one day, and, when he complied, he realised he had inadvertently 'surrendered'. Now, like more than a million other Filipinos, Raphael is on the kill-list database. Being on it doesn't necessarily mean he will be taken out, but the chance of there being a bullet with his name on it is always there. That name would not be 'Raphael', though: giving him an alias was the first condition I agreed to when we met.

'But if I've been killed by the time your book comes out, feel free to use my real name,' he told me, with exemplary Filipino gallows humour.

'Oh, please, come on, don't say that!' I winced.

He shrugged. Both of us knew that this was entirely possible. This was a man who now spent his life glancing over one shoulder and listening out for motorbikes.

Assassins wear smoked-visor helmets over black balaclavas; black t-shirts, black jeans, the barrel of an unholstered Colt .45 'Duterte pistol' jammed into the pillion's belt; the uniform of the Philippine army of freelance executioners tasked with interpreting the dog-whistles of their godfather-president. It's lucrative enough work — the going rate is rumoured to be at least 10,000 pesos (US$200) for a hit on an addict or local pusher, the money divvied up among the kill-team. Each night's handiwork faithfully reported in the media within a day or two, a paragraph here or there, and then nothing. No investigation. No risk of getting caught. As if the pot-holed, back-alley shanties had become the setting for a bloodthirsty action-packed TV box set.

Raphael had been willing enough to meet me, although it took a while to work out where. He was being monitored, and didn't want me coming to his city — which he refused to let me even name. And, knowing I was to meet a marked man, I wasn't that keen on bringing him to my apartment in Manila. We decided to meet on neutral territory, in a crowded place — hiding in plain sight, as the saying goes. We ate well and had a couple of Red Horse beers to take the tension down a notch, though at no point did Raphael look relaxed. In better days, he might have had a rakish charm. But these were not good days. He came with very strict conditions of total anonymity — which was a shame because, in real life, he was a compelling character, with an intriguingly unlikely job and an equally unusual and colourful story. As often happens, at times I felt more shrink than journalist listening to his extraordinary life.

He had had it rough. Raphael grew up with his grandmother in Tondo, that sprawling Manila slum, before accidentally killing his violent, drunken uncle with a karate kick and then wisely moving far away. His aunt, possibly grateful for this intervention, had not pressed charges, although money did change hands. But the odds on Raphael having a long life himself had recently got a lot shorter. He had been informed by a couple of friendly cops that his name was not only on the watch list, but also on the police high value target (HVT) list, identifying him as a purveyor of methamphetamines and licensing the henchmen of Duterte's war on drugs to shoot to kill. He was now even more likely to be dispatched in one of the notoriously fatal buy-bust operations, with alleged dealers entrapped by police, or liquidated by 'vigilantes' who are actually off-duty cops.

Raphael had also come to discover that, once his name was on a list, it would stay there, for as long as Duterte was president, or for as long as Raphael survived. Though in the *barangays*, drugs watch lists pre-date Duterte's administration, he has used them to instil fear and to impose a paranoiac's version of social order. Despite a reported spike of over 50 per cent in the national murder rate, Filipinos are said to feel safer with President Duterte's nationwide 'peace and order project' in full swing. The government has claimed there has been a 42 per cent drop in crimes like carjacking and theft. The police have said the number of crimes overall has dropped by 30 per cent. The reality is that nearly eight out of 10 adult Filipinos fear that they or someone they know will be taken out by men in black on motorbikes.

These sinister dark riders bear Duterte's unmistakable branding, his grisly *modus mortis*. Some of the killings have been caught on CCTV and have occasionally been posted online. The black-and-white, low-resolution clips run like silent snuff-movies, cold and brutal. In the course of my reporting for Channel 4

News, I found footage that showed the murder of a 'suspect' who, realising what is about to happen, attempts to make a run for it. He is no match for the hunter-killers, who chase after him on their motorbikes and shoot him down. The pillion then dismounts and fires again, point-blank, into the kneeling man.

'How am I supposed to live like this?' Raphael asked, *sotto voce*.

He is no exception: hundreds of thousands of people in the Philippines have lived like this since the day Duterte was inaugurated, having found themselves on one list or another. Every single *barangay*, in every single town, in every single city, has drawn up watch lists and HVT lists, and Duterte himself has his own 'kill list', a voluminous sheaf of papers he brandishes during threat-laden after-dinner speeches. With two exceptions, the only other Filipinos I had knowingly encountered who had been on one of these lists were already dead by the time I set eyes on them.

'I lie awake at night,' said Raphael. 'I don't know when they will come ... But I know they will. Every time I hear a motorbike, every time my dog barks, I think it's them. I can get shot any time.' He paused. The stress had placed unsustainable pressure on his relationship. He and his partner of 20 years no longer talked. His eldest son was a *shabu* user, he told me, and was also on the watch list, making the strain unbearable.

'I've done a lot of bad things in my life,' he said. 'But it's my son I'm worried for. I'm old. He's just 19. He is frightened. I don't want him going out at night. I'm used to living with danger, but he's not, and I'm concerned about my family's safety.'

Raphael claimed that a local community leader bore a personal grudge against him and this was their revenge; that it had nothing to do with drugs, but was rather about Raphael's family home, a handsome property for a city shanty. Raphael had shown me pictures of his house as he'd swiped through photographs of his children on his phone, and I could see that, relatively speaking, it was indeed an enviable house.

I had heard stories of how the drugs war was being used as a pretext for settling personal vendettas. In late 2017, the Philippine National Police adopted a sinister new tactic: deploying public drop-boxes outside police stations into which anonymous informants could post the names of their neighbours in the hope they would be placed on drugs watch lists. This practice began in Quezon City, part of Metro Manila, but was soon reported to have spread to towns and cities in two other provinces. Although there was nothing I could do to verify Raphael's allegation that he had been stitched up by his neighbour, he was insistent that, although he had once been involved in the drugs world, he had long ago left it behind; that he hated *shabu* and hadn't smoked the stuff in 20 years. In the late 1990s, he had used it for two months, but each time he had been unable to sleep or eat for days on end. Finally, he said, he had overdosed and nearly died, and hadn't touched it since.

'I also didn't like to be around users unless they were really close friends,' he said. 'And even then, they would turn into something I didn't recognise. They get paranoid when the high starts to wear off. And then they get violent.'

The destructive, character-warping effects of crystal meth on users' personalities are matched in intensity only by the psychological and social damage it inflicts on those around them. As a foreign correspondent, I had reported on the plague of methamphetamine addiction in other countries, too, among them South Africa and Thailand. In Cape Town, I interviewed Ellen, a mother who had strangled her only son, who smoked the drug. He had stolen and sold almost everything she owned to fund his insatiable habit, and had attacked her with scissors, a breadknife, and an axe. Finally, early one morning, she throttled him as he lay comatose. Charged with murder, she had been handed a three-year suspended sentence; the judge had ruled that she, not her junkie son, had been the victim. Ellen is a gentle, thoughtful woman, who remained deeply distressed and seemed unlikely to ever recover from the trauma.

While reporting on the crystal meth epidemic in Cape Town's murderous townships, I had filmed with hardened gang members and addicts who brazenly smoked the little white crystals in pipes called lollies even as I interviewed them. Within a year, one of those addicts, a meth-crazed former prison gang leader called Fabian, would be shot dead in a fight. As I sat questioning and cross-examining Raphael, it was clear to me that he was not a *shabu* junkie.

'Most people in my *barangay* know I'm clean and straight and wouldn't touch it again,' he said.

I heard resignation in his voice: any indignation he might have felt was gone. Overwhelmed by feelings of his powerlessness, he had taken to self-medicating with Red Horse beer, he said, to counter what he called the well of 'deep, black depression and rage'.

Raphael said the number of people he knew who were using *shabu* had increased dramatically over the previous decade. Many, like his own son, were teenagers, and changed the atmosphere in the *barangay*: 'The kids are all stealing.'

And with the petty crime came violence.

In the early days, crystal meth was mostly coming in from China, dropped off at sea, off the Philippine coast, in plastic containers which Filipino drug lords and dealers would salvage and bring ashore. That was 'the stuff that kept you awake for days' Raphael said. But, as the years went by, small labs began to spring up everywhere; the *shabu* increasingly being locally produced, with the quality and potency decreasing. Scores of labs have been raided by the Philippine Drug Enforcement Agency (PDEA) in recent years, with regular big busts since Duterte became president. By the end of the first year of the drugs war, police said they had dismantled nine labs and confiscated nearly 2.5 tonnes of *shabu* with a street value of US$250 million. The labs all contained the tell-tale equipment — drums and pressure tanks, tubes and packing facilities — familiar to anyone who ever watched *Breaking Bad*.

The labs were, and are, disguised as legitimate factories, hidden in warehouses, abandoned mines, remote poultry farms, and inner-city apartments. Their discovery has almost always been accompanied by the arrest of Chinese nationals. In one case, police seized a floating *shabu* lab aboard a converted fishing boat in Subic Bay — northwest of Manila, the site of a former US naval base — with 11 Chinese crew, all from Hong Kong, arrested. Another lab was uncovered in a village piggery two miles from the new Central Luzon Drug Rehabilitation Center and a regional police training centre. Seven Chinese nationals were arrested there. Determining the precise source of synthetic drugs can be difficult, but data from seizures and arrests in the Philippines suggests — as Duterte has openly alleged — that organised-crime syndicates originating in southern China, and possibly Taiwan, are today involved in trafficking precursor chemicals, and sometimes the drugs themselves, into the Philippines. One leading source of *shabu* now is the autonomous Muslim region of Maguindanao, west of Davao City.

Raphael grew aware that crystal meth was destroying the social fabric of his community. 'Our *barangay* was considered a hotspot ... The number one dealer is in my neighbourhood. He was selling drugs to my son, who started stealing from [us].'

A growing sense of despair set in, particularly now that his son was hooked on meth, and Raphael crippled by regret. Back in 2012, he told me, he had been arrested and charged with dealing drugs, but when his case had finally come to court (after he had spent two-and-a-half years in jail on remand), he was acquitted. He had documents to prove this. He confided that he had, in fact, been an irregular, small-time dealer, but claimed to have stopped years ago for the sake of his family.

'Aha, so he was a dealer', I surprised myself by thinking, as if Raphael's inclusion on two kill-lists was somehow justified because of this. Of course, this is exactly what has happened in the minds of many Filipinos, as killings have been normalised, and Duterte's deadly and distorted views have gone mainstream.

If I regretted thinking that, Raphael's own regrets about his former life were striking, and reminded me again of someone I had worked with all those years ago in Cape Town, where crystal meth is known locally as *tik*. My fixer there, who had been my team's passport into those dysfunctional, broken, and violent communities in the Western Cape, had once been a major dealer. He had, he told me, been among those primarily responsible for introducing *tik* to several townships. He took me around the homes of those whose lives had been destroyed by the drugs he had once peddled. He had converted to Christianity and changed his ways, seeking to remedy the mess he had created, but he lived in a state of permanent remorse.

Raphael, too, said dealing *shabu* was something he wished he had never done, adding that it had 'heaped trouble' on his family. His honesty — despite the court acquittal — and his clear, reasoned account of the impossible situation he now found himself in seemed to add weight to the credibility of other, unverifiable, aspects of his story. Although I only had his word to go on, I have since been sent a signed affidavit he had drafted with lawyers, presenting an identical account, which he hopes to use as part of a legal challenge to remove his name from the two lists.

Raphael painted a bleak picture of his own drug-infested *barangay*, a place where neighbours spied on neighbours, and where small disputes found lurid means of resolution. Drugs war dropboxes began to appear at police stations for informants to post the names of suspects. If you had influence, or could convince someone else who did, death sentences could be handed to your enemies, Raphael alleged, simply by adding names to lists. Raphael was not alone, it seemed, in tracing his troubles to personal antipathy. He said he knew of two other men on his community drugs watch list who had nothing to do with drugs, but, like him, had had the misfortune to have found themselves on the wrong side of those who wielded influence.

During the five hours I spent with him, Duterte's name came up frequently. Raphael had followed the campaign for the presidency, and, a month before the election, had written a post on Facebook about a premonition.

'Everything was red,' he said. 'I saw blood, everywhere, even before he came to power ... Duterte doesn't make any sense,' he said. 'I don't know how to make any sense of any of this so I don't know how to behave.'

He sank into a thousand-yard stare.

'Shit!' he suddenly exclaimed, as though struck by the insanity of the situation he was in. 'Duterte is crazy, man. Crazier than I am. He's a psychopath.'

Whose name is on which list is fairly common knowledge. List compilers are leaky, as are the police. The listed become socially toxic and are publicly ostracised: months of stigma and exclusion generally precede violent death. Several listed individuals Raphael knew had already been shot dead. The first to die in Raphael's *barangay* was a dealer he had known, who was killed on the very day of Duterte's inauguration. The man had served 20 years for murder, and, on his release in 2014, had set up as a *shabu* 'distributor', as Raphael called him, and tried to recruit him as a dealer. Raphael said the man had been supplied by the police, who took most of the profit. The *barangay* sounded like a typical, poor urban district. It could have been anywhere in the Philippines; a place where everyone knew everyone else, but where community spirit had been shattered by suspicion and consumed by fear since Duterte had been elected president. Many, including children, had witnessed the regular street assassinations.

Raphael related in detail two chilling encounters with masked men on motorbikes, both right outside his house. The Grim Reaper had come calling, checked his address, and moved on, as though on a recce. But the Reaper now definitely knew where HVT Raphael lived. Once, two men who had not bothered to remove their helmets or balaclavas, stopped in front of his house and asked for him by his full name. On hearing the motorbike idling, Raphael was already tense — he had been peering down into the street from an upstairs window. He saw his tenant talking to the men and pointing up; there was no avoiding it, so, heart in mouth, he had gone down.

The riders claimed to be working for a courier company, he said, although neither wore a uniform, nor did they have any company IDs. Then, to his horror, one reached into a sling bag, strapped across his chest, and went to pull out what Raphael was sure would be a Duterte pistol, the bullet with his name on it sitting in the chamber. In that moment, he'd reckoned he was as good as dead. The man hadn't pulled a gun, though. It had been an envelope, addressed to him, with a label identifying its sender as his aunt, who lives abroad. He hadn't been in contact with her for months … and, no, it wasn't the same aunt whom he had inadvertently widowed years earlier. As Raphael showed proof of identity and scribbled his signature, he'd wondered whether he'd just signed his own death warrant, confirming for his would-be assassins that he was indeed their local HVT. Nervously, he made a joke of it and said to the riders: 'You know, I really thought I was going to die! I thought you were riding in tandem!'

'When I explained this,' Raphael told me, 'they just laughed! Then they roared off.'

The terror of the experience was written all over his face, even in the telling of the story. It had really spooked him.

The envelope turned out to contain a pre-paid Visa card — a common means by which Filipinos receive remittances from family members working overseas.

'But when I tried to use it, there was no money on it,' he said. This had made him feel distinctly queasy again, and when he eventually called his aunt to thank her for her 'gift', she'd had no idea what Raphael was on about.

This was one of several similar incidents.

The main reason it had proved so complicated working out when best to meet Raphael was that his time was not his own. Once your name is on a list, you're busy. But he was keen to talk, and reckoned that, for once, he could push it with an evening out, then back on a bus at dawn. He was required to sign in once a week at his local police station and attend lengthy state-run and church-run drug-rehab programmes three times a week, all after-noon. These 'rehab' programmes involved addicts hooked on meth attending lectures; there was no medication on offer, Raphael said, and no other form of psycho-social intervention. Narcotics Anonymous sessions took place every weeknight ('except they weren't anonymous') and in the community hall every Sunday afternoon. Missing even one of these sessions would be a problem. On completion of these compulsory pro-grammes, it was promised that the names on the lists would be submitted to the city mayor and police chief for 'de-listing'. It never happened. New requirements were always drawn up. No one was de-listed. That was when Raphael realised he was on the lists for life.

I have remained in regular contact with Raphael. The good news is that, at the time of writing, I still have to use his pseudonym. He has remained unable to get himself de-listed. Finally, having toughed it out for a year, he recently messaged me to ask whether I could put him in contact with someone who could help him disappear. He wanted to go into hiding with his 19-year-old son and hole up in a safe house somewhere far away, in the hope that one day their nightmare would be over. A nascent network, operating by word of mouth, had begun to provide sanctuary and protection for people who have found themselves on Duterte's death lists. But the safe houses, it turned out, were all full.

One Sunday evening, in a noisy, crowded cafe on the University of the Philippines campus in Manila's Quezon City, I met Jose Manuel 'Chel' Diokno, the country's best-known human rights lawyer, and one of Duterte's most daringly outspoken critics. Diokno has publicly disparaged the president's war on drugs, condemned the surge in EJKs, and lamented the erosion of the rule of law. He is incensed by Duterte's murderous threats to human rights activists and lawyers. Dean of the College of Law at De La Salle, another university, Diokno had discovered a thing or two about Duterte's lists. He was not a man to beat about the bush, and his opening salvo set the tone for our conversation.

'When he was king of Davao, Duterte didn't keep his lists a secret. And if you look at how his government is conducting its drugs war now, it's based on these watch lists. There is no difference between what is happening here today and how the Japanese operated, with their Secret Police, or how the SS operated in Nazi Germany,' he said, fixing me with a steady, solemn glare over the rims of his glasses, as though imparting urgent, need-to-know information to someone he felt needed to comprehend the gravity of the crisis of democracy unfolding in the Philippine Republic.

'The police are operating that same kind of machinery now. They are becoming the Gestapo. The more I see, the more disgusted I am. The way Duterte's government has been operating is very similar to the way the Marcos government operated, in that it uses fear and violence to impose order. During the Marcos regime, they exploited fear of communism: "You are not human so you don't have any human rights." All you have to do is substitute "communist" with "drug addict" or "dealer" and it's exactly the same thing.'

Diokno chairs the Free Legal Assistance Group (FLAG), which for years has handled cases dating back to martial law under Ferdinand Marcos, as well as those linked to Duterte's kill squads. He represented Arturo Lascañas, who'd run the DDS and had testified against the president in the Senate. Diokno's late father, Jose 'Ka Pepe' Diokno, also a distinguished human rights lawyer and a senator, was widely regarded as a legendary opponent of Marcos. When military rule was declared in 1972, Diokno senior was arrested without charge and held incommunicado in solitary confinement. The young Chel, then not even a teenager, spent two years not knowing if his father was alive. Ka Pepe founded FLAG when he was released, and, four decades on, his son was following in his footsteps.

Diokno sipped his strong black coffee and continued, as, pen racing through my notebook, I scrambled to keep up. He mentioned the 2008 UN report into summary executions in the Philippines — and Davao in particular — by the special rapporteur Philip Alston. I had noticed, when I read it, that Alston had cited

FLAG as a source. Diokno was well versed in Duterte's patterns of behaviour. Now, he confirmed exactly what I'd heard from Raphael.

'Part of [Alton's] recommendations was that the practice of compiling watch lists by *barangay* officials had to be abolished.'

They hadn't been, of course. Successive governments had failed to rein in the excesses of the mayor of Davao.

'There are several kinds of lists … Names on the typical watch list are supplied by local *barangay* officials. They're required to supply names. There are allegations that this is done on a quota basis. Then there are the HVT or 'wanted' lists. Those names come from the PDEA [Philippine Drug Enforcement Agency, which for many years had been trained by the US, the EU, and Australia] and Philippine National Police agents monitoring drug activities. I don't know it for a fact,' he said, 'but it's not beyond this government to compile a list of human rights activists and lawyers, too. What I do know is that, once your name is on a list, it's pretty much impossible to get off it.'

Diokno told me about two lawyers he knew, one in Mindanao, one in Luzon, who had sought to have their clients' names removed. The first had a transgender client who had gone to the lawyer with a drugs-test certificate to prove to the police that she was clean. They went to the PNP, he said, asking them to please remove her, but were told: 'Sorry, the list is now at police HQ in Manila and we don't have the power.'

In Luzon, it had been exactly the same story, he said, with another client.

'The long and short of it is that, unless you know someone high up in the PNP or in Malacañang, it is impossible to get de-listed. Some people have approached lawyers who have gone to inquire into whether someone's name is on a list. They too have been refused. It's a closely guarded secret. If I file a case to ask whether my client's name is on the list, the judge will say, "What's your proof your client's name is on the list?" And because we have no proof, it will not fly. It is impossible to question in court.' Those who have managed to get themselves de-listed are about as rare as survivors of riding-in-tandem hits or police buy-bust operations.

In late September 2016, Duterte did something very out of character: he publicly apologised to a congressman and former provincial governor whom he had maligned as a named kingpin of what he'd called a 'drugs matrix', which supposedly ran operations in and out of the country's biggest prison. Unsurprisingly, Duterte's critic-in-chief, Senator Leila de Lima, who was named as 'boss' of this drugs ring, received no such apology. But the president said he was 'very sorry' to have implicated Representative Amado Espino Jr and two other senior provincial officials in this supposed 'matrix'. He called the mistake a 'lapse' and said 'somehow we were negligent in counter-checking'.

It was Raphael who had reminded me of this incident.

'If Duterte can mistakenly put a congressman's name on a list, and makes it public, and then admits it and says sorry, how much more uncertain is it for ordinary people?' he had said. 'Even if they do say sorry, what's the point when you are dead?'

Those documenting the spiralling death toll believe that, among the thousands killed by either police or hitmen, there are likely to have been scores of cases of mistaken identity. Many of those killed in police buy-bust operations are known to have had falsified evidence — sachets of *shabu* or .38 homemade revolvers, often both — planted on their bodies. A priest I got to know who'd had dealings with the police — but was not complicit with them — said they joked about how clever the *shabu* suppliers and dealers were in never leaving any evidence. 'So we provide it for them!' the cops had laughed. A source in counter-narcotics, who did not wish to be identified, but who claimed to be familiar with specific incidents in the drugs war told me: 'They're not even trying to cover it up. Guns with identical serial numbers turn up in different incidents; shells don't match the calibre. Revolvers are found in the right hands of left-handed people.'

According to US online campaign StoptheDrugWar.org, 49 people were killed in the United States in police drug-bust operations during 2016, although not all were shot by police — one suspect died after swallowing his stash. Deaths during American counter-narcotics operations have averaged just under one a week over the past six years. The organisation's 'Drug War Chronicle' blog has also kept a tally of the number of police officers killed in anti-narcotics operations, which works out at about one cop killed for every 10 dead civilians. In the US, being part of the drugs taskforce is a highly dangerous job; in the Philippines, according to government statistics, just 36 police personnel were killed during more than 50,000 drugs operations in Duterte's first 10 months in power. While confusion over the figures means it is not possible to work out the ratio of police deaths to civilians, it is evident that, compared with the US, counter-narcotics operations in the Philippines are not particularly dangerous for police, but all-too-often fatal for the suspect.

In addition to the watch lists and HVT lists, Duterte has his own personal 'Narco List', which he waves around during live televised addresses. This list began with 158 government officials whom he named and shamed, accusing them of involvement in illegal drugs right across the country. They included more than several serving or former congressmen, and seven judges, as well as mayors, governors, scores of senior police officers — including generals — and military officers.

Speaking at the central command of the Philippines army

camp in Cebu in July 2016, the president said: 'These drug lords, these mayors, these governors — don't be complacent with me. I will have you killed.'

Later, speaking to reporters, he again warned those on his list: 'If you show the slightest violence in the resistance, I will tell the police: "Shoot them."'

He had presented no evidence against those whom he accused. It quickly transpired that two of those on this initial list had already died. One, a former judge, had actually been dead for a decade; of the other six judges named, two had retired from the bench.

In legal circles, the president's evidence-free allegations were a cause of growing concern. Father Ranhilio Aquino, dean of the San Beda Graduate School of Law, where Duterte earned his law degree, said: 'The only thing that is against them is the fact that they were mentioned by the president. There is no basis for removing them from office.'

Then the Philippines' Supreme Court chief justice, Lourdes Sereno, entered the fray, defending the accused judges. In a letter to Justice Minister Vitaliano Aguirre, Sereno said: 'The Court would consider it important to know the source and basis of any allegation ...' She took Duterte to task for what she called his 'premature announcement', pointing out that, given the number of judges who had been assassinated over the years, the president had rendered those he had named 'vulnerable and veritable targets ... in the war on drugs'. Her letter was firm, but polite.

The next day, clearly feeling challenged and undermined by a judiciary for which he had no respect, the president lashed out: 'I'm giving you a warning,' Duterte said. 'Don't create a crisis ... don't order me. I'm telling you. I hope you are listening. You want me to be frank? You're interfering. Please don't order me. I'm not a fool. If this continues [that] you're trying to stop me, I might lose my cool. Or would you rather I declare martial law?'

This was the first time the president had publicly threatened martial law; it wouldn't be the last. Sereno hit back, saying the thousands of brazen and unresolved killings of suspects on these lists had severely eroded perceptions of justice in the Philippines. In September 2017, Congress began the process to impeach Chief Justice Sereno. This came as no surprise at all.

As the months went by and the drugs war plumbed new depths of brutality, Duterte's 'Narco List' lengthened — dramatically. He began to unfurl large drugs war diagrams that looked like genealogies, complete with photographs, annotations, and flow-chart arrows connecting the accused. The number of alleged narco judges grew to 40; numbers in all the other categories also rose relentlessly. Duterte repeatedly asserted that 'the problem is now all-encompassing, it is destroying our nation'.

By early 2017, the Philippine Drug Enforcement Agency announced that the president's 'Narco List' contained the names of more than 6000 'suspects' although *The New York Times* would soon report that there were anywhere between 600,000 and more than a million names on the list, which is hardly surprising given that Duterte claimed there were more than 3 million addicts. One of the names on the presidential list was the mayor of Albuera, a town in Leyte province in the eastern Visayas region, Rolando Espinosa. His son, 'Kerwin' was also named.

'I have ordered people to look for him and shoot on sight like a dog,' Duterte said. 'That is how I see him. A dog.' And that, a few weeks later, is exactly what happened. The mayor and his son had voluntarily surrendered within 24 hours of the president's initial ultimatum; there had been no warrant out for him, but police had raided his family home, shot dead six of the mayor's bodyguards, and apparently discovered a stash of 11kg of *shabu*.

Espinosa made a personal plea to Duterte and said he was confident that the justice system would uphold his innocence. He was released, then re-arrested, and, while in jail, was shot four times, three of them in the head, inside his cell, by police who claimed he had a gun and had shot at them, that they had fired in self-defence. They also claimed they had found sachets of *shabu* in Espinosa's cell and in those of an alleged accomplice, who was also shot dead in a neighbouring cell. Malacañang Palace described Mayor Espinosa's death as 'unfortunate', and, in a televised interview, Senator 'Ping' Lacson, the former national police chief and ally of Duterte, suggested the police had been over-eager to comply with the president's instructions. 'They got emboldened,' Lacson said, with his Senate committee concluding the killings had been premeditated.

Superintendent Marvin Marcos, the police chief whose men had killed the mayor, was relieved of his duties by PNP director 'Bato' dela Rosa, but later quietly reinstated on the direct orders of President Duterte, a move opposition senator Leila de Lima branded as 'sinister'. In March 2017, a gutsy judge in Leyte issued arrest warrants for murder against Superintendent Marcos and 18 other policemen for Espinosa's killing; they surrendered to their own police unit. In July, Bato dela Rosa ordered them to return to work.

While in jail, Espinosa had signed an affidavit, without a lawyer present, implicating 226 police officers, as well as Senator de Lima, in a drugs ring allegedly run by his son, Kerwin, who had meanwhile fled the country. Three weeks after Espinosa senior's 'unfortunate' death, Kerwin was tracked down in Abu Dhabi, where he was arrested, then deported. Within days of his return, Kerwin was paraded, wearing manacles and a bullet-proof vest, before a Senate hearing where he confessed to being a drug lord; however, he also accused de Lima of bankrolling her senatorial election campaign with the proceeds of drugs trafficking, testifying that she had received three separate tranches of *shabu* cash. De Lima claimed she had never met him, and dismissed his testimony as a 'nice script', advising Kerwin that his 'cooperation' would not save his skin. 'May God forgive you for all your lies about me — and I forgive you,' she said to him in the Senate.

I happened to be in Davao that very week, and so was Rodrigo Duterte. At a news conference, I raised with the president the dramatic escalation of the killings; he countered by raising the case of Mayor Espinosa, warning that other mayors involved in illegal drugs would suffer the same fate. He often uses his responses to journalists' questions to threaten those on his kill-list.

'There are still mayors, still there,' he said, 'playing the narco-politics game, and I'm warning them again. You might not want to hear it. You will not only lose your funds, you will lose your life.' He then berated me for my impertinence in asking the question in the first place. I got the feeling we were falling into a pattern.

A week before Espinosa's death, another mayor was gunned down in the autonomous Muslim province of Maguindanao, west of Davao City. Samsudin Dimaukom was the popular mayor of a town called Datu Saudi-Ampatuan, known for its extraordinary pink mosque, and as a hotbed of Islamist insurgency. Dimaukom had been named by Duterte in his initial list as a leading *shabu* trafficker. He told local media in Mindanao that he supported the president's crackdown, and was the first of five provincial mayors on the list to surrender. He had said he was willing to face investigation. He had also been to see PNP chief Ronald dela Rosa in a bid to clear his name.

Before dawn one morning in late October 2016, Dimaukom, accompanied by staff and bodyguards, was travelling home from

Davao City in a convoy of three vehicles when he was flagged down by anti-narcotics police at a checkpoint. The police had reportedly received intelligence that Dimaukom had been planning to move a 'huge' amount of methamphetamine from Davao City into his home province of Maguindanao. Police said his convoy had failed to stop and that those in the vehicles had opened fire. In all, 10 men, including the mayor, were killed in a hail of bullets. Not one policeman was killed or injured. The police claimed to have recovered 13 small sachets of *shabu* from the vehicles, not the haul they had expected. They also claimed to have found a shotgun, four handguns, and a rifle: a standard arsenal for night-time travellers in Maguindanao. Local journalists who had covered the convoy killings said silencers had been used on the weapons fired by police, and millions of pesos allegedly being transported by the mayor had mysteriously gone missing. I passed the spot a couple of months later. It was right outside a local school.

At the end of July 2017, a third mayor, also on Duterte's list, was killed. Reynaldo Parojinog, mayor of Ozamiz City in Mindanao was shot dead, along with his wife and thirteen other people, in a series of simultaneous pre-dawn raids at several of the family's properties, during 'shootouts' with the police. CCTV cameras had been disabled, and not a single policeman was injured. Ronald dela Rosa warned more such deaths would follow.

Conspiracy theories swirled around these killings. In the cases of mayors Dimaukom and Espinosa, there were rumours that both men knew secrets Duterte did not want out. Once, while waiting for the president to arrive at one of his late-night news conferences, I was chatting to a Filipino reporter about the deaths of these two mayors. He gave me a raised eyebrow: 'Dead men don't tell tales.'

One of the biggest names on the original list was Peter Lim, a

Cebu City based Chinese-Filipino businessman accused of masterminding *shabu* trafficking in the central Visayas region. He had been repeatedly named in past congressional investigations into the trade. Lim went straight to Malacañang for what was described as a 'cordial' meeting. In a video of this encounter posted on the palace Facebook page, Duterte told Lim: 'I warned you that I will have you killed. I will really have you killed if I'm able to prove you're a drug lord.'

Lim responded by instantly pledging his absolute allegiance to the president, and, by the end of the meeting, Duterte asserted that he had quite clearly got the wrong Peter Lim. The Bureau of Immigration later chipped in to say that there were at least 4000 Filipinos with that name. That particular Peter Lim walked out of the palace and promptly vanished.

By the first anniversary of Duterte's 'Narco List', one thing stood out: apart from some murdered mayors, there had only been a tiny handful of arrests, and the only alleged narco-politician to face charges was the former human rights commissioner, justice secretary and Duterte-inquisitor, Senator Leila de Lima, now a recognised Amnesty International prisoner of conscience. Prior to her arrest, de Lima had traded accusations with Duterte about the other's involvement in the drug trade, with Duterte calling the former justice secretary 'the mother of all drug lords', and de Lima repeatedly alleging that Duterte was the drug lords' 'number-one protector', citing Peter Lim as evidence.

The president's list served a key purpose, however, by allowing a cloud of suspicion to hang over those he so publicly accused, all of whom were then forced to live in a state of perpetual anxiety, imagining they could be hit by an assassin's bullet at any time.

———————

In September 2016, the daughter of a British hereditary peer was shot dead in the Philippines. Her late father, Lord Anthony Moynihan, had lived a racy life, before fleeing the UK for the Philippines in 1971 rather than face 57 charges of fraud in his home country. In Manila, 'Rock'n'Roll Tony', who was married to a belly-dancer, ran a string of brothels, and was a known heroin trafficker as well as a US DEA informant. His daughter, Maria, who had dual British-Filipino citizenship, had been a dealer, too. The ABC-CBN TV network aired CCTV footage showing her body being pushed from a vehicle on a Manila street, and a sign was propped up next to her: 'Drug pusher to celebrities'. No one argued that she wasn't a dealer, but the drug she dealt was not *shabu*. Manila's glitterati were scared to death that Duterte's drugs war would end their cocaine nights, but her death proved to be an aberration, though her boyfriend — another suspected dealer — was also killed in an alleged gun battle with police a few weeks later. For the scions of Manila's rich and powerful, the party started up again, fuelled by Bolivian marching powder, their drug of choice. *Shabu* was cheap and nasty. It was for the poor, the drug of last resort.

Another kill-list — unlike the others, this one was *post facto*, listing actual hits, not potential targets — was published by the *Philippine Daily Inquirer*, a leading national newspaper available online and in print. From the very beginning of Duterte's presidency, it documented the names, locations, and circumstances of all the killings in the war on drugs. The list is thousands of names long and includes several hundred who remain unidentified or were known only by an alias. It is a depressing catalogue of targeted hits on men and women who, like Raphael, had all doubtless lived in fear of motorbikes. The refrain 'killed by unknown hitmen' echoes down the kill-list, top to bottom. But the *Inquirer*'s kill-list suddenly stopped being updated shortly after Duterte temporarily suspended the drugs war at the end of January 2017. The newspaper noted that the killings by unknown hitmen had not let up just because the PNP had been briefly taken off the case, but did not respond with an official answer as to why its kill-list had been killed off. It must have been a traumatic daily column for anyone to compile.

The top of the kill-list web page features what is, beyond doubt, the most iconic image from the war on drugs: a picture taken by Raffy Lerma, a *Philippine Daily Inquirer* night shift photographer. It features a weeping woman, Jennelyn Olaires, barefoot in the street, her arms and legs wrapped around the half-upright, but limp, body of her partner, 30-year-old Michael Siaron. Siaron had been a pedi-cab driver in Pasay, Metro Manila, and, at 1 am on 23 July 2016, he was shot dead by killers riding in tandem. A crowd is gathered behind Olaires, but is held back by yellow police tape. In the foreground, you can make out the scrawled word 'PUSHER' on a flap torn from a cardboard box, which was left on Michael's body. The rest of the sign read: 'I'm a drug pusher. Do not emulate me.' A chalk circle on the tarmac rings the spot where police found a bullet casing. There are what looks like blood stains on the road. The caption under the photograph is headlined 'LAMENTATION'. To many, the image evoked Michelangelo's *Pietà*, the sculpture depicting Christ's limp body lying in his mother's lap after he was taken down from the cross.

Lerma's tragic, but beautiful, photograph went viral, published on the front page of the Sunday edition of the *Philippine Daily Inquirer* and in newspapers around the world. It seemed to capture the shockwave reverberating around the Philippines over the sudden rash of killings. It gave a face to victims who the president had said were scum, not even human. One newspaper commentator wrote of how the picture of Jennelyn and

Michael had 'immortalised their powerlessness'.

Duterte was not happy. In his first State of the Nation address, he railed against the melodrama of the photograph, and mocked Siaron's bereaved partner as a parody of *Pietà*: 'There you are, sprawled on the ground, and you are portrayed in a broadsheet as Mother Mary cradling the dead cadaver of Jesus Christ.'

Jennelyn went into hiding. It took time to track her down, but, working on a report for Channel 4 News less than a month after Michael Siaron's death, we found her. The *Philippine Daily Inquirer* had photographed the 'home' she had shared with Michael, a dilapidated patch-board, tin-roofed shack, about eight feet by 10, built on rickety stilts above a disgusting canal of stagnant water, surrounded by a carpet of floating rubbish. It was in the district of Santo Niño, Pasay City, very close to where I would later meet Elizabeth, the widow of another bicycle sidecar driver, Domingo Meñosca, who was killed in his home along with his five-year-old son Francis a few months later. They really were the poorest of the poor.

We met Jennelyn at the Pasay cemetery, where all three had been buried.

It was threatening rain when she arrived, by sidecar. She was wearing a white t-shirt with a Mickey Mouse print on the back and a black sparkly-spangled baseball cap embroidered with a disco-dancer. Her long, black hair was tied up in a ponytail and threaded through the back of the cap. The contrast between her get-up and her mood could not have been starker. Jennelyn was still fragile, and teary from the start. She had come with Michael's father and little sister, and brought some yellow lilies to place on the grave. We meandered together between the cluttered tombs to the 'Duterte Compound', the high-rise matrix of graves on the back wall where the remains of many of the victims of his drugs war are interred. Halfway along the wall of concrete box-graves, and three layers up, a plaque with as-yet unfaded gold-leaf lettering read:

RIP

MICHAEL C. SIARON

OCT. 26, 1985

JULY 23, 2016

FAMILY REMEMBERANCE

Jennelyn lit a tall, white votive candle, reached up, and placed it in a pool of melted wax, then stood in silent prayer, lost in her memories and crying quietly. After a few minutes, she gathered herself and wandered over to a nearby tomb. At the invitation of the Pasay graveyard watchman, she plonked herself on top of one, and it was right there, among the dead, that we sat and talked. She told me how her life had disintegrated, how she felt completely crippled by what had happened, and that she had been scared by Duterte's mocking of her. She said that Michael had occasionally smoked *shabu* for exactly the same reasons Elizabeth would later tell me that Domingo smoked it: to keep him going as he worked ever longer hours to try to make ends meet. Jennelyn denied he had been a pusher or a dealer, and said that (just like Domingo) he had even voted for Duterte. I asked her about the famous photograph and she started to cry again.

'I couldn't think of anything else to do but to cradle him, to find out if somehow he might still be breathing and whether we could still save him,' she sobbed, dabbing her eyes with a thin, white Good Morning towel. 'I just wish these killings would stop. If only his death had ended all this. He's gone. He cannot speak for himself any more.'

But this was only the beginning. My graveyard interview with Jennelyn Olaires was brought to a sudden stop by an ear-splitting crack of thunder. Fat, heavy raindrops began to hit us and splatter like water bombs on the tops of tombs. I looked round at Julian, my cameraman, who raised his eyebrows, shook his head, grabbed his gear, and ran for cover. Within another minute, it was tropical-torrential. The anvil-headed storm clouds, which had been building all afternoon, had welled to bursting and the deluge could no longer be contained. The rain cascaded down onto the pitiful paupers' graves in the Duterte Compound, extinguishing the candles.

11

THE DRUGS WAR, PART (II): LIES, DAMNED LIES

Ten days before Trump's inauguration, the contents of a private intelligence dossier, containing mostly unverifiable allegations of collusion between his presidential campaign and the Kremlin, were leaked to online news website *Buzzfeed*. This report, compiled by a former British MI6 agent called Christopher Steele, had initially been funded by the Republicans, and later by the opposition Democrats. It contained a mixture of politically explosive and salacious claims that Trump angrily dismissed as 'fake news'.

I wondered if a similar intelligence document might be floating around in the Philippines, and, sure enough, a 'dirty dossier' of sorts ended up in my possession. It lacked the licentious details of Steele's dossier, but the 24-page document claimed to be the work of 12 serving and five retired police intelligence officers determined to expose the *modus operandi* of Duterte's war on drugs. It was titled: 'Special Report: The State-Sponsored Extra

Judicial Killings'. My trusted source — a respected authority on drug war EJKs — told me the dossier had also been given to senior leaders of the Catholic Church and to the government's Commission on Human Rights. Diplomatic contacts confirmed they had also seen it, but that it proved hard to obtain an impartial steer on the document's plausibility.

It was packed full of detail so dense that it took me some time to decipher all the acronyms and work out exactly who it claimed did what, but at its heart was the description of how the Davao Death Squad had allegedly been upgraded and transplanted, on Duterte's orders, into a 'Presidential Death Squad'. This, it said, had been placed under the aegis of PNP leadership and covertly funded through key individuals in the president's inner circle. The report did not back up its assertions with evidence, but it detailed exactly what Raphael and others — including the former Davao Death Squad cop Arturo Lascañas — would later tell me about how watch lists and HVT lists worked, and it set out the methods by which kill orders targeting pushers and users were made by PNP commanders from the database of those who had surrendered as part of Operation Tokhang.

Supposedly legitimate police operations ran in parallel to vigilante killings, the dossier said, but in reality both were hoaxes — 'a blatant lie', designed to facilitate a form of 'social cleansing' initiated, directed, and sustained by Duterte, aiming for the 'eradication of drug pushers' through EJKs.

The report set out in black-and-white how liquidation teams, riding in tandem, were organised, the hitmen drawn from the ranks of PNP personnel. PNP station commanders were required to hold a weekly tactical assessment of progress, after which fresh targets would be selected from the database of those who had surrendered. EJK teams would coordinate with *barangay* officials, and the target house would be located. On determining the time and place of each hit, streetlamps and CCTV cameras would be shut down, as the hit-team, usually comprising four assassins, 'executes the target suspects'. The dossier noted three different variations of EJK techniques, including riding in tandem, assassinations by masked intruders, and abduction/torture/execution. Killings are followed by what the report called 'a scripted forensic investigation', including the planting of recycled *shabu* and .38 calibre home-made handguns.

The intelligence document outlined command structures, as well as how EJKs were carried out, including a detailed break-down of reward scales for assassinations. These payments were higher than kill-rates I'd been quoted from those who lived in the *barangays* in Luzon, Visayas, and Mindanao. They ranged from 10,000 pesos (US$200) for unlisted targets — including pickpockets, rapists, swindlers, snatchers, troublemakers, and alcoholics — to 20,000 pesos for targets on watch lists. *Barangay* Kapitans whose names were on watch lists, it said, earned the killers 100,000 pesos, while those higher up the chain carried bounties of between 1 million and 5 million pesos. 'In all police districts ... the so-called "Firer" is designated to kill the drug suspect. The Firer, whether he is riding on a motorbike or a member of an abduction team, is usually given half of the EJK payment.'

It was difficult to know what to make of the dossier. Its pages read like something from a convoluted thriller, but it was clearly written by someone familiar with the inner workings of the PNP, with intimate knowledge of command structures and named individuals. Trusted sources I showed it to, with authoritative knowledge of the drugs war, read it with varying degrees of curiosity and scepticism. The document was clearly politically motivated, but only in so much as it implicated the president and his cronies in what amounted to a vast alleged criminal conspiracy. Some felt its credibility was undermined by what they considered over-stated or even fanciful assertions about just how close the links were between Duterte and the Communist Party of the Philippines (CPP).

The second half of the document alleged that the main vehicle for the covert supervision and implementation of Duterte's 'bloody purge' at the local community level was a grassroots intelligence network linked to organs of the CPP. The mastermind, it said, had been Leoncio Evasco Jr, the former communist rebel priest who Duterte had prosecuted in Davao and then employed, first in the mayor's office and now in Malacañang. Duterte's self-declared leftist sympathies have long roused suspicions, part-icularly among members of the armed forces. The dossier drew a strong parallel with Mao Tse-tung's brutal war on opium and heroin addiction in China after 1949, which, it said, had 'decap-itated the entire narcotics pipeline' when tens of thousands of dealers were allegedly executed.

Most of the contacts I shared the document with thought it credible. Though the detail was impossible to verify, much of the content reinforced what was already known. Persistent, but careful, inquiries eventually yielded the identity of this dirty dossier's author: a retired police intelligence officer, as he had claimed.

In April 2017, Reuters published its own special report in which it said it too had obtained a copy of the document, and had confirmed its authenticity with two senior officials, one retired, one active, who had reiterated the claims in the dossier. Reuters described the report's contents as 'the most detailed insider accounts yet of the drug war's secret mechanics'.

As the Philippines marked 18 months of Duterte's rule, statistics on the number of people killed in the president's war on drugs were as confusing as they were contested, due mostly to the PNP's decision to stop publishing data relating to Operation Double Barrel Reloaded. The Philippine Center for Investigative Journalism accused the government of wilful obfuscation, saying official statistics were 'writ in riddles'. In January 2018, the PNP claimed that 3968 suspects had been killed in what it called 'legitimate police operations' since July 2016. The International Drug Policy Consortium, together with an alliance of Philippine non-governmental groups, put the total number of drug war deaths at 'more than 12,000'. By August 2017, the leaders of protests opposing the drugs war claimed the death toll had topped 13,000. This was also the estimate of the Catholic Bishops' Conference of the Philippines. In March 2018, Leila de Lima and her allies were asserting that the body count from what she branded 'state-sanctioned extra-judicial killings' had topped 20,000.

When Human Rights Watch (HRW) cited the 12,000 figure, the government demanded an apology. Alan Peter Cayetano, the foreign secretary, said: 'To make such sweeping accusations without being able to support these claims with facts is not just misrepresentation, it is outright deception.' HRW called for an independent UN-led investigation to help clarify what it called 'the glaring disparity' between official and independent estimates, in line with an assurance from Cayetano to the UN secretary general in October 2017 that the government would 'fully cooperate and work with' UN independent experts. One of these experts, Agnès Callamard, the UN special rapporteur on extra-judicial killings, had been subjected to expletive-riddled ridicule by Duterte. The president's government did not make good on Cayetano's commitment, and the killings did not stop, contradicting the PNP's public pronouncements that the war on drugs would become less deadly. Between the beginning of December 2017 and the beginning of February 2018, the PNP conducted

3253 raids in which it claimed 46 people had been killed, none of them police. This number did not include what *The New York Times* reported were 'the hundreds of victims killed nightly, in attacks the government attributes to vigilante groups'.

I met a counter-narcotics expert who — like many others I spoke to — wanted to remain anonymous. He talked of 'the austere simplicity' of Duterte's deterrence policy; however, the ones who were dying weren't the ones making the money. The illegal drugs trade was said to be worth US$8.4 billion a year in the Philippines — a figure cited by Joseph 'Erap' Estrada, who was president of the country from 1998 to 2001.

'Busts — real busts — are built on surveillance, building a case, intelligence, and analysis,' my narco-expert said. 'If they are really after the people who are actually controlling the narco state, then they are killing the wrong people. This is the elimination of the dumb, the slow, and the weak. It's Darwinian. The real guys are going to own the police.'

The kill-rate has given the impression that the Philippines is like the Wild West, with guns galore, but, conversely, the number of privately owned firearms in the country is miniscule in comparison with the US. In the Philippines, there are half as many guns in circulation as there are in Thailand, a country two-thirds of the size. Australia has more than three times as many privately owned firearms per capita. Until Duterte arrived, the Philippines' murder rate was the highest in East Asia, according to the World Bank, but dwarfed by homicide figures in Latin America.

Duterte's war on drugs had been launched by his chief of police, Ronald 'Bato' dela Rosa, in a document dated 1 July 2016, the day after the presidential inauguration. 'Command Memorandum Circular No. 16' presented the plan for Operation Double Barrel, and is unique in the annals of law enforcement in the Philippines because it expressly authorises EJKs, directing police to 'neutralise' drug personalities. Three months into his neutralisation programme, Bato announced that he would visit Colombia to see for himself how they 'won the war on drugs'. Perhaps he had become hooked on the Netflix drama *Narcos* because, as the *Philippine Daily Inquirer* reported, Bato was 'in awe' of what he found on his police jolly to Bogota. When he returned to Manila, the PNP chief told reporters that Colombia had poured unlimited resources into their war on drugs.

'I'll make an even stronger version of Colombia's Search Bloc,' he boasted, referring to the special police units created in 1989 and, whose core remit, under the presidency of César Gaviria, was the arrest or killing of the leader of the Medellín cartel, Pablo Escobar. In an opinion piece that appeared in *The New York Times* in February 2017 entitled 'President Duterte Is Repeating My Mistakes', ex-president Gaviria said that throwing more soldiers and police at drug users was not just a waste of money but could make the problem worse. 'Trust me,' he said, addressing Duterte directly, 'I learned the hard way ... the war on drugs is essentially a war on people.'

Gaviria, who founded the Global Commission on Drug Policy, said repressive policing was not the answer, and added that the smartest way to tackle drugs was to decriminalise consumption. His commission has long declared that wars on drugs and coercive campaigns have always failed, and recommends investment in treatment rather than detention. It says that countries that have viewed citizens dependent on drugs as patients in need of treatment have demonstrated far more positive results.

Experts I spoke to, some in Manila, some abroad, were unequivocal in their judgement of rehabilitation and treatment centres in the Philippines as ineffective, ill thought-out, and inadequate. There are 50 rehab centres in a country of more than 100 million people. A controversial 'Mega-Drug Rehab Center' at a fort in central Luzon that President Marcos used to detain and torture political prisoners was designed for 10,000 addicts, but, by mid-2017, six months after it opened, it housed only 300. The government would later confirm that it is drawing up plans for the construction of two other huge rehabilitation facilities in the central Visayas region and on Mindanao, reportedly to be bankrolled, like the one in central Luzon, by Chinese billionaire philanthropists. Most of the 1.3 million Filipino drug-users who had surrendered to police were held in jail cells so unimaginably congested that photographs of the incarcerated flashed around the world, causing widespread disbelief and horror. The maximum capacity of the Philippines' 466 prisons is 20,400, but, according to the Bureau of Jail Management and Penology, the national jail population was running at 142,000 by May 2017. Sixty-four per cent of inmates were awaiting trial or sentencing on charges of violating the illegal drugs law as a result of arrests and of addicts surrendering after Duterte came to power.

When I met the president's sister Jocelyn, I commented on how strange I thought it was that, as city mayor, her brother had opened a drugs rehab centre, which many people thought enlightened and progressive, and how this contrasted with his draconian campaign.

'He's not really hopeful about rehabilitation,' she admitted. 'The mayor, one time, had an autopsy performed on a drug addict who died on the street. When they opened his brain, it was totally like cigarette ash. So what would this whole country be like? Once a person is hooked, you would be very lucky if they could ever be totally free. And that treatment will really drain the economy because drug rehab centres would eat up all the resources.'

There wasn't much danger of Duterte allowing drugs rehab facilities to drain his budget. His government ordered the Department of Health to slash its rehab budget for 2018 by

75 per cent while asking Congress to approve a 40-fold increase in the year's police budget for anti-drugs operations.

Duterte does not respond well to being lectured, and, after Gaviria's article was published, he lambasted the former Colombian president, calling him an 'idiot'. Elsewhere in Southeast Asia, Duterte's put-down had impressed at least one other head of state. In July 2017, President Joko Widodo of Indonesia declared that his archipelago was also in the throes of a methamphetamine pandemic. Drug-dealing would not be tolerated, he warned. 'Shoot them!' he said, beginning to sound a lot like Duterte.

Gaviria is not the only outsider to have predicted that Duterte's drug war won't work. Jeremy Douglas, the head of the UN Office on Drugs and Crime for Southeast Asia and the Pacific, watched events in the Philippines unfold with disbelief. For him, Duterte was a serious case of déjà vu. The UNODC's regional headquarters is in Thailand, where, in 2003, the then prime minister, Thaksin Shinawatra, launched a vicious, violent war on drugs. The man who now runs regional operations for the UNODC had just taken up his first posting with the agency in Bangkok.

'I was thrown in the deep end,' he told me. 'We now recommend the authorities in the Philippines take a look at the result of the Thai war on drugs. It's the closest comparative example of the approach currently underway. It was also focused on methamphetamine and thousands died as a result of extra-judicial killings.'

Thaksin, a telecoms tycoon, turned populist politician, who was overthrown in a coup in 2006 and now lives in exile, drew much of his support from the poor. He stood on an anti-elitist platform and presented himself as Thailand's Mr Fixit, promising political stability through authoritarian governance. As a BBC correspondent based in Bangkok in the mid-1990s, I had reported on the former policeman's political rise. Looking back now, the comparisons with Duterte are uncanny. The seemingly affable Thaksin had just been appointed deputy prime minister and assigned the impossible task of solving Bangkok's legendary gridlock. In 1997, I spent a day filming with him as he flew around the city inspecting its clogged arteries and declaring war on traffic. He pledged to solve the problem in six months. Both he and Duterte liked to give themselves impossible deadlines requiring repeated extensions.

Thaksin's war on drugs would have to wait until early 2003. By then, he had become prime minister, and the late King Bhumibol Adulyadej called on his government to bring what he called 'the methamphetamine problem' under control. For Thaksin, it meant he could declare open season on what he cast as the pandemic of what Thais call *ya ba* and Filipinos know as *shabu*. Crystal meth, he said, had ravaged poor communities across the country; as in the Philippines, there was truth in this.

As with Duterte, Thaksin's strongman approach was welcomed by the masses. He too enjoyed widespread support, with reported approval ratings as high as 70 per cent. Thaksin's firm hand quickly became a clenched fist. He clamped down on the media, hounded civil society groups, and did not shy from violence. An influential privy councillor called on the government to use its parliamentary majority to set up a parallel court system just to handle drugs cases. 'If we execute 60,000 the land will rise and our descendants will escape bad karma,' he said.

But Thaksin saw no need for any sort of courts. He launched his first salvoes, supposedly at traffickers and dealers, as the world was looking the other way: George W. Bush and friends were about to invade Iraq. In Thailand, Thaksin had some shock-and-awe tactics of his own planned, with local government officials required to draw up blacklists based on an incentivised quota system, and police instructed, Duterte-style, 'to act decisively and without mercy'. Those on the lists were contacted, and, if they admitted to a *ya ba* habit, were dispatched to treatment centres — in reality, boot camps for users. For those who denied involvement in drugs — including those who really did have no involvement — other means were used. In many cases, they were just shot dead — with the police claiming the spiralling body count was the result of feuding between rival cartels operating out of the forested mountains along the Thai-Burma frontier. The government claimed that only a few dozen deaths had been down to the police. Human rights groups disagreed, citing eyewitness testimony and forensic evidence that police were directly involved.

In the first three months, more than 2500 were killed. The Thai Narcotics Control Board said 17,000 dealers were arrested, and more than a quarter of a million pushers and addicts surrendered for rehabilitation. But concerns quickly began to grow. A nine-year-old boy was shot dead by undercover cops in a sting operation, and the blacklists, it was said, were being used to settle personal, political, and business grudges.

Phil Robertson, a human rights activist in Thailand at the time, and now the Bangkok-based deputy Asia director for Human Rights Watch, told me: 'For many officials and their crony backers in local business and politics, Thaksin's war on drugs was a convenient way to settle scores with political enemies and business rivals. Just by including their enemies on the lists drawn up of people allegedly involved in drugs, an official could ensure that a rival faced the full weight of state security forces, with death waiting in the wings if they denied the accusations. If, out of fear, they admitted involvement in drugs, and reported to treatment centres, they faced humiliation and physical abuse.'

The widespread reporting of the nine-year-old's death triggered a backlash led by the press, which, despite Thaksin's best efforts, remained free. International human rights groups were quick to condemn the drugs war, and, in response to expression of alarm from the UN, the prime minister berated the organisation, saying defiantly: 'The UN is not my father.' Thais loved this, just as Filipinos cheered when Duterte swore at his UN critics.

The year after Thaksin was overthrown in one of Thailand's clockwork coups (his younger sister, Yingluck, who became prime minister later, at her brother's instigation, was also ousted, in 2014), an official investigation conducted by independent experts and backed by the military junta found that half of those killed between February and April 2003 had nothing to do with drug dealing. Those who did have links were mostly low-level dealers. The expert committee that authored the report accused Thaksin's administration of operating a shoot-to-kill policy that drew on flawed blacklists. Many of the dead were later proved to have been innocent. No one was held to account.

Douglas, the UNODC head, says Thailand's experience under Thaksin is a clear illustration that a state-sponsored policy of killing and incarcerating addicts and dealers doesn't work: 'The data from Thailand show that, after a temporary disruption of distribution at the street level, supply was still available and kept increasing, demand was still high and ended up rising, and, for years after, Thailand filled prisons with low-level users and dealers. Actually, Thailand has had 40 per cent of the Southeast Asian prison population due to drug crime even though it only had 10 per cent of the population.'

Although Thaksin claimed victory in his war, meth-amphetamine consumption quickly returned to alarming levels and continued to worsen. The UNODC reported a huge increase in the number of *ya ba* labs operating in Thailand, and Thai anti-narcotics police said the number of new users grew by more than 100,000 a year. In 2015, the new military government announced that the country now had around 1.3 million 'drug addicts', 2 per cent of the population.

The following year, in a policy proposal Gaviria might have considered remarkably enlightened, General Paiboon Koomchaya, the junta's justice minister, announced plans to decriminalise methamphetamines on the grounds that prohibition, the jailing of addicts, and the brand of violent drug wars launched by Thaksin and Duterte was an approach that obviously didn't work. In 2017, the Thai military regime declared, for the first time, that Thaksin's war on drugs had failed.

But in the Philippines, Duterte's war was gathering momentum, reinforced by government statistics leading Filipinos to believe their nation was about to be subsumed by a tsunami of *shabu*.

When he authorised Operation Double Barrel on 1 July 2016, the national police chief put the number of drug users in the Philippines at 1.8 million. *Shabu*, he asserted, was by far the most prevalent illegal drug. The 1.8 million figure derived from a nationwide survey by the Philippines' Dangerous Drugs Board (DDB) survey, completed in February 2016, which stated that this number included occasional users and consumers of other drugs. Fewer than half were *shabu* smokers, and around a third had only taken drugs once over the course of the previous year. The drugs board said marijuana use far outstripped that of *shabu*.

During his presidential campaign, Duterte put the number at 3 million 'addicts' and after just a month in office this became 3.7 million addicts. He declared this figure 'quite staggering and scary', and in a national address stated: 'I have to slaughter these idiots for destroying my country.'

By early 2017, the number had grown to 4 million, then '4 or 5 million', and by way of explaining such an inexplicably inflated figure, Duterte said the extent of the problem had been greater than even he had expected, so he now needed more time to tackle it.

A Reuters investigation into Duterte's war on drugs concluded that most of the government's statistics — whether for the number of users, the number of police being killed in drug busts, or the prevalence of drug-related crime — were either 'exaggerated, flawed or non-existent'.

Even employing the most creative mathematical chicanery, by applying the maximum possible margin of error to the DDB's figures, President Duterte's fictional figure was more than 60 per cent higher than the very highest number its statisticians considered possible. The government has failed to explain this discrepancy.

Feeling the heat as reporters continuously asked whether he could confirm Duterte's 4 million figure, and not wanting to appear treacherous, the chairman of the DDB, Dr Benjamin Reyes, had a brainwave: he widened the margin of error of his survey from plus or minus 0.9 per cent to plus or minus five per cent, which, he said, brought the president's numbers 'within the realm of possibility'.

On 24 May 2017, the president, aware of his diaphanous attire, summarily terminated Dr Reyes' career, dispatching him in Trump-like fashion. 'You're fired. Get out of service,' Duterte told him angrily. 'You do not contradict your own government ... you're just a civilian member of a board.'

Reyes' DDB report had shown a significant decline in drug addiction rates in the Philippines, and, casting around for international comparisons, it turned out that, per capita, Australia's crystal meth addiction crisis was much worse. Although statistical and anecdotal evidence clearly shows the Philippines does have a serious drugs problem, Duterte deliberately ignored expert opinion that contradicted his assertions. He knowingly exaggerated the scale of what he called the drugs 'pandemic', the foundation on which his policy was built.

Duterte's war on drugs was based on a lie.

12

SLAVES AND TYRANTS: THE AUTHORITARIAN PROJECT

Five hundred years ago, Nostradamus predicted the rise of Rodrigo Duterte. Well, that's if the viral cyber-babble churned out by the Davao king's troll army is to be believed. 'The power of 16 million forsaken souls will give birth to a messiah in the pearl of the orient seas,' these cod-philosophers enthuse, citing 'expert interpretations of the sacred texts' to explain how Duterte's election was apparently prophesied in days of yore. They hail the arrival of 'the Glory of all Glory, the Hope of all Ages', physically manifest in the form of the ex-mayor. News that even the late, great French seer had seen Duterte Harry coming triggered febrile debate online.

The multi-millionaire pastor of an evangelical cult foretold his coming, too. Apollo Quiboloy, a golfing partner of the president, who also claims to be the Appointed Son of God, said that even before the turn of the millennium, he had had a vision of Duterte playing golf in the presidential place. Quiboloy, who lent his friend a helicopter and use of his personal executive jet during his campaign, shared this prophesy with what he claimed were 'hundreds of thousands of supporters' at a rally in Manila just before the presidential poll.

'He destroys the destroyers of lives,' the Davaoeño prophet said, sounding like a voice from the Bhagavad Gita. He then accurately predicted Duterte's apocalyptic war on drugs, although by that stage the soon-to-be president had provided a smattering of clues as to how things might pan out.

The messiah's coming brought chaos and disequilibrium to the Philippines, and very quickly the landscape began to change. As an outsider, Duterte had no interest in the traditional architecture of power — he burst in like a bull in a china shop, akin to the fire and fury with which Trump seized the White House just a few months later. As with Trump, there was no fidelity to anything that had come before, no sacred cows, but Duterte took things ever further. He was possessed of a medieval mind-set: might was right. He sanctioned killing, and, within a year, a culture of impunity had taken root and the national police force had become indelibly tainted, top to bottom. Duterte threatened martial law and, again, within a year, had declared it in the south after a city there was overrun by militants claiming allegiance to the Islamic State group. He began to re-write history, rehabilitating the memory of Ferdinand Marcos and ordering the ex-president's re-burial at the Cemetery of Heroes in Manila.

Policy-wise, he is winging it. For a politician known for his straight-talking rhetoric, Duterte's stance on critical issued has remained muddled and unclear. He may have his own private agenda, but there is an absence of strategic vision: there is nothing much that he is for, but plenty he is against. He has declared war on drugs and, supposedly, corruption; then on Islamist insurgents;

followed by the communist New People's Army. And, for Duterte, the ends always justify the means. Exactly what those ends are is not clear, and history is full of despots who lost track of the ends in pursuit of the means. As president, his motivation is the same as it was as mayor of Davao — to be the centre of attention, playing to the gallery, ever the iconoclast, enthralling his audiences by saying the unsayable. He jokes about rape and insults the US president, the Pope, and the Catholic Church.

Among his first acts of governance was to fulfil a campaign promise to push for the re-introduction of the death penalty — in case, Duterte reasoned, there was no God. This threatened to make the Philippines the first country ever to withdraw from the UN agreement to abolish capital punishment. The death penalty bill was calculated as a shot across the bows of the Catholic Church, seemingly to warn the bishops that the president intended to take them on. It sailed through the lower house, and, in March 2017, a dozen congressmen and women were summarily stripped of their committee chair positions in a purge designed to punish those who had voted against the bill — including former president Gloria Arroyo. The Liberal opposition said this move betrayed the Duterte administration's intolerance of dissent, which it condemned as 'a disturbing indicator of a dangerous slide towards authoritarianism'. But the legislation later stalled in the Senate. To the exasperation of the president's allies, it remains implacably opposed by a handful of opposition Senators. Bringing back the death penalty would be a particularly contentious move because it involves rescinding the Philippines' ratification of a UN protocol, considered a treaty under international law.

While threatening serious damage to international law, Duterte Harry also threw down the gauntlet to the Philippines' chief justice, and began to stuff the Supreme Court with loyalist appointees, just as he stuffed his cabinet with cronies. He now owns both houses of Congress, after the liberal elites took fright and his political opposition disintegrated then joined him — save for a handful of outspoken critics, whose ringleader he jailed to send a chilling signal. His overwhelming support in Congress was startlingly apparent when, in a joint session on 22 July 2017, the Senate and the House of Representatives voted 261–18 in favour of the president's request to extend martial law and suspend *habeas corpus* in Mindanao until the end of the year. In December 2017, Congress approved the extension of martial law in Mindanao until the end of 2018. In the Philippines' winner-takes-all political system, he demonstrated that he could do as he liked, and, although the fetters of state were a greater restraint than when he was simply mayor, his allies easily fended off an impeachment attempt as Duterte basked in presidential immunity from prosecution.

His first year in office was a master class in populist author-itarianism. As Walden Bello, a former congressman and respected Filipino political analyst put it: '*L'état c'est moi* may well be the most fitting description of the way Duterte views his relationship to the Philippine state.' He rather strikingly branded Duterte 'a fascist original'.

The 2018 Worldwide Threat Assessment, published by the US intelligence community, declared Duterte a 'regional threat'. The report, released by Daniel R. Coats, director of US national intelligence, represents the views of the CIA and 16 other US intelligence agencies. It predicted that Duterete would 'continue to wage his signature campaign against drugs, corruption and crime' as part of a general deepening of autocratic tendencies across a 'fragile' Southeast Asia. It observed that 'Duterte has suggested he could suspend the Constitution, declare a "revolutionary government", and impose nationwide martial law.'

The appointment of cronies to cabinet posts and other senior positions is not simply down to Duterte's mistrust of people not from Davao — although this is indeed the case. From day one, Duterte set out to block any possible investigation into his criminal liability for killings, either as mayor or as president, by surrounding himself with a cast-iron team of lickspittle legal henchmen. If his enemies couldn't get him as mayor, he could be confident they weren't going to get him as president. Vitaliano 'Vit' Aguirre, his old law school classmate, who had faithfully represented him during the inconclusive Davao Death Squad investigation by Leila de Lima, was appointed justice secretary. Duterte's chunky enforcer, Salvador 'Bingbong' Medialdea — another lawyer who had worked with Aguirre as counsel to Bienvenido Laud, the owner of the Laud quarry — was appointed executive secretary, a cabinet post and the highest-ranking position in the president's office. Duterte appointed another Davao lawyer, Dante Gierran, to head the National Bureau of Investigation. The self-confessed DDS hitman Edgar Matobato said under oath that he had worked with Gierran for 15 years, and that, as an NBI agent, Gierran had been part of an abduction team that had fed an alleged kidnapper to a crocodile. Duterte put Gierran in charge of the Matobato manhunt. Another of Duterte's former Davao lawyers, Salvador 'Sal' Panelo, was appointed his chief legal counsel, and attorney Jose 'Jun' Calida, his former chief assistant as Davao City mayor, was named solicitor general. Duterte's former top cop from Davao, Ronald 'Bato' dela Rosa, became national police chief, and, on his retirement in 2018, Bato's successor is likely to be his deputy, Ramon Apolinario, another ex-Davao City police chief. These are the president's men, although not all of them.

To the despair of foreign (and many Filipino) diplomats, Duterte has adopted a devil-may-care approach to international affairs, in some cases upending years of painstaking negotiations, baffling policy analysts everywhere. This has disrupted the fragile equilibrium in a region whose stability is critical to global trade. His reckless 'new foreign policy' appears to be informed by ignorance of international relations, and driven by Trump-like mood swings — and the big chip on his shoulder over the United States. Duterte views the US as a source of past and present humiliations, personal and national. In October 2016, announcing a 'separation' with Washington, he turned his back on an alliance dating back 70 years, perplexing the State Department and causing great disquiet among US regional allies. He began to flirt openly with China and Russia, whose authoritarian leaders, he boasted, were his new friends. Unlike their western counterparts, they would not interfere in how he ran things back home. Meanwhile, he continually rebuffed those who did, swearing at EU leaders who criticised the barbarity of his drugs war, cursing the UN, and — in one press conference I attended — threatening to withdraw from the International Criminal Court, whose chief prosecutor has expressed 'deep concern' over extra-judicial killings. (In April 2017, a Philippine lawyer delivered a bundle of evidence to the ICC accusing the president and 11 associates of mass murder and crimes against humanity. Three months later, Duterte was conspicuously not invited to a G20 summit in Germany, which as the then chairman of the ten-member ASEAN group, he should have been, and this was interpreted by many as a very pointed snub.) Even after the ICC had announced its preliminary investigation, Duterte's foreign affairs secretary was dispatched abroad to candy-coat the drugs war for international consumption. De Lima called this 'death squad diplomacy' and lamented that these 'barefaced lies' would take the foreign ministry years to recover from.

At home, Duterte's new foreign policy has raised concerns that the ex-city mayor is out of his depth, spurning his country's long-standing alliances and trading national sovereignty for short-term economic gain. Nothing has illustrated this better than his *volte face* over the disputed sovereignty of islands and reefs in the South China Sea. In a fit of bravado during his presidential campaign, Duterte gallantly declared himself 'ready to die' to defend his country's claims, and said he would ride a jet-ski to plant a Philippine flag on a Chinese man-made island to reinforce Manila's claim to a contested reef. The Philippines is one of five countries that dispute Beijing's sweeping territorial claim to almost all of the South China Sea. The US and its allies also challenge this claim, citing rights to freedom of navigation over and through what is a strategic seaway for an annual US $5.3 trillion in trade. The South China Sea is also thought to be rich in oil, gas, and minerals.

Once president, however, Duterte suddenly veered off-course, announcing that he would instead engage with China in an effort to resolve these disputes through talks, even though a UN-backed tribunal had just ruled, in a case brought by the previous Philippine government, that there was no legal basis to Beijing's claim and that it had no historic territorial rights. Duterte's change of tack was a dramatic reversal of policy, which some viewed as capitulation to China and *de facto* acceptance of its military occupation of remote reefs and islets. The two countries have since been in talks about jointly developing oil fields in the disputed waters.

After visiting Beijing in October 2016, the president triumph-antly announced that his improved ties with China had reaped US$24 billion in promised investment. A year later, virtually none of this had materialised. In April 2017, Duterte suddenly altered course again, ordering Philippine troops to occupy disputed uninhabited islands in the Spratly archipelago — a move guaranteed to antagonise China. This caused great consternation, with analysts unsure whether it amounted to a policy statement or was just another of Duterte's off-the-cuff provocative quips. The following month, in a speech to the Philippine coast guard in Davao, Duterte said China's president, Xi Jinping, had warned him that, if he continued to force the issue, China would go to war. Beijing's remorseless militarisation of the South China Sea had clearly begun to rattle Duterte again, but questions were raised at home and abroad as to whether he had an adequate grasp of just how high the stakes were.

If this was conflict-management, Duterte-style, it came across as naïve and hopelessly confused. By January 2018 he was publicly talking about asking China to conduct anti-piracy operations in the Sulu and Celebes seas. Meanwhile, former president Fidel Ramos publicly bemoaned Duterte's failure 'to assert the Philippine legal victory, preferring loans, investments and development assistance from China'. From her prison cell, Leila de Lima accused Duterte of selling out to Beijing because it did not criticise his human rights record. 'Our foreign policy is now reduced to one man's inexplicable lust for blood and his disregard for the value of human life,' she wrote.

For all the doublespeak, nothing the president could say or do could dent his popularity at home. A Social Weather Stations survey on the eve of his first anniversary in power found 78 per cent of Filipinos satisfied with Duterte's performance. He was even more popular in the central Visayas region and Mindanao (both 83 per cent). It didn't waver much between cities and the countryside, or between young and old; women loved him a little bit more than men; and college graduates awarded him an approval rating of 83 per cent. His popularity proved highest among the very poorest Filipinos, despite their being the primary victims of his war on drugs. Subsequent surveys dipped a bit, then rose again. By and large, it seemed he could do no wrong.

You might have thought a bloodbath would be bad for business. Not so. When Standard & Poor's, a US credit rating agency, predicted that Duterte's war on drugs and the policy chaos of the Philippine administration might lead to a downgrade, the president shrugged and asked 'So what the hell?' He reckoned he could just as readily turn to his new friends in Beijing and in Moscow for investment. Commentators in the business pages deemed his reaction injudicious and not particularly reassuring, especially as the US remains the Philippines' largest foreign investor. Meanwhile, the wildly fluctuating Philippine stock market averaged a flat line throughout Duterte's first year in office and the peso hit a 10-year low against the dollar, with Bloomberg Markets branding the currency 'Asia's ugly duckling'. Yet, just as the business community in 1990s Davao City had embraced and even helped bankroll Duterte's dystopia, so investors in the Philippines — local and foreign — were, it seems, prepared to look the other way when it came to the ugly realities of Duterte's law-and-order.

They were impressed by a two-year forecast that predicted that economic growth in the Philippines would average close to seven per cent — which, according to the World Bank, would make the country the world's 10th fastest-growing economy. Investor confidence was also buoyed by Duterte's populist pledges to build US$16.8 billion worth of roads, railways, ports, and airports, which, it was promised, would generate 2 million jobs a year during his six-year administration. This initiative, launched in April 2017, finally constituted a really ambitious, forward-looking policy, which underpinned what the government ludicrously labelled 'Dutertenomics'. It heralded, they crowed, 'a golden age of public infrastructure investment'. This economic policy hinges on tax reform and enhancing national competitiveness but at its heart is the aspiration to build, build, build.

No one questioned the need for all this spending; transport

links within and between cities in the Philippines are awful. What has worried critics is how the administration will pay for it — *Forbes* magazine has predicted that the country will be saddled with generations of debt bondage to China and Japan.

Nonetheless, by late 2017, infrastructure projects across the Philippines were being contracted out. However, the country does not necessarily have Duterte to thank for this. The president has had very little to do with Dutertenomics personally; it is managed by technocrats, and he rarely takes much interest. This detachment is apparent in what was omitted from speeches he gave to the business community at the time of the launch. In October 2017, for example, in a speech to a national business conference, he barely mentioned the economy at all, other than boasting that growth had hit nine per cent. Instead, he predictably railed against drugs, communists, and jihadists, and condemned foreign interference in his country. He has always been more focused on waging his wars than on anything else, but the boom — which independent economists have said continued 'despite Duterte' because he inherited a strong economy — has bolstered his stranglehold on the country. The Philippine stock exchange ended 2017 on a record high and the peso bounced back too. The progressive economic agenda Duterte had promised to pursue in the course of his presidential campaign — aimed at tackling poverty through tax reform — failed to live up to its billing, however, as did the agrarian reform he promised.

The president has cast himself as everybody's friend, exactly as he did as mayor, courting warring insurgent groups, and turning Davao into a 'city of respite' in which all rebel factions — communist or Moro separatist — were welcome, as long as they didn't bring their guns. Since his landslide election victory, he has set about harvesting all the good will he has planted over decades, with capitalists, communists, progressives, conservatives, separatists, federalists, environmentalists and mining tycoons. But Duterte is a political chameleon, with that populist knack of making everybody feel he is 'their guy'.

'Truth is, he's nobody's guy,' a straight talking seasoned observer of Duterte told me. 'He's just a master-manipulator, an instinctive politician, capable of saying anything that suits him and capable of turning on anyone. He will make friends with those that he finds useful, only to later turn round and crush them. He has no qualms about biting the hand that feeds him. Everything centres on him. It's all about control.'

Duterte has masterfully wrong-footed both the political establishment and the rebels. He remains beholden to absolutely no one.

While clearly no ideologue, Duterte claims to be a socialist and has appointed three members of the hard left to his cabinet, all the while edging ever closer to absolute power and cosying up to the Marcos clan. In the May 2016 elections, Ferdinand 'Bingbong' Marcos Jr narrowly lost his bid for the vice presidency, and Duterte encouraged him to contest the victory of the liberal candidate, Leni Robredo. Bongbong accused her of cheating, and Duterte, who repeatedly demeaned her in public, banned Robredo from attending cabinet meetings. If the Supreme Court overturns the vice presidential election result, another Ferdinand Marcos could find himself a heartbeat from the presidency. Perhaps Duterte reasoned that having Ferdinand Jr as his potential heir, no one would dare impeach him.

Duterte's links to the hard left are difficult to disentangle, but his political moorings were put in place in his early days as mayor of Davao by Leoncio 'Jun' Evasco, the former communist rebel priest he first had sent to jail then recruited as his chief of staff. Evasco, together with communist activists in Davao, helped consolidate Duterte's declared socialist beliefs. But there is no evidence that the president was ever a card-carrying member of the Communist Party of the Philippines (CPP), as some of his political enemies have claimed. His past associations with revolutionary organisations — including commanders of the New People's Army — are known to have caused alarm in military circles, particularly when comrade Evasco was appointed cabinet secretary in Malacañang. Evasco has since masterminded the formation of Duterte's political support base, a grassroots organisation called *Kilusang Pagbabago* — Movement for Change — from which the rank and file of the president's army of trolls is drawn. KP has active youth wings throughout the archipelago.

On a beautiful winter's day in early 2017, I travelled to Utrecht in the Netherlands to meet José Maria 'Joma' Sison, the exiled Maoist founder of the CPP, now in his late seventies. Although once hugely influential, he is struggling to remain relevant in his homeland. Joma, as he's known, had been professor of political science at Lyceum University, Manila, and Duterte had studied under him before he took his law degree. Duterte would have been well schooled in the evils of American imperialism by Joma, but the ex-professor remembered his former student as being an undergraduate who 'didn't apply himself too seriously' and played a lot of billiards. Duterte, Joma said, had joined his leftist 'patriotic youth' movement in the 1960s, but he denied he had ever tried to recruit the future president to the CPP, as Duterte has claimed.

Their relationship continued after Duterte was elected in Davao, when, Joma said, the mayor made a deal with the CPP's armed wing, the New People's Army (NPA), promising no more manhunts. The CPP, Joma claimed, had considered him 'our man'. Duterte's former professor had never thought his student 'presidential timbre', he admitted to me, but when Duterte was elected, Joma released a video message in which he said the president offered the best hope of peace in 50 years.

'For the first time in the history of the Philippines,' the ageing communist announced, 'a president has emerged by denouncing the abuses of the oligarchy and the folly of servility to foreign powers and by using the street language and methods of the mass movement.' It was as if he was already imagining the CPP in a coalition government. But when I met him in a Utrecht cafe, Joma was scathing of Duterte's supposed socialist convictions, repeatedly referring to him as 'a bundle of contradictions' and laughing that 'probably what he means by socialism is providing social services'.

As negotiations got underway between the government and 'the Reds' — as the communists are still referred to in the press — Joma had already been involved in several late-night slanging matches with Duterte over the phone and Skype, but he told me he still considered him a friend. Joma had called him a '*butangero*' — Tagalog for hoodlum — and, never one to be outdone, the president shot back a few choice insults himself. Joma considered the president uncouth, although he had clearly enjoyed the verbal jousting.

'But do you trust him?' I asked.

He took a moment to answer, but when he did, it startled me.

'I know very well the story of Mussolini. He came from the [Italian] Socialist Party and he flipped! Because, as Hitler said in *Mein Kampf*, the point is to steal the colour red.' At this, Joma began to laugh heartily, as if he had cracked a joke, although when he continued, his tone was deadly serious. 'In building a fascist movement, the youth factor is very important, no? The youth are the most vigorous, open to ideas. A counter-revolutionary can harness this energy, this open-mindedness, to do anything exciting that he wants. You have to be very alert with Duterte. He is capable of saying anything that suits him.'

After being widely feted for initially pursuing peace with

communists and Islamist insurgents in Mindanao, in 2017 Duterte declared all-out war on both, and, in doing so, appeased the army top brass, who had been deeply mistrustful of the president's supposedly leftist leanings. His cabinet included neo-liberal economists — led by school chum turned finance secretary, Carlos Dominguez — who leftists accused of spearheading an elitist agenda. Yet the three most prominent communists in his government were assigned to the ministries of agrarian reform (which had been paralysed for decades by corruption, bureaucracy, and inefficiency) and social welfare, and to the anti-poverty commission. The left found itself in an impossible position, associated with a bloodthirsty regime that, on the other hand, had held out the prospect of peace and promised progressive social reforms.

'Duterte plays everyone off against each other,' another contact, who declined to let me name him, said. 'It's what he's always done. Progressive groups need him more than he needs them — in terms of political trade-off. He values the links with the communists, but he's a political dynast, if not an oligarch, paying lip service to progressive politics, but only because it suits his purpose. He's a tricksy pragmatist.'

Duterte's proclivity to sow confusion through his often contra-dictory statements extends to pronouncements on his personal state of health — if only to keep everybody guessing. Rumours abound, from time to time, that the septuagenarian president is terminally ill and at death's door, press speculation fuelled by his absence from the public eye for periods of up to several days. Advancing age is one of the president's few disadvantages, although he is working hard to create a legacy that many fear will be hard to erase when he is gone. But Duterte has also worked out how to use his age to his advantage. When he extemporises in speeches, he will often make gloomy reference to his life expectancy. A typical comment, made during a rambling speech in Davao that I attended, was: 'I have a six-year window. I really do not know if I will last that long.' He has made many similar remarks, talking about how his presidency is 'my last hurrah'. In another speech, in which he said 'I doubt if I can finish', he added that if he died in office and was carried out of Malacañang horizontal, he would at least enjoy a state funeral.

Evidently fed up with Duterte's dismal pronouncements on his imminent demise, former president Fidel Ramos appealed to him to refrain. In February 2017, Ramos, who was about to turn 89, in a commentary published by the *Rappler* digital news site, wrote: 'Pardon me for saying this Mr President Duterte, but you must be at peace with yourself and do not talk about dying soon or being killed or not caring for your life ... You were elected for six years. And you [must] fulfil it.' Ramos said he was offering this as unsolicited advice and added that he thought Duterte's fears were borne of insecurity.

Cynics roll their eyes at Duterte's morbid musings. Some dismiss the intrigue surrounding his long absences as the antics of a schemer who is actually interested in seeing whether vultures start to circle. At least four powerful, competing factions are represented in his cabinet, all of them aware that the whimsical, erratic king will not live forever. But the lugubrious talk has stirred genuine concern among Filipinos of all persuasions, for different reasons. While his fan club is in awe of the president's patriotic selflessness, a human rights activist I met said: 'Every time this guy says he's going to die, part of me believes him. A dying person has nothing to lose and that's exactly how he's behaving.'

Sam Zarifi, who heads the Geneva-based International Commission of Jurists (and was previously the ICJ's Asia-Pacific director) told me that Duterte presented 'a prosecutor's dream' and that 'he didn't even have a moment of plausible deniability', but he lamented that his age makes it unlikely a criminal case against him could be built from scratch as such cases take years, sometimes decades. This is unlikely to have escaped the attention of the former Davao public prosecutor, surrounded by his coterie of pugnacious lawyers. As though he had nothing left to lose, Duterte's boasts cut ever closer to the bone. In a speech in February 2018 he ventured that, if it weren't for his 'dictatorial' style of governance, nothing would ever get done. 'If you say "dicator", well, l am really a dictator. Because if I don't [act like a] dicator,' he postured, 'nothing will happen to our nation.'

Opposition politicians have demanded transparency from Malacañang on the question of the president's health, calling it a matter not just of public interest, but also of national security, and citing constitutional provisions obliging the government to inform the public of their commander-in-chief's health. On each occasion, the palace has eventually released proof-of-life photographs, reassuring the country that Duterte is well and simply exhausted from his gruelling schedule, all amid rumours that range from his suffering everything from kidney failure to cancer. In mid-June 2017, the president dropped out of view for days, failing to show up at Independence Day celebrations. Five days later, he resurfaced, joking that he had 'had a circumcision'. Duterte has candidly admitted that he suffers from migraines as a result of nerve damage following a motorcycle accident and from Buerger's disease, a narrowing of the arteries, caused by heavy smoking in his youth. He uses an oxygen converter at night and has talked of his dependence on Fentanyl, a powerful synthetic opiate as addictive as heroin.

Duterte has also spoken of his fears of being assassinated — by Filipino drug lords, the political opposition, and, more recently, the CIA. In an interview with the Kremlin-backed Russian broadcaster RT in May 2017, Duterte said that, while 'Trump is my friend', he mistrusts the US political establishment and the intelligence services in particular.

'If I survive the CIA, I still have five years to go,' he told the RT interviewer, who commented that he seemed to talk a lot about the possibility of assassination.

Duterte replied: 'They do it. Does it surprise you?'

He said he had shifted his foreign policy away from 'the Western world' because of conditions America and the EU placed on improvements in human rights, and he railed against what he called US double standards and interference.

'Me, I'm just fighting the criminals,' he said. 'I never invaded a country.'

Duterte clearly sees a difference between the US political establishment and his friend, the American president. But despite the developing bromance between Duterte and Trump, their first alpha-male exchange of invective did not bode so well. While still on the campaign trail, Trump, proposing his immigration ban on majority Muslim countries, said the US was letting in 'animals' from 'terrorist nations', and specifically mentioned the Philippines. It was never clear what he meant by this remark, which caused great offence in a country where Trump has extensive business dealings, having licensed use of his name for branded property developments, including a Trump Tower in Manila. Amid calls from a Philippine congressman to deny the US presidential contender entry to the Philippines because of this slur, Duterte appeared on national TV and invited Trump to Manila so they could slug it out, 'man to man'. If Trump was too scared, Duterte volunteered to take him on in Las Vegas or in the MGM Grand Arena, where his friend and political ally Manny Pacquiao would shortly contest (and win) the WBO welterweight title.

'I will not take any insult on my Filipino people sitting down,' a furious Duterte said, clearly relishing the fact he too had a new US sparring partner. 'Let's settle this once and for all, extra-judicially.'

Personal relations between the two men were to improve immeasurably when President Trump congratulated Duterte on the 'unbelievable job' he was doing in his war on drugs. He returned the compliment in true Duterte Harvey style: 'He is a billionaire, his wife is very beautiful. I envy him ... that's his edge over me,' he said at a birthday party for his chief of police in the company of his girlfriend, Honeylet. (Her view of her partner's remark is unrecorded.)

But Duterte's newfound rapport with Trump has done nothing to diminish his visceral hatred of the United States — and it is Duterte himself who terms it 'hatred'. His bitter anti-Americanism is out of step with the tens of millions of Filipinos who love America more than many Americans themselves. Since early colonial days, when thousands of Filipinos were lured across the Pacific to the US west coast by promises of jobs, there has been a large community of Filipino expats in America. The Philippine government now estimates their number at 3.4 million, a quarter of a million of them undocumented migrants. Of the US$26.9 billion in cash remittances repatriated by overseas Filipino workers in 2016, by far the largest tranche came from the US, with 43 per cent either going through the US or originating there. Any large-scale deportation of large numbers of Filipino illegals as part of Trump's proposed crack-down would be a flashpoint.

A survey by the US-based Pew Research Center conducted across 37 countries, published in June 2017, showed 78 per cent support for the US in the Philippines, against a global average of 49 per cent. This was down, however, from the 92 per cent of

Filipinos who said they held America in high regard the previous year, a figure that far outstripped even Israel and South Korea. Globally, Trump has tarnished the American brand, but in the Philippines they still like the US president almost as much as they love the USA. Of all the 37 countries surveyed, Trump was by far the most popular in the Philippines, with 69 per cent of respondents expressing trust in him, compared with a global average of 22 per cent.

Strangely, this level of confidence in Trump is despite a large majority of Filipinos disagreeing with his polices — including his proposals to build a border wall with Mexico, pull out of the nuclear weapons agreement with Iran, and withdraw from the Paris Agreement. Neither does it bother Filipinos that their own highly popular president expresses such a discordantly hostile view of the US. They like Trump because he is perceived as a strong leader, and they like Duterte for the same reason. Their own president appears to stir a sense of national pride when he is seen to stand up to the Philippines' former colonial master as no other president has ever done. 'Deferential' is not a word associated with Duterte. In private, he has thanked the US ambassador for American support, and, from time to time, he says that there remains a bond of friendship, but in public he has relished grandstanding to his domestic audience. Many of his compatriots have squirmed, however, at his indelicate diplomacy.

'As long as I am here, do not treat us like a doormat because you will be sorry,' Duterte raged against the US, early in his presidency, weeks before he called Barack Obama *'putang ina'*. In broadside after broadside, he spoke of 'separation' from Washington, telling the US not to treat his country 'like a dog on a leash'. He abruptly cancelled joint US-Philippine military exercises and threatened to evict the US military from Philippine soil – although in the end the joint exercises did continue. But even as the front page of a leading newspaper in the Philippines ran a headline 'Duterte sparking international distress — US,' Duterte proclaimed 'America has lost', and said he would 'break up with' the US. He said Washington could forget their bilateral defence deal if he stayed in power long enough.

'I am very emotional because America has certainly failed us,' he said in a speech on national TV. On another occasion, he said: 'You know, I did not start this fight.'

Perceived rejection has long led Duterte to lash out and behave in a rash manner; he has a similar level of emotional maturity to Trump and, in his personal life, he has been known to act impetuously when his fragile self-esteem takes a battering. His younger sister Jocelyn told me that, while at law school in Manila, Duterte had a long-term girlfriend called Jeannette — a Mestiza, half-American, half-Filipina. Jocelyn told me Jeannette had grown weary of his indecision when it came to marriage and had left for the US.

'Three weeks later, he went to the States,' she said, 'to get her back, only to find out that she had married ... probably out of spite.' They'd had a fight, she said, and he came back. 'It was the only time I saw him cry! Yup!' She laughed at the reminiscence. 'I remember there was a song he was playing over and over. "MacArthur Park ... is melting in the dark". La la, la la la la.' It was voted the worst song of all time by the *Miami Herald* in 1992, but the future president wallowed in its bewildering lyrics. 'I remember telling him "Now you've got your karma!"' Jocelyn said. Three months later, Duterte met Elizabeth (who Jocelyn described as from the Davao slums — 'a social and economic mismatch') and promptly married her. 'It was on the rebound ... the marriage was very turbulent from the beginning.' She agreed her brother had a propensity to act rashly.

Duterte's anti-Americanism is as rooted in perceived personal humiliation as it is in his Mindanaoan historical resentment. Those who know him best say the refusal of a US visa was the straw that broke the camel's back. Mounting concern in the US Congress about his human rights record as mayor of Davao City is likely to have been the reason Duterte was denied a visa to visit his girlfriend Honeylet Avanceña and their daughter, Veronica 'Kitty' Duterte, who was born in the United States. Many years on, the snub still rankles, and he has sworn he won't be going there in his lifetime. 'I've seen America, and it's lousy,' he is reported to have said.

But what made Duterte incandescent with rage was an incident in Davao shortly before that visa was refused. It involved the mysterious case of a 67-year-old American, Michael Terrence Meiring. On 16 May 2002, a small bomb exploded inside room 305 on the third floor of an ugly, sleazy, low-budget hotel called the Evergreen, in Davao City's Chinatown, a stone's throw from the mayor's favourite Magsaysay durian vendors. Estrella and Celes, a mother and her daughter who have been selling caramelised deep-fried bananas for years at a stall just across the street from the Evergreen, witnessed what happened. The city was already on edge after a succession of bombs elsewhere on Mindanao and bomb threats in the oasis of peace otherwise known as Davao City.

'It blew up just before noon,' Estrella told me. 'There was a loud bang, like the sound of a tyre exploding, and then black smoke came pouring out of the room. We never actually saw the foreigner, but we learned from the TV it was an American guy and the mayor got really angry about it.'

This was an understatement.

The explosion mangled Meiring's legs and left much of the rest of his body badly burned. As he was rushed to hospital, questions were already being asked about what an American was doing with explosives in Davao. Police described the device that exploded as powerful and high-tech, and filed charges of illegal possession of ammunition. Duterte personally added a further charge of arson. Meiring had stayed in the Evergreen on several occasions over the previous decade and had passed himself off as a treasure hunter and a mining engineer.

Over dinner in Manila, Duterte's sister Jocelyn admitted to me that she had met Meiring in Davao — on four separate occasions, she said, over several months.

'He was very arrogant. He showed me his papers and said, "You see? I can go in and out of the country, no questions asked. Not even from the president." I saw the documents. It was true. It was a foreign policy agreement between the Philippines and the US. I said to him, "What do you do in the Philippines? Are you messing with the mayor?" I said, "Be careful. The mayor, my brother, is not stupid. If you are a CIA agent ..."'

'You actually said that to him?' I asked.

'Yes! And he was laughing. He was arrogant.'

Newspaper reports from the time alleged that Meiring had close ties to government authorities in Mindanao, the Philippine National Police, and both Moro nationalist and communist insurgent groups. It was also reported that he was originally a South African of British extraction who had worked undercover for the African National Congress before fleeing the apartheid regime for the US. Documents filed as exhibits in the case against him included a copy of a Moro National Liberation Front identification card bearing his name and picture, and other documents appearing to corroborate his claim to have been a treasure-hunter, searching for sunken gold bars in wartime shipwrecks. In the aftermath of 9/11, US forces were operating elsewhere in Mindanao in support of Philippine army operations against the jihadist Abu Sayyaf group. American intelligence agents were widely rumoured to be active on the island, allegedly posing as business consultants.

Three days after the bomb went off in the Evergreen hotel, Meiring vanished. Mayor Duterte later alleged that an aircraft had landed in Davao and US FBI agents had headed to the hospital where the wounded American lay. Flashing their FBI cards, they took him from the hospital, spiriting him out of the country to the fury of the mayor. Press reports later had Meiring in Manila, Singapore, and San Diego. Duterte said he had been 'shanghaied' to the USA.

'They think and act nonchalant [sic] as if they own the place,' he was reported as saying by online paper *MindaNews*. 'I don't give a shit who they are. Those metal badges do not have any value to me. If FBI agents do that again, I will have them eat their badges ... Sovereignty does not come cheap.'

The US embassy in Manila reportedly paid Meiring's hospital bills in Davao, but the US was — and remains — dismissive of the conspiracy theories surrounding this not-so-quiet American. In 2005, the US ambassador called the mayor of Davao 'misinformed' and denied that Meiring had been whisked out of the country in the dead of night. But Duterte, clearly believing that nothing is credible unless it has been officially denied, has never let the matter go, and, 15 years after Meiring disappeared, on becoming president, he raised the issue with another ambassador. The ambassador once again explained the American position. By then Meiring was long dead. Inquiries through journalist friends of mine in the US established that he had passed away in California in 2012.

A few months after my own testy encounter with Duterte in Davao — when he had conferred on me the Order of Son of a Whore — I attended another late-night press conference inside Malacañang Palace. As it wound up, I joined a handful of

Filipino colleagues who had gathered round the president. He often ended up having long informal conversations with reporters. One of these journalists had earlier told me that, following my run-in with him in Davao, a still furious Duterte — who had mistaken me for an American — had told the gathered cluster of reporters that he was convinced that I was working for the CIA. We laughed at this, and I suggested that next time I had better tell the president that British nationals were barred from working for US intelligence.

That particular night, having already made his threats and exorcised some demons, the president was in a more magnanimous frame of mind. My colleague decided it was a good moment to inform Duterte that I was the one who, in his words, he had '*putang ina'd*'. This caused much amusement, not least for the president. He looked me in the eye and made a hangdog face. For a moment, I thought he was going to say sorry for defaming my late mother.

I said, 'I think I need to clarify that I am British.'

'In that case,' he responded, holding out his hand in mock contrition, 'I owe you an apology.'

For Duterte, impugning a Brit by branding him American constituted a far more grievous insult than calling somebody's mother a whore.

Having sat through several of Duterte's anti-American diatribes, I met his elder sister, Eleanor, in Davao and asked her why he harboured so much rage towards the US. It turned out she shared his animosity. She began by quoting from Manuel L. Quezon, the pre-independence wartime president of the Philippines, who lent his name to a city, a province, and a famous bridge.

'I prefer a government run like hell by Filipinos to a government run like heaven by Americans,' he had said.

Deftly skipping over the 'government run like hell by Filipinos' bit, Eleanor told me this anti-imperialist anger was 'ingrained in the Duterte blood'; anger against the Spanish colonisers and their abusive Catholic priests, and anger against America.

'All of us,' she said. 'Not just my brother. All of us. Colonisers colonise. They enslave people. [Ask] any country that was colonised. Ask the Vietnamese … and do you think the children do not remember it? Terrible. Who was the enemy?' She was shrill and shouting at me now. 'The United States of America! It behoves us to just let it go because it is not right to hold a grudge … The person holding the grudge is going to suffer. In Mindanao especially.' The official portrait of her brother hung over her shoulder like her menacing guardian angel. 'You expect respect, but you don't respect people yourself? It's impossible! You are breaking a cosmic law … so I'm telling you right now, America, they had better go down on their bended knees and ask forgiveness from the Lord if they want their souls saved because I think they are all the walking dead.'

Eleanor, who had lived and worked in the US for many years herself, paused for a moment before spitting out the words her brother could have uttered: 'America is the number one hypocrite.'

During my interview Eleanor became increasingly irate and began yelling about anti-Zionist conspiracies encompassing the Rothschilds, Rockefellers, George Soros, the Pope, the mainstream media, as well as various former and serving heads of state who were collectively denounced as members of a satanic cult — as were senators de Lima and Trillanes. She was visibly consumed with anger, leaning forward, jabbing her finger at me, and reserving an even more passionate tongue-lashing for the conquistadors.

'The Filipino nation suffered a lot. A lot and I mean A LOT. On a scale of one to 10, I would say nine point nine under Spanish rule. We have Spanish blood whether we like it or not, in our family. José Rizal's ancestry is purely Spaniard.' She was referring to the most revered of all Filipino nationalists, the poet, writer, and philosopher, executed for rebellion by the Spanish colonial regime in 1896, two years before the US kicked them out. In one of his classic texts, *El filibusterismo* (*The Reign of Greed*), Rizal wrote 'There can be no tyrants where there are no slaves.' At the end of the novel, one of his characters, the pacifist Filipino priest Padre Florentino, asks the dying revolutionary, Simoun: 'What is the use of independence if the slaves of today will be the tyrants of tomorrow?' Filipinos often cite these, and other poignant quotations from Rizal's works, in their analysis of their troubled colonial past, and sometimes their troubled present, too.

But Eleanor Duterte wanted me to understand that Rizal's 'martyrdom' was more to do with his exposing 'the corruption of the Roman Catholic hierarchy of the Spanish-ruled Philippines at that time'. The corruption, she said, was not about the money. 'It was about the killing of unborn children who are the product of illegitimate sex between priests and nuns. You cannot get deeper than that. They did not break the laws of man. They broke the laws of God. The nuns who went to the convents to be the brides of Christ became the brides of priests. That is what every Filipino knows from history. That is what every one of us knows. Not just Rodrigo.'

Outside on the street, a cock was crowing.

When the most prominent Catholic Archbishop of the Philippines, Socrates Villegas, urged Filipinos not to vote for Mayor Duterte, the die was cast.

'What the world desperately needs now is leadership by example,' Villegas said in a statement, six months before the presidential poll. 'Corruption, like a monster, is a devil with many faces. Killing people is corruption ... Adultery is corruption ... Vulgarity is corruption ... When a revered and loved and admired man like Pope Francis is cursed by a political candidate and the audience laugh[s], I can only bow my head and grieve in great shame ... Is this the leadership by example that Mayor Duterte excites in us?'

Unfortunately for the archbishop, it was, and, being the unforgiving type, President Duterte has pursued his freshly rekindled — but longstanding — grudge against the priesthood with a vengeance. He not only attacked Villegas, but views the entire Catholic Church as a threat to his rule, calling bishops corrupt 'fools' and 'sons of whores'. These castigations reached a crescendo during a speech in Malacañang in January 2017 (bizarrely, to the bereaved families of police commandos killed in a massacre in Mindanao), when he said: 'I challenge you now. I challenge the Catholic Church. You are full of shit. You all smell bad.' He accused them of corruption, child abuse, homosexuality, and hypocrisy. Concluding this presidential homily, Duterte urged the grieving relatives to read the book *Altar of Secrets: Sex, Money, and Politics in the Philippine Catholic Church*, whose author, the late journalist Aries Rufo, had alleged that in many dioceses, 'priests having affairs or siring children ... has become the norm rather than the exception'. That day, Duterte singled out one bishop as a particular target of his ire — a protégé of the revered late cardinal, Jaime Sin, Teodoro Bacani, whom he called 'that monkey' and a 'son of a bitch' The president claimed Bacani had two wives — just like him, he said. The bishop, who had been forced to resign in 2003 following an accusation of sexual harassment, denied Duterte's allegation, and said he would give the president 10 million pesos (which, he added, he would have to borrow) if he could prove it.

It seemed no coincidence that the ageing cleric, by then long reinstated as Bishop Emeritus of Novaliches, had been among the notably few Church leaders to speak out against Duterte's war on drugs. In August 2016, Bacani had told Veritas, the Catholic radio station, that the killings had become so common and so widespread that the situation in the Philippines was worse than during the Second World War or under martial law. He denounced the national police as a 'bringer of death'.

In the days after his outburst in Malacañang, the president continued to ridicule the Church for questioning his war on drugs. The killings would only stop, he said, when the last pusher was off the streets. He even suggested priests try *shabu* themselves so they could understand what goes on inside the mind of an addict and grasp the gravity of the problem. Meanwhile, he co-opted a biblical lexicon himself — talking of sacrificing himself to cleanse the nation of this evil.

Duterte has never had a problem with priests who do his bidding, and he is always nice to nuns. In Davao, there were priests among the mayor's disciples. Monsignor Paul Cuison, who baptised Duterte's daughter Kitty (born out of wedlock) was brought to Manila to bless the presidential quarters in Malacañang when he became the president. Cuisson — who refused to meet me — went there with another Davao priest, Father Emmanuel 'Bong' Gunzaga, whose parish was at Ma-a, just down the road from the DDS's execution ground, Laud Quarry. It was in Gunzaga's parish that the 'Duterte for President' movement had been launched. One day, I went to find him. He spent a long time scowling at my Philippine and British press cards before he reluctantly agreed to speak. A dead gecko lay belly-up on the table next to where I sat, inside his front room. The priest made no attempt to move the lizard: the smell of death did not appear to bother Father Bong.

'Those who criticise him do not understand the real person,' he said. 'He is misunderstood because of his mouth. I have been privileged to know him since 1987. He asked me to open every City Hall council meeting with a prayer. If he knows I am in the room he will not curse. He is strong, but he is humble and compassionate. He knows the struggles of the people, of those who are unfortunate, and he will lay down his life.'

As he spoke, Gunzaga chain-smoked a brand of cigarettes called Hope; between his breathless, messianic plaudits, he blew his smoke straight at me.

'What about the Davao Death Squad, though?' I asked.

'Not true!' the priest exhaled indignantly. 'The killings are the drug lords fighting. He established a drug rehabilitation centre! He wants to save people and to save souls. I went to bless the rehab place and all the residents.'

Gunzaga told me he had also blessed the Davao City ambulances and garbage trucks at the invitation of the mayor.

'During the blessing in Malacañang I told him, "This is your destiny. Now is your time." He was crying and I said, "Mayor, there are a lot of people who are praying for you. If you walk hand in hand with God, you can do this thing, the presidency, to the glory of God."'

And Father Bong Gunzaga unwaveringly believes he has.

With priests who cross his path, however, Duterte has a long record of playing dirty and hitting hard, below the belt. It is his way of silencing the church. In Davao, a popular local priest called Father Pedro 'Pete' Lamata had used his pulpit to relentlessly attack the mayor for the vigilante killings, accusing him of masterminding them. Duterte's Sunday morning TV show was the mayor's own pulpit, and he would use it to ruthlessly attack his critics, as well as to extol the virtues of his Old Testament-style eye-for-an-eye justice by selectively quoting scripture, his favourite being Ecclesiastes chapter three: 'To every thing there is a season, and a time to every purpose under the heaven: A time to be born, and a time to die ... a time to kill.'

One Sunday, the mayor gave Father Pete Lamata both barrels. Live on air, Duterte revealed that, as a young priest, two years after his ordination, and nearly 30 years earlier, Lamata had violated his vow of clerical celibacy by secretly getting married. This covert marriage had later been legally dissolved and a penitent Lamata had long ago been restored to the priesthood, but the matter was reported by the mayor's network of spies and Duterte confessed that he had sat on the intelligence for years. Lamata was a shame to the Catholic Church, the mayor said, recommending that the archbishop conduct a 'morality probe' and exile the padre 'to Somalia or Afghanistan'. Lamata's sexual life, Duterte said, 'shamed bedtime stories in porn tabloids'.

'I hope Father Lamata [can] become a cardinal and stay in the Vatican so that he can spare the women of Davao from his womanising,' he said.

Duterte's exposé of the priest scandalised Davao in 2009, and the mayor kept on attacking Lamata during press conferences, taunting him, according to Jesus Dureza, who knows both men well. Dureza told me Duterte had placed a giant poster in front of Lamata's church, St Mary's in downtown Davao, depicting a man's face with an index finger pulling down one lower eyelid. In a dictionary of offensive Bisayan gestures this might top the list, the local cultural equivalent of an upright middle finger. Dureza said Duterte had finally agreed to bury the hatchet after Lamata pleaded with the mayor to stop.

Little was reported about Lamata after that. He remains a priest in Davao, and, in December 2016, a front-page story carried a photograph of him in a wheelchair holding midnight mass in St Jude Thaddeus parish church and praying for 'the success, safety and good health of Pres. Rodrigo R. Duterte', with whom, the story said, the priest was reconciled.

'When you hit him,' Dureza said, 'be sure you have a clean soul because he will send someone to research you and he will expose you. But he has never done anything to anyone who has not provoked him.' It felt a little like a warning.

Although more than 80 per cent of the Philippine population self-identifies as Catholic and many indulge in passionate, pious public displays of devotion, regular church attendance has declined dramatically in recent decades — from 64 per cent in 1991 to 37 per cent in 2013. Abortion, divorce, and same-sex marriage are still illegal in the Philippines, where the median age is 23, and the views of the Church are widely regarded as out of kilter with those of young Filipinos. The only other country in the world which still outlaws divorce is the Vatican itself. In 2012, the bishops vociferously opposed a law guaranteeing universal access to contraception and sex education. This didn't do them any favours, and exposés such as *Altar of Secrets* have served to undermine them further. Duterte, who has claimed he was abused by a priest as a child, contends that the Church has no moral authority at all.

He knew that the election that brought him to power was also a referendum on the Catholic Church — and he had won.

Unlike in the 1980s, when Cardinal Jaime Sin led the charge against Marcos, the Church today is a paper tiger, too slow to find its voice and publicly oppose the drugs war killings as the numbers rose. Some clergymen believed that openly challenging Duterte would be a mistake, however — the Church had already locked horns with him over his efforts to bring back the death penalty and lower the age of criminal responsibility from 15 to nine. It was not until February 2017, that the Catholic Bishops' Conference of the Philippines issued a pastoral letter, to be read out in Sunday sermons, decrying what they called a 'reign of terror' among the poor. 'Many are killed not because of drugs. Those who kill them are not brought to account,' the letter said. 'An even greater cause of concern is the indifference of many to this kind of wrong.' It did not mention Duterte by name. At a press conference the following day, the president responded.

'You Catholics, if you believe in your priests and bishops, you stay with them,' he said. 'If you want to go to heaven, then go to them. Now, if you want to end drugs … I will go to hell. Come join me.'

In more recent months, members of the clergy have quietly set up an alternative witness protection programme, providing safe houses and sanctuary to the former DDS members who have testified against Duterte, and to others on various kill-lists. In the heart of Tondo slum, a place on the front line of the war on drugs, I met the auxiliary bishop of Manila, Broderick Pablo. He was distressed by what was going on around him every night, and depressed by what he saw as the failure of the Church to take a moral stand.

'The response of the Church came late,' he conceded dolefully. 'Duterte is not opposed by other institutions. The politicians want his endorsement. Businesses want his protection. We should have responded earlier because what he is saying is that it is all right to kill! He is killing to give the impression he is in control. When your leader says "Kill! Kill! Kill!" they will kill, kill, kill. This is the culture of death, believing that death is the solution to our problems. Killing is not the solution.'

With his enemies crumbling one by one, the first president from Mindanao turned his attention to the military battlefields 500 miles to the south. In November 2016, Duterte had surprised many Filipinos by inviting Nur Misuari, founding chairman of the rebel Moro National Liberation Front (MNLF), to Malacañang and embracing him in front of cameras, despite his being a wanted man. Misuari praised the president as the one man who could bring 'peace and order in our homeland'. Peace in Mindanao had eluded every previous president, and the island's 5 million Muslims — on average nine times poorer than Christian Filipinos — were in constant rebellion, believing they had been left to rot and were the victims of a war against Islam. Peace talks had dragged on for decades, with the five predominantly Muslim provinces of western Mindanao demanding the creation of a Bangsamoro homeland. Eventually, the MNLF signed a Final Peace Agreement in 1996, which formalised the Autonomous Region of Muslim Mindanao, but this had only led to the further splintering of the MNLF and its rival breakaway, the Moro Islamic Liberation Front, into ever more radical jihadist factions. These included the Abu Sayyaf group (ASG), Ansar al-Khilafa Philippines, the Bangsamoro Islamic Freedom Fighters, and the Maute group, most of them sustained by extortion rackets and an lucrative kidnap-for-ransom trade.

By the time Duterte became president, this fractious jumble of jihadists had begun to coalesce under the black flag of the self-declared Islamic State group and the loose command of the Philippines' most wanted man, Isnilon Hapilon, a former MNLF insurgent, then Abu Sayyaf commander. Also known by his *nom de guerre*, Abu Abdullah al-Filipini, the Arabic-speaking Hapilon had had a US$5 million bounty on his head from the US Department of Justice since 2002, and, four years after that, he made it onto the FBI's most wanted list. By 2016, he had been anointed *emir* of Islamic State forces in what its leaders hoped would be the Southeast Asian *wilayah* (province) of the self-proclaimed IS caliphate — which at that stage was still ascendant. Several verified IS videos and statements acknowledged this appointment, so it was not an idle claim, and the threat posed to the Philippines by Hapilon's Salafist insurgents was real enough.

At first, the IS link was thought overblown and tenuous, but Hapilon's group, it would later be revealed, was joined by foreign fighters from elsewhere in the region and beyond, and reportedly received funding from IS in Syria, routed through Indonesia and coordinated by a Malaysian jihadist. By early 2017, as the beleaguered caliphate in Syria and Iraq was making its last stand in the cities of Raqqah and Mosul, Hapilon's alliance was seeking to expand the IS presence on Mindanao, rather than limiting itself to the offshore island fiefdoms of the ASG. The jihadist coalition included the ASG and several smaller bands of militants, among them the Maute group (named after the two brothers who lead it). The insurgents revelled in their IS branding and the fear it struck into Filipino Christian hearts. They waved black flags and guns in videos, shouting '*Allah-hu akhbar*', and from time to time would wreak local havoc, raiding, bombing, kidnapping, and beheading.

Then, in late May 2017, after what some senators and a Supreme Court judge later said had probably been a serious failure of government intelligence, clashes broke out between the Philippine armed forces and fighters of the Maute group in Marawi City, the provincial capital of Lanao del Sur in northwestern Mindanao. The military had been attempting to arrest Hapilon, who was known to have entered Marawi, but had failed to gauge the scale of the jihadists' build-up in the lakeside city of 200,000 people. They also failed to capture him, and, within a few hours, the Islamists had secured control of several districts of Marawi, sprung prisoners from the jail, taken hostages at the cathedral, and raised their black flag over the city hospital. The Philippines had become the first country in Asia to have one of its cities fall to gunmen linked to the IS caliphate.

As Marawi's residents fled, ground troops moved in, and, at 10 pm on 23 May, Duterte declared martial law in Mindanao, as he cut short a trip to Russia. Filipinos everywhere sat up and took notice as the president conjured the spectre of the dead dictator. Marcos' imposition of military rule had been preceded by violence blamed on communists. Now it was Islamists.

Before leaving Moscow, Duterte said martial law in Mindanao would be no different to martial law under Marcos, and he warned he would be harsh. Arriving back in Manila, he held a televised news conference and sought to justify the move amid widespread mistrust of his motives. He said he might have to declare military rule throughout the country 'to protect the people' and revealed, to the horror of all those listening, that IS militants had stopped a local police chief at a checkpoint near Marawi and beheaded him on the spot. 'They decapitated him then and there,' he said.

This chilling claim made headlines everywhere — but, two days later, Senior Inspector Romeo Enriquez turned up — head still securely attached to his shoulders — and confirmed to journalists that reports of his gruesome death had been exaggerated. Duterte, it was said, had just been misinformed — but, as *The Washington Post* pointed out, 'the inaccurate report shaped how the martial law news was covered — and potentially how it was received by the US government'. It was fake news, plain and simple, but by the time the truth came out, it was too late. The deed was done.

Days later, it emerged that Duterte's defense secretary Delfin Lorenzana had told senators that, in his opinion, the Philippine armed forces could contain the crisis in Marawi without recourse to martial law. The former president and ex-armed forces chief, Fidel Ramos, meanwhile questioned why it had been necessary to declare military rule across the whole of Mindanao, an island of 22 million people (a fifth of the country's population), when in reality the army was in pursuit of a few extremists holed up in one small city. He appealed to government officials to stop talking about the extension of martial law to the rest of the Philippines as this was creating 'a sense of fear and foreboding'.

But, as the weeks went by, the small insurrection in Marawi proved hard to crush and the Maute fighters difficult to dislodge, despite the Philippine armed forces unleashing an array of weaponry against them, in what became the country's biggest battle since the second world war. The armed forces bombed and strafed and launched air-to-ground rockets while armoured fighting vehicles moved into the city. The army chief of staff, General Eduardo Año, declared that his forces were engaged in 'Mosul-type, hybrid urban warfare' and warned that rebellion could spread to other cities on the island. The Iraqis' costly victory over IS in Mosul — which took nine months and left much of the ancient city in ruins and unknown thousands dead — had been in the news that very week, and what was happening in Marawi bore no comparison. After two months of sustained military assaults, assisted by the deployment of US and Australian surveillance aircraft, 421 militants, 99 soldiers and 45 civilians had been killed. But an estimated half a million people had been displaced from the city and its hinterland.

It would take until the middle of October 2017 before the city of Marawi was declared 'liberated' — although, even as Duterte did so, on one of several visits to the city, gunfire could still be heard, with up to 40 militants still holding out. But the Philippine armed forces had killed Hapilon and one of the two Maute brothers in a gun battle, and police presented pictures of their bloodied bodies as proof of death. Hapilon had been shot in the head. Duterte thanked President Xi Jinping for supplying his army with Chinese-made 'Armalite look-alike' sniper rifles which took out the two militant leaders who were standing a kilometre away, he said, to great applause. He also thanked the US and Israel, whose equipment the Philippines had 'borrowed' and would return.

In all, the five-month standoff had killed around 1100 people, including 165 soldiers, most of them said to be Islamist fighters. No one expected the demise of the two leaders to herald the end of hostilities in the south. A week later, General Eduardo Año retired and Duterte declared the battle for Marawi 'the crowning jewel' of his career. In reality, the military's failure to quickly recapture Marawi from the militants handed the Philippine IS franchise a propaganda coup and suggested that militant Islamism might be more prevalent in Mindanao than many had feared. Sidney Jones, an expert in the Southeast Asian jihadisphere, said it had 'inspired young extremists from around the region to want to join' and 'lifted the prestige of the Philippine fighters in the eyes of [IS] Central'.

But if the prolonged Marawi crisis played well for the jihadists, it also played into the hands of Duterte, who had his own plans.

With his presidential declaration of martial law limited to 60 days by the post-Marcos anti-dictator constitution, Duterte sought congressional approval for its extension. In a letter to both houses, he said that, of the 600 militants still known to be there, about 220 remained in the heart of the city, holding 300 people hostage. This contradicted General Año's assessment that there were only about 40 gunmen in Marawi. Duterte said they were armed with high-powered, military-grade weapons. His request for an extension until the end of 2017 was virtually uncontested — 245–14 in the lower house and 16-4 in the Senate — but his critics said Duterte's true intention had been unmasked and that nationwide martial law was no longer a matter of if but when.

The one opposition senator notably absent from this vote was former justice secretary Leila de Lima, who remained in detention at national police headquarters. In a statement, she had condemned Duterte's request for an extension as 'egregiously excessive' and 'unconstitutional'. Unable to visit her in person, I asked that a list of questions be taken in to her, and, within a day, I had received a long reply, painstakingly handwritten in blue ink on senatorial notepaper. De Lima was seething about Duterte, who she told me was 'surrounded by sycophants and fanatics', and said that he would only be remembered as 'a madman who enraptured a nation with a forked tongue and an evil charm'. He would 'leave behind not a legacy but a most bitter lesson that hopefully the Filipino people will never forget'.

'Martial law is his way of seducing the armed forces of the Philippines back to the dark side, his recruitment tool for the army to join his authoritarian project,' she wrote. 'His endgame is the imposition of authoritarian rule. It's just a question of whether the army will allow itself to be seduced.'

De Lima said the commander-in-chief needed his troops on side. 'The imposition of martial law is undeniably a discretionary power of the president,' she wrote, 'as long as he can justify the existence of a state of rebellion or invasion. However, an authoritarian leader will always find martial law as his first option. A democratic leader will postpone its use until the last possible moment because of its effect on civil liberties. The constitution envisions its use as an emergency measure of last resort, not as a development paradigm.'

If Duterte was going to successfully beguile the Philippine top brass and complete his grand seduction of the armed forces, one more inducement would be necessary. The president had to convince his generals — first among them the rabidly anti-communist Eduardo Año — that his game plan would not involve handing the Reds the keys to Malacañang. After I had met José Maria 'Joma' Sison, Duterte's old professor and founder of the CPP, peace talks had been on and off for months, with occasional clashes breaking out, shattering ceasefires between the army and the 4000-strong NPA. This had prolonged one of the world's longest-running insurgencies, which over five decades had left 30,000 dead. Duterte had said he wanted to 'walk the extra mile' to achieve a settlement, but he and his negotiator, Jesus Dureza, seemed increasingly convinced that Joma no longer called the shots of what Dureza described as 'the only remaining Marxist-Leninist-Maoist insurgency in the world'. In parts of Mindanao in particular, the fractious movement's armed wing, the New People's Army, was now little more than an extortion gang, imposing 'revolutionary taxes' on mining companies which, according to the military, earned them US$25 million a year.

At 6 am on 19 July 2017, a vehicle containing members of the Presidential Security Group (PSG) en route to meet Duterte was riddled with bullets in an ambush northwest of Davao City. The attack — in which five of the president's bodyguards were wounded and a local militiaman killed — was immediately blamed on the NPA; the communists had denounced the imposition of martial law in Mindanao and there had been a number of skirmishes with government troops. As Duterte sought the extension of military rule from Congress, Joma accused him of being 'obsessed with martial law and mass murder' as the means to solve the country's problems. He told the *Philippine Daily Inquirer* that the president had gone mad.

'It's really hard to talk with a lunatic who takes pride in extrajudicial killings,' Joma said. 'There can be no peace negotiations if ... the other side is drunk with power.'

Duterte then solemnly addressed his old professor, agreeing that negotiations were a waste of time.

'Let us stop talking. I am tired,' he said, from Davao. 'Let us renew the fighting for another 50 years. It's what you want.' A couple of days later he declared categorically: 'No more talks.'

The president's annual State of the Nation address presents the country with a moment to stand back and take stock. The Philippines downed tools at 3.30 pm on the fourth Monday of July 2017, and gathered to watch their ever-entertaining strong-man boast of his achievements and set out his plans. He was running late, just for a change, so while they waited, commentators picked over the sartorial display as the nation's political peacocks strutted down the red carpet and cameras snapped and whirred. For the Duterte clan, this was a major family outing. First daughter, Sara, mayor of Davao, wore a flouncy pink Maria Clara dress with shoulder pads worthy of a *Star Wars* wardrobe, the style once favoured by Imelda Marcos. Paolo Duterte, eldest son (and at that point vice mayor of Davao), was sporting a daring jungle-print *barong*; his younger brother, Baste, opted for an intricately embroidered version. Their mother Elizabeth skipped the event, but Honeylet, the president's first girlfriend attended, as did her teenaged daughter Kitty. The arrival of Duterte in the cavernous Congress session hall sparked a feeding frenzy as the president swaggered through, glad-handing loyal allies from both houses who snapped selfies as the tough-talking president of the Philippines made for the podium, dwarfed by a gigantic national flag. He wore a simple, white, what-you-see-is-what-you-get *barong tagalog*, in marked contrast to his choice of clothing while visiting Mindanao days earlier, where he was photographed, for the first (but not the last) time, wearing camouflaged military fatigues — albeit in a comically rakish manner. He had looked comfortable in his role of commander-in-chief, the Philippines' new martial lawyer.

Three former presidents were in attendance at the State of the Nation address, including Fidel Ramos, as was the increasingly edgy chief justice of the Supreme Court, the Vatican's *apostolic nuncio* (dean of the diplomatic corps), and the ageing Imelda

Marcos herself, former first lady of the Philippines. The rehabilitation of the Marcos clan was by now nearly complete; two
days later, the government would announce plans to abolish the
agency tasked with recovering the billions plundered by the
dictator and his cronies. It had only recovered US$3.4 billion of
the estimated US$10 billion they had looted. But the Duterte
regime was suddenly more interested in going after the previous
president, Benigno Aquino III, who did not attend the State of
the Nation address. He had just learned that he was to face
charges of criminal negligence over a botched assault on Muslim
insurgents the year before he left office. Duterte doesn't do irony.
It is a time-honoured tradition for each incoming resident of
Malacañang Palace to lock up the previous occupant.

Duterte's speech was a two-hour marathon — long, but still
less than half the length of the longest State of the Nation speech
on record, delivered by Ferdinand Marcos in 1969. True to form,
Duterte repeatedly deviated from his teleprompter script with
random quips and impromptu remarks. The tone was combative,
but he opened by noting that there was 'euphoria in the air'
because the multitude of grave problems which he said the
Philippines had been reeling from the previous year, were being
beaten by those with 'unflinching and tenacious determination'.
It only took a couple of minutes for the law-and-order president
to launch into a robust defence of his signature policy — his
government's proudest achievement.

'I have resolved that no matter how long it takes, the fight
against illegal drugs will continue because that is the root cause
of so much evil and so much suffering' — at this point a ripple of
applause spread through the auditorium, led by Ronald dela
Rosa, the national police chief — 'that weakens the social fabric
and deters foreign investments [sic] from pouring in. The fight
will be unremitting as it will be unrelenting.'

But in his address, he vowed his war on drugs would continue in the face of international and domestic criticism by those he said were 'trivialising' the campaign by raising human rights concerns. 'The beasts and vultures' preying on Filipino youth would end up either 'in jail or hell'. 'You harm the children in whose hands the future of this republic is entrusted, and I will hound you to the very gates of hell,' he said.

The meandering, expletive-heavy speech — in which he attacked the US and took sideswipes at the media — was also dominated by the president's security-related obsessions — jihadists and communists. He said there was no point in talking to communist insurgents who attacked his security convoy while making unreasonable demands in peace talks. 'They said I'm a bully. You're all fools. I am really a bully, son of a bitch. I am really a bully, especially to the enemies of the state.'

Later, Duterte held a press conference and told reporters that the government offensive in Mindanao would not stop 'until the last terrorist is taken out'. He threatened airstrikes on schools for indigenous children on Mindanao that he alleged were teaching subversion and communism. Over the next two years, he said, 45,000 new troops would be added to the armed forces so that they could 'fight all fronts, everywhere'. How the army must have loved it.

Outside, on the streets of the capital, 10,000 people were marching in a huge and colourful demonstration towards the plenary hall in Quezon City, Metro Manila, holding placards of protest against the drugs war, martial law and calling for peace in Mindanao. The demonstrators placed more than 1000 pairs of shoes along Commonwealth Avenue. This time it wasn't a dig at Imelda Marcos; these empty shoes represented the thousands killed in the war on drugs. Many of those demonstrating were leftists who felt betrayed.

One effigy depicted the president with a toothbrush moustache, right arm raised in a *sieg heil* salute; another, which had Duterte dressed in combat fatigues, was torched.

Following his news conference, Duterte went outside — against security advice — to 'listen' to the protestors. As he stood on a stage, they chanted 'Never again to martial law', and when he tried to speak they heckled him.

'Shut up,' he said, threw away his microphone, and left.

Barely six weeks after Rodrigo Duterte delivered that 2017 State of the Nation address, threatening to hound to the gates of hell those harming children, the murders of three teenagers — the youngest just 14 — exposed the president's hypocrisy. Once again, the police themselves were the prime suspects. In the point-blank extra-judicial execution of 17-year-old Kian Loyd delos Santos, CCTV pictures had actually caught two plain-clothes officers red-handed as they dragged him off before he was shot in the head and the chest, a pistol planted in his hand. Months later, they were still maintaining that Kian was a courier, as though this unproven allegation somehow justified his killing. They hung around in the neighbourhood long after they had shot the boy, their nonchalance attesting to their misplaced confidence that their sins would never find them out.

The night before Kian Loyd delos Santos died had been the bloodiest in Duterte's war. In Bulacan province, north of Manila, 32 suspects were shot dead in encounters with police in 67 separate operations, most of them attempted buy-bust stings.

'Beautiful!' said Duterte, next day. 'We could kill another 32 every day. Then maybe we could reduce what ails this country.' He chided human rights activists for getting in the way of his campaign and said police would shoot them if they obstructed justice.

Police officers described the raids as part of a 'one-time, big-time' operation, and claimed that all those who died had chosen to put up a fight. The president's wishes were not quite fulfilled, but the police did their best: in the end, more than 80 suspects were killed over four consecutive nights. Bato, the national police chief, told reporters: 'The president did not instruct me to kill and kill.'

But he had.

Days earlier, while reporting for Channel 4 News, I had attended a PNP anniversary parade inside Camp Crame, Manila, where the president had come to pin medals on chests. The parade ground was within easy earshot of the cell where Senator Leila de Lima was held. Duterte addressed the rank and file and the officer corps of his police force, as well as the heads of the other armed services, former president Joseph Estrada, cabinet ministers, foreign ambassadors, and the press. He started by boasting of his command responsibility.

'This will be handy, if Duterte ever ends up in the Hague,' I was thinking.

'I am your commander-in-chief,' he asserted, 'and for the police, you are under the local governments which I direct and supervise and control.' He referred to himself as 'the chief of all the police because the constitution says the president shall be commander-in-chief of all armed forces in the country'.

He told them that the 6 million margin of his electoral victory freed him from what he called the vagaries of politics, whatever that meant. 'I thank God that I was elected president,' he said, before doing his usual dog-leg straight into his flagship policy. All the cops, thousands of them, sweating in their starched uniforms and hats, knew exactly what was coming.

'If you have to shoot, shoot them dead,' the president advised his police force, crammed into the stadium or standing dutifully to attention down on the parade ground in the searing afternoon heat. 'And this is what the human rights idiots are trying to complain [sic],' he said, as officers tutted and rolled their eyes in shared indignation. 'You know, when I say "I'll shoot them dead", I'd prefer they'd shoot them in the heart or in the head. That's the end of the problem.'

'If you insist on a drug war, I will kill you all. I will kill you,' he said, this time addressing any listening dealers or addicts, none of whom had insisted on a drug war. 'I have shown it and I will do it, and do it again and again until I shall have wiped you from the face of the earth.' He had his Dirty Harry face on, grand-standing in the grandstand, live on national TV.

I was meanwhile cutting a rather lonely figure, a toxic foreign correspondent — who, unfortunately, all the president's security men had recognised — in a bank of seats reserved for the press, but into which a few senior police officers had spilled. These seats were immediately adjacent to the VIP stand where Duterte was extemporising violently from the podium. I glanced round at the cops in peaked caps and gold braid just behind me, and then turned to watch Al, my cameraman, as he sweated it out on an uncovered gantry filming the kill-kill-kill speech. There surely could not be anywhere else on the planet where you could listen to a democratically elected leader talking like this. The police, who made up the vast bulk of the audience, were drinking it in, laughing at Duterte's jokes and asides, basking in his presidential munificence. He would watch their backs, he assured them. Even the foreign diplomats, sitting to the president's right, just stared straight ahead as he confided that while, as mayor, he had been 'charged' with killing (he hadn't), he had never actually executed anyone as they knelt on the ground. No, he said, he had never allowed that. But the police had to preserve their own lives.

'If there is a shootout, if they offer the slightest violent resistance, if you have to shoot them, shoot them in the head. That is my order.' Not that the police needed encouragement: 97 per cent of suspects shot in drug operations are killed.

When the 'one-time, big-time' killing spree started days later, it did not strike me as entirely unconnected.

When you fly in or out of Manila, the vast expanse of Manila Bay, a perfect natural harbour, presents a magnificent view. It's a historic vista: it was in these waters that, on 1 May 1898, the US Navy routed the Spanish Pacific fleet, ending more than three centuries of Spanish colonial occupation. Filipinos had expected to be granted independence, but instead the Americans helped themselves to the Philippine archipelago and launched a scorched-earth policy to pacify the natives. Half a century later, the Republic of the Philippines was finally granted independence, but US bombing of Japanese occupation forces had levelled Manila the previous year, leaving 100,000 Filipinos dead. From the plane, the shanties and the post-war high-rises that now make up the jumbled urban sprawl, appear on the eastern fringe of the bay. In-shore are waters dotted with the neat rectangular pens of fish farms. Poor fish. Manila Bay is described by Greenpeace as 'a reeking cesspool of sludge, human sewage, industrial waste and garbage'. Today, it is one of the most polluted bodies of water in the world, and now, just as Duterte predicted, it is also polluted with bodies.

Long before he had even launched his campaign to be president, Duterte warned that if Filipinos were to vote him into power he would dump the bodies of 100,000 criminals in these waters. 'You will see the fish in Manila Bay getting fat,' he said. It was a headline-grabbing Dutertism that has been recycled by reporters ever since as quintessential Duterte.

Navotas is a ramshackle city within a city, extending along the coast from Tondo slum at the northern fringe of Metro Manila, its rickety lean-tos stretching out on rotting stilts into the black water of the Navotas River, one of several which empty their fetid liquid waste directly into the bay. There are better places to be a fish in the Philippines, but, remarkably, Navotas is still known as the country's fishing capital, and boasts of what it claims is the biggest fishing port in Southeast Asia. Colourful outrigger trawlers, slung with nets and laden with cold-boxes, set out to sea from its riverbanks at dawn and dusk. Navotas has seen its share of the killings that came with Duterte's war on drugs. Residents told me there had been many shootings, with bodies found dumped along North Bay Boulevard. Sometimes corpses just float down the river — one had washed up the very morning I battled through the congested streets to get there. I met a man who told me he had watched another body being hauled out of the water, face wrapped in packing tape, a hallmark of the drugs war. Trawlers out in the bay had found bodies tangled up in their nets. These, I was assured, were not just fishermen's tales.

The bodies, those I spoke to in Navotas insisted, 'were not from around here'. The random dumping of dead 'disappeared' people had become a new trend, a new phase in the drugs war. The PNP had stopped publishing numbers of those killed, and revised previously published figures downwards, making it impossible to collate detailed drugs war statistics. It also emerged that the police had, for months, been taking gunshot victims directly to hospital following supposed buy-bust operations — most were reportedly dead on arrival. Suspicion grew that this was a deliberate policy enabling the police to bypass scene-of-crime investigations and awkward questions about extra-judicial executions.

Ten miles down the coast of Manila Bay from Navotas stands the Catholic Baclaran Church, in Parañaque City, also part of

Metro Manila. It can cram in thousands of worshipers every Sunday and Wednesday, and it does — on the hour, every hour, its vast, vaulted roof echoing to the hymns and supplications of the faithful. It is known as the National Shrine of Our Mother of Perpetual Help, and, true to its name, it's open for business 24/7. It is the home of Father Amado 'Picx' Picardal, a Redemptorist priest, who celebrates mass at the shrine and takes confessions — sometimes from killers.

'We get police here with guilty consciences, seeking confession and absolution because they have been involved in EJKs. One used to be an altar boy. "What could I do?" he asked me. "I had been ordered."'

Father Picx, as he's affectionately known, is suffering a severe case of *déjà vu*. For 16 years, he had a ministry in Davao City during Duterte's tenure as mayor. It was he who began documenting the murders of the Davao Death Squad. One of the victims was even shot dead in the car park of a church while he was holding mass. Father Picx had been one of my first ports of call in Manila when I began work on this book. I had stumbled across his website and blog which, if you spool back through his poems and writings, accurately foretold what has come to pass. He had seen Duterte coming, and warned, very specifically, of what would happen. And lo, it had all come to pass.

One sweltering Sunday towards the end of 2017, I went to see Father Picx again, between Baclaran services. The church's pastoral hinterland includes impoverished urban ghettoes in Parañaque and Pasay cities, where many hundreds have been killed by police or masked assassins. In the dappled light of a modern stained-glass rose window high above the congregation, Father Picx stood in his white robes and reflected on the dramatic events that had unfolded in the months since we had last met. The priest has a gentle, self-effacing manner, and that, combined with his shaved head and round, metal-rimmed glasses, lent him a distinctly Gandhian demeanour. But Picx Picardal was not feeling very Gandhian about what was happening in his country.

'It's a disaster,' he said. 'It has been a horrible year. A bloody year. We started monitoring the killings in Davao from 1998 and there were 1424. Duterte said he would replicate Davao, but the only thing he has replicated is the killing. He is addicted to it. Now, in one year, there have been more than 10,000! This is mass-murder!'

'I believe there is no more rule of law,' he went on. 'It is the rule of a person. It's authoritarian, dictatorial rule without a formal declaration of martial law all over the country. He controls all the institutions — Congress, the judiciary, the military, the police. And now the police are a killing machine. He is doing terrible damage to our institutions and the repercussions will be felt long after he has left power.'

In the church nave down below, celebrants had packed in for the 4 pm mass, and songs of worship were being carried up to our gallery on the faint breeze made by overworked fans mounted on the faux-Gothic columns.

'So how has he done it?' I asked. 'How has he got away with it?'

The priest paused briefly then replied: 'You know, I believe he reflects the worst version of ourselves as Filipinos. There is a Duterte in many of us. Someone who lacks mercy and compassion, who is rude, brutal, and does not respect the law. I think he really represents the worst version of ourselves as Filipinos. That is why he is popular.'

ACKNOWLEDGEMENTS

Among those worst afflicted by the prevailing paranoia that has settled on Duterte's Philippines are those who have dared to oppose his vindictive regime. They include journalists, writers, lawyers, human rights workers, priests, politicians, and, increasingly, ordinary people sickened by the killing. Sadly, I am unable to publicly acknowledge Filipino friends who have helped me greatly with this book, for fear of possible repercussions. For me, it's disappointing that I cannot thank them all by name because I owe them a ton of gratitude. Anonymity may improve their life expectancies, however, and also means they will escape bombardment by Duterte's malicious social media trolls, whose unpleasant hounding and — sometimes violent — threats cannot be taken lightly. To all of you, thank you for helping me to better understand the insidious nature of what began the day Duterte Harry set his sights on Malacañang.

There are many friends, colleagues, and sources I cannot name, but one person in particular committed to working with me from the very start and, to you, my heartfelt thanks: *lubusan po akong nagpapasalamat*.

I want to acknowledge the work of many Filipino journalists, which I have drawn on in my research; I have also been deeply impressed by the Philippine Center for Investigative Journalism and by the work of journalists at *Rappler*, an independent Philippine digital news network whose standards are high and whose reporting is invariably reliable and gutsy, which is why, as I write, Duterte is trying to close it down.

Also in the Philippines, I owe a debt of gratitude to an under-lit speakeasy bar, entered through a fire door marked 'Exit' at the back of an anonymous building in Manila, which from time to time (and unbeknownst to staff there) made it easy for me to speak to some of those who did not wish to be seen to speak to me.

Outside the Philippines, thank you to my wonderful coterie of friends in Bangkok for your persistent encouragement, your willingness to be my sounding board and throw around ideas, in particular Anna-Lisa Fuglesang, Michael French, Philip Sherwell, Roque Raymundo, Alastair Thomson, and Chanchaya 'Mix' Hadden. Thank you to my editors at Channel 4 News in London for backing this endeavour and enabling me to take the time to work on this book at short notice. And to my colleagues Lindsey Hilsum, Thom Walker, and Matt Frei: your encouragement and assistance was particularly appreciated, as was the work of Girish Juneja and Kathryn Milofsky, who did some digging in the USA. Invaluable tuition in the art of getting started, from fellow foreign correspondent Colin Freeman, got me started.

Thank you to Cory Dobb for your thought-provoking and revelatory insights into what makes people tick, not least myself, and to Zoë Ciara Miller for buoying me up with your endless encouragement and love. To Peter Dobb: I offer fathomless gratitude for your attentiveness to my convoluted etymological abuseage. And to my dad: thank you for your support, but most of all, for bringing me to Southeast Asia aged seven and making it my home.

At the 'number one' Asia Literary Agency, a huge thank you to the indefatigable Kelly Falconer: you coached and coaxed, advised and edited, with boundless energy and optimism. To Philip Gwyn Jones, editor-at-large at Scribe UK in London, another big thank you, and to your team, particularly Molly Slight, for your scrupulously careful copy-editing. And in Melbourne, Australia, my thanks to Henry Rosenbloom, founder and publisher of Scribe, for sharing, with Philip, my conviction that the story of Duterte needed telling.

More thanks, this time to Steve Crawshaw, former advocacy director of Amnesty International; Brad Adams, executive director of the Asia division of Human Rights Watch; and Sam Zarifi, secretary general of the International Commission of Jurists, for giving me both time and inspiration. I would also like to thank Mark Ellis, executive director of the International Bar Association, for your unwavering support of my journalism over many years.

And Iman Ehinger: I could have done none of this without you.

INDEX